Responsive Web Design by Example Beginner's Guide

Discover how you can easily create engaging, responsive websites with minimum hassle!

Thoriq Firdaus

[PACKT]
PUBLISHING

BIRMINGHAM - MUMBAI

Responsive Web Design by Example Beginner's Guide

First published: March 2013

Production Reference: 1140313

Published by Packt Publishing Ltd.
Livery Place
35 Livery Street
Birmingham B3 2PB, UK.

ISBN 978-1-84969-542-8

www.packtpub.com

Cover Image by Arief Bahari (ariefbahari@gmail.com)

Credits

Author

Thoriq Firdaus

Reviewers

Kevin M. Kelly

Shawn McBurnie

Volkan Özçelik

Chad Adams

Abhishek Bhardwaj

Acquisition Editor

Erol Staveley

Lead Technical Editor

Neeshma Ramakrishnan

Technical Editors

Prasad Dalvi

Varun Pius Rodrigues

Copy Editors

Brandt D'Mello

Insiya Morbiwala

Alfida Paiva

Ruta Waghmare

Project Coordinator

Amey Sawant

Proofreaders

Lynda Sliwoski

Maria Gould

Indexer

Rekha Nair

Production Coordinator

Nilesh R. Mohite

Cover Work

Nilesh R. Mohite

About the Author

Thoriq Firdaus is a graphic and web designer living in Indonesia. He has been working in web designing projects with several clients from startup to notable companies and organizations worldwide for over five years.

He is very passionate on HTML5 and CSS3 and writes on these subjects regularly at `http://www.hongkiat.com/` and at his own blog `http://creatiface.com/`. Occasionally, he also gives presentations on web design at some local colleges and institutions.

Outside of work, he enjoys watching movies with his family and trying out some good food in a new cafe or restaurant nearby.

First, I would like to thank the team at Packt Publishing for giving me a chance to write this book and also to the editors and reviewers for their help on improving this book with their valuable feedback and comments.

I also thank my friends Arief Bahari (`www.ariefbahari.com`) and Ferina Berliani (`http://nantokaa.tumblr.com/`) for allowing me to use their artwork for this book.

Lastly, I thank my family, especially my wife and daughter, for giving me support during the process of writing this book.

About the Reviewers

Kevin M. Kelly is an experienced web craftsman specializing in interface development, producing in areas such as ad agencies, e-commerce places, and government bodies. He has worked with companies such as Canadian Tire, Rogers, The Toronto Star, Nissan, and Mazooma. He is the cofounder of the coder-focused meetup, #devTO, and member of Multimedia Design and Production Technician Program Advisory Committeee at Humber Institute of Design and Advanced Learning. Kevin is passionate about the industry as well as his community.

> My special thanks to Packt Publishing, my friends, family, and every person that I have dealt with in regards to my amazing career.

Shawn McBurnie has been developing websites since the late 1990s. He is the principal developer at Nettercap, a promotion and development shop focused on traditional music and arts, and is a frontend developer for The Nerdery. He was also a technical reviewer for Sang Shin's *HTML5 Mobile Development Cookbook*.

When he's not programming, Shawn can be found performing with his band, Rumgumption, or teaching at the Center for Irish Music in Minnesota.

Volkan Özçelik is a frontend engineer living in Mountain View, in the middle of Silicon Valley. Since 2003, he has been creating client-heavy AJAX web applications. He loves to architect responsive and intuitive web components, driven by amazingly well-organized JavaScript code. He dreams of the death of Internet Explorer, and shudders at the horror of thousands of people still using the crazy thing, but tenaciously works around its quirks and gently aligns it with its more modern peers.

Volkan has a blog (`http://o2js.com/`) where he shares peculiarities, intricacies, best practices, patterns, use cases, and implementations of reusable, cross-platform, optimized JavaScript. He is also the author of a book *JavaScript Interview Questions* (`http://o2js.com/interview-questions/`).

Other than JavaScript, Volkan has experience with NoSQL data stores, ASP.net, C#, PHP, Java, Python, Django, Ruby, Objective C, and a variety of other languages and frameworks.

Volkan is currently a Software Engineer at Jive Software (`http://www.jivesoftware.com`); prior to that he was a JavaScript hacker at SocialWire (`http://socialwire.com`). He was the VP of Technology at GROU.PS (`http://grou.ps`) and also a JavaScript Engineer at LiveGO (a social mash-up that's gone to dead pool, R.I.P). He was the CTO of Turkey's largest business network `cember.net` (which got acquired by Xing A.G.).

When he's not satisfying his never-ending appetite to experiment with cutting-edge technologies and frameworks, Volkan loves to be with nature spending days away from anything digital; he's a trekking and camping enthusiast, and a keen lover of parrots.

www.PacktPub.com

Support files, eBooks, discount offers and more

You might want to visit www.PacktPub.com for support files and downloads related to your book.

Did you know that Packt offers eBook versions of every book published, with PDF and ePub files available? You can upgrade to the eBook version at www.PacktPub.com and as a print book customer, you are entitled to a discount on the eBook copy. Get in touch with us at service@packtpub.com for more details.

At www.PacktPub.com, you can also read a collection of free technical articles, sign up for a range of free newsletters and receive exclusive discounts and offers on Packt books and eBooks.

http://PacktLib.PacktPub.com

Do you need instant solutions to your IT questions? PacktLib is Packt's online digital book library. Here, you can access, read and search across Packt's entire library of books.

Why Subscribe?

- ◆ Fully searchable across every book published by Packt
- ◆ Copy and paste, print and bookmark content
- ◆ On demand and accessible via web browser

Free Access for Packt account holders

If you have an account with Packt at www.PacktPub.com, you can use this to access PacktLib today and view nine entirely free books. Simply use your login credentials for immediate access.

Table of Contents

Preface

Responsive web design is one of the most discussed topics on web, and a very demanding feature for today's websites. It lets the website to adapt in difference viewport sizes nicely. But, if you think that building a responsive website is hard, wait until you have finished this book.

It will also show you how to use some development tools that allow you to build responsive websites faster, more efficiently with lesser number of hurdles.

What this book covers

Chapter 1, *Responsive Web Design*, explains the basics of responsive web design, explores the development tools to build it, and highlights some good examples of a responsive website.

Chapter 2, *Constructing a Responsive Portfolio Page with Skeleton*, introduces Skeleton, discusses how to use its responsive grid, and starts the first project by constructing the webpage with HTML5.

Chapter 3, *Enhancing the Portfolio Website with CSS3*, introduces some additional features in CSS3 like Transforms and Transitions, and discusses how to incorporate them to enhance our responsive portfolio website.

Chapter 4, *Developing a Product Launch Site with Bootstrap*, introduces Bootstrap framework, and explores some of its components to build responsive websites.

Chapter 5, *Enhancing the Product Launch Site with CSS3 and LESS*, explains several LESS functions to author CSS3, and discusses how to use them to make our responsive Product Launch site look stunning, yet also maintainable. In this chapter, we also test our website to see how it looks in several difference viewport sizes.

Chapter 6, A Responsive Website for Business with Foundation Framework, introduces Foundation framework, and walks through the key features. We also start the third project to build responsive website for business purposes.

Chapter 7, Extending Foundation, explores the Sass CSS preprocessors, SCSS and Compass, and discusses how to extend the website appearance by configuring several Foundation framework variables.

What you need for this book

You will need, at least a basic understanding in HTML and CSS, a code editor, and modern browsers.

Who this book is for

This book aims for beginners who are quite familiar with HTML and CSS, and want to extend their skills to develop responsive websites that virtually fit on any screen size.

Conventions

In this book, you will find several headings appearing frequently.

To give clear instructions of how to complete a procedure or task, we use:

Time for action – heading

1. Action 1
2. Action 2
3. Action 3

Instructions often need some extra explanation so that they make sense, so they are followed with:

What just happened?

This heading explains the workings of tasks or instructions that you have just completed.

You will also find some other learning aids in the book, including:

Pop quiz – heading

These are short multiple-choice questions intended to help you test your own understanding.

Have a go hero – heading

These practical challenges and give you ideas for experimenting with what you have learned.

You will also find a number of styles of text that distinguish between different kinds of information. Here are some examples of these styles, and an explanation of their meaning.

Code words in text, database table names, folder names, filenames, file extensions, pathnames, dummy URLs, user input, and Twitter handles are shown as follows: "You may notice that we used the Unix command `rm` to remove the `Drush` directory rather than the DOS `del` command."

A block of code is set as follows:

```
<meta name="viewport" content="width=device-width, initial-scale=1">
```

When we wish to draw your attention to a particular part of a code block, the relevant lines or items are set in bold:

```
<picture alt="responsive images">
  <source src=big.jpg media="min-width:768px">
  <source src=medium.jpg media="min-width:320px">
  <source src=small.jpg>
  <img src=medium.jpg alt="responsive images">
</picture>
```

Any command-line input or output is written as follows:

```
compass watch
```

New terms and **important words** are shown in bold. Words that you see on the screen, in menus or dialog boxes for example, appear in the text like this: "On the **Select Destination Location** screen, click on **Next** to accept the default destination."

Warnings or important notes appear in a box like this.

Tips and tricks appear like this.

Reader feedback

Feedback from our readers is always welcome. Let us know what you think about this book—what you liked or may have disliked. Reader feedback is important for us to develop titles that you really get the most out of.

To send us general feedback, simply send an e-mail to `feedback@packtpub.com`, and mention the book title through the subject of your message.

If there is a topic that you have expertise in and you are interested in either writing or contributing to a book, see our author guide on `www.packtpub.com/authors`.

Customer support

Now that you are the proud owner of a Packt book, we have a number of things to help you to get the most from your purchase.

Downloading the example code

You can download the example code files for all Packt books you have purchased from your account at `http://www.packtpub.com`. If you purchased this book elsewhere, you can visit `http://www.packtpub.com/support` and register to have the files e-mailed directly to you.

Errata

Although we have taken every care to ensure the accuracy of our content, mistakes do happen. If you find a mistake in one of our books—maybe a mistake in the text or the code—we would be grateful if you would report this to us. By doing so, you can save other readers from frustration and help us improve subsequent versions of this book. If you find any errata, please report them by visiting `http://www.packtpub.com/submit-errata`, selecting your book, clicking on the **errata submission form** link, and entering the details of your errata. Once your errata are verified, your submission will be accepted and the errata will be uploaded to our website, or added to any list of existing errata, under the Errata section of that title.

Piracy

Piracy of copyright material on the Internet is an ongoing problem across all media. At Packt, we take the protection of our copyright and licenses very seriously. If you come across any illegal copies of our works, in any form, on the Internet, please provide us with the location address or website name immediately so that we can pursue a remedy.

Please contact us at copyright@packtpub.com with a link to the suspected pirated material.

We appreciate your help in protecting our authors, and our ability to bring you valuable content.

Questions

You can contact us at questions@packtpub.com if you are having a problem with any aspect of the book, and we will do our best to address it.

1
Responsive Web Design

The number of users and features for mobile devices have been increasing exponentially in the last few years. Mobile browsers can now render web pages as good as desktop browsers can, so it is now a common sight to see people enjoying browsing through websites from their phones or tablets. The number of mobile users will grow even larger in the future; Cisco predicts that there will be about 788 million mobile-only users by 2015 [http://www.cisco.com/en/US/solutions/collateral/ns341/ns525/ns537/ns705/ns827/white_paper_c11-520862.pdf].

This event surely comes with a consequence on the other side. Designers are forced to think of new ways to deliver web pages for mobile users; we can definitely no longer rely on the static grid, since the sizes of mobile devices are too varied. In 2010, Ethan Marcotte [http://ethanmarcotte.com/] *coined a new answer to this situation called* **responsive web design [RWD]** *that now has become a popular practice in web design to deliver web pages in varying viewport sizes* [http://www.alistapart.com/articles/responsive-web-design/].

 John Allsopp (http://johnfallsopp.com/) had actually foretold the adaptability of web pages twelve years earlier in his post *A Dao of Web Design* (http://www.alistapart.com/articles/dao/).

In this first chapter we will:

◆ Take a glance at the basics of responsive web design and its current limitations
◆ Take a look at the responsive frameworks that we are going to use to build responsive websites
◆ Look into CSS preprocessors and their syntax to compose styles
◆ Prepare the tools to build responsive websites

Let's get started.

Basic responsive web design

RWD basically allows a website to respond or adapt to a different viewport size, smaller or larger, without your having to set a specific domain/subdomain for people using mobile devices. The look and feel of the website can be maintained as to have similar experiences across different device sizes. This is possible with the use of viewport meta tag and CSS3 media queries.

Viewport meta tag and CSS3 media queries

A responsive website is primarily built with two components. The first component is the viewport meta tag (`http://developer.apple.com/library/ios/#documentation/AppleApplications/Reference/SafariWebContent/UsingtheViewport/UsingtheViewport.html`). This tag is placed inside the `<head>` tag and is used to control the scale of the web page.

For example, adding the following viewport meta tag with `initial-scale` set to `1` will allow the web page to be scaled by 100 percent of the viewport size upon opening it for the first time.

```
<meta name="viewport" content="width=device-width, initial-scale=1">
```

 Ian Yates (`http://www.snaptin.com/`) has exclusively covered the use of the viewport meta tag in his post at Webdesigntuts+ (`http://webdesign.tutsplus.com/tutorials/htmlcss-tutorials/quick-tip-dont-forget-the-viewport-meta-tag/`).

The second component is the CSS3 media queries (`http://www.w3.org/TR/css3-mediaqueries/`), which specify the styles for specific viewport sizes. For instance, the following code snippet shows how we can hide images when the viewport size is between 321 px and 480 px:

Downloading the example code

You can download the example code files for all Packt books you have purchased from your account at `http://www.packtpub.com`. If you purchased this book elsewhere, you can visit `http://www.packtpub.com/support` and register to have the files e-mailed directly to you.

```
@media screen and (min-width: 321px) and (max-width: 480px) {
    img { display: none; }
}
```

The SmashingMagazine website (`http://www.smashingmagazine.com/`) is a good example to illustrate how responsive web design is executed; the following screenshot shows how it is displayed in two different viewports. Note how the search button text changes from **Search** to **Go!** in the smaller viewport size.

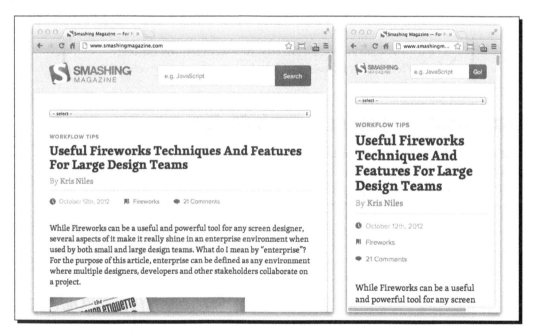

The website `http://www.barackobama.com/` is also a good example of a responsive website:

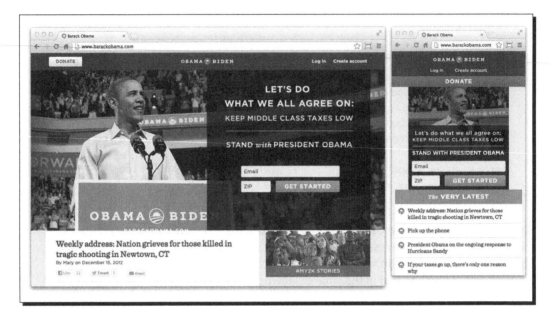

 For more inspiration on responsive websites, you can visit `http://mediaqueri.es/`.

Limitations of responsive web design

At this point, RWD is not quite perfect; there are several issues to be resolved, including making the image responsive. The current practice for making the image responsive is to scale it to fit the viewport with `max-width: 100%`, or possibly to hide it with `display: none` when the image is not needed.

The problem with this practice is that it only alters the image presentation on the surface, while the actual image on the HTML document remains unaffected. This means that the users will still be downloading the same image resolution with a larger size regardless of their device and viewport size, which will result in wasted bandwidth consumption and could also hurt website performance particularly for mobile users.

From the preceding screenshot, you can see that the image is resized responsively to the viewport size, however the image resolution and size has not changed.

Responsive image with picture element

Recently at **World Wide Web Consortium (W3C)**, a group called Responsive Image Community Group (`http://www.w3.org/community/respimg/`) proposed a new element called `<picture>` to address the situation. This `<picture>` element enables the delivery of a proper image size and resolution based on a particular situation. It is worth noting that this new element, at the time of the writing, is still in the draft stage, which means that it is yet to be implemented by the browser vendors. This specification may be changed or even removed in the future.

Now let's take a look at the following code example:

```
<picture alt="responsive images">
  <source src=big.jpg media="min-width:768px">
  <source src=medium.jpg media="min-width:320px">
  <source src=small.jpg>
  <img src=medium.jpg alt="responsive images">
</picture>
```

The preceding code snippet will deliver the `big.jpg` image file with a high resolution and probably a wider width only when the viewport is at a minimum of `768px`, while the `medium.jpg` image file with a lower resolution and file size will be delivered when the viewport is at a minimum of `320px`.

Then, when these conditions are not met, the smaller image `small.jpg` will be delivered. Lastly, at the bottom of the list, we also have one more image with the `<img>` element; this is additionally used to provide a backup image for the browsers that do not support the `<picture>` element.

Let's see how we can use this element in a situation where scaling down the image is not the suitable approach.

Let's say we have an extremely wide image like a panorama and want to use it as the header on our website. When we'll view this image on the desktop's screen, we most likely won't find any issue, and the image will be clearly viewable.

However, when we view this image in a smaller viewport, the image is now too narrow and the people in the image are barely viewable. If there is text in the image, reading it will be hard on the eyes.

In this case, it will be more sensible to display different image proportions rather than scaling down the image, and using the `<picture>` element, this scenario would become possible. The following screenshot shows how we replace the image with the cropped version for a smaller viewport. Do you notice the difference? The people in this image look closer.

 If you can't wait to implement this ideal responsive image as demonstrated with the `<picture>` element, you can use a server-side solution with Adaptive Image (`http://adaptive-images.com/`) created by Matt Wilcox (`http://mattwilcox.net/`); technically, it will detect the user's screen size and deliver the appropriate image based on the screen size.

Or you can also use a polyfill (`http://remysharp.com/2010/10/08/what-is-a-polyfill/`) to mimic the `<picture>` element functionality (`https://github.com/scottjehl/picturefill`).

Furthermore, at .NET magazine (`http://www.netmagazine.com/`), James Young (`http://offroadcode.com/`) has done a survey for his fellow designers to understand the common problems with responsive web design and how to avoid them. You can head over to the post at `http://www.netmagazine.com/features/top-responsive-web-design-problems-and-how-avoid-them` and join the discussion.

Learn more about HTML5 and CSS3

Having a fairly good understanding of basic HTML5 or CSS3 would be really helpful to follow the projects in this book. You shouldn't be afraid though, as we will explain what the code in this book does, in order for you to understand what is happening in each step of building responsive websites.

Additionally, Packt Publishing has published a book covering these subjects in depth; it is called *Responsive Web Design with HTML5 and CSS3* (http://www.packtpub.com/responsive-web-design-with-html-5-and-css3/book) written by Ben Frain (http://www.benfrain.com/). It is a good book for you to start digging into HTML5, CSS3, and responsive web design.

Just in case this is your first time of dealing with HTML5 and CSS3, there are many good resources to help you understand these subjects in more detail.

- *Dive Into HTML5* (http://diveintohtml5.info/)
- *Write Semantic Markup* (http://css-tricks.com/video-screencasts/100-lets-write-semantic-markup/)
- *Sitepoint CSS Reference* (http://reference.sitepoint.com/css)
- *Using CSS3* (http://css-tricks.com/video-screencasts/57-using-css3/)

Or else, if you are still puzzled with what RWD is all about, at this point we suggest you watch the screencast *Braindump on Responsive Web Design* (http://css-tricks.com/video-screencasts/102-braindump-on-responsive-web-design/) by Chris Coyier that is available at CSS Tricks (http://css-tricks.com/).

Introduction to RWD frameworks

Certainly, whether you are a beginner designer or an expert, creating a responsive website from the ground up can be convoluted. This is probably because of some indispensable technical issues in RWD, such as determining the proper number of columns in the grid and calculating the percentage of the width for each column, determining the correct breakpoint, and other technicalities that usually appear in the development stage. So in this book, rather than creating responsive web design from scratch, we will be using frameworks to help us out and make things a little easier in the process.

Many threads regarding the issues of creating responsive websites are open on StackOverflow:

♦ *CSS Responsive grid 1px gap issue* (`http://stackoverflow.com/questions/12797183/css-responsive-grid-1px-gap-issue`)

♦ *@media queries - one rule overrides another?* (`http://stackoverflow.com/questions/12822984/media-queries-one-rule-overrides-another`)

Why use frameworks?

Following are a few reasons why using a framework is considered a good option:

♦ **Time saver**: If done right, using a framework could obviously save a lot of time. A framework generally comes with predefined styles and rules, such as the width of the gird, the button styles, font sizes, form styles, CSS reset, and other aspects to build a website. So, we don't have to repeat the same process from the beginning but simply follow the instructions to apply the styles and structure the markup. Bootstrap, for example, has been equipped with grid styles (`http://twitter.github.com/bootstrap/scaffolding.html`), **basic styles** (`http://twitter.github.com/bootstrap/base-css.html`), and user interface styles (`http://twitter.github.com/bootstrap/components.html`).

♦ **Community and extension**: A popular framework will most likely have an active community that extends the framework functionality. jQuery UI Bootstrap is perhaps a good example in this case; it is a theme for jQuery UI that matches the look and feel of the Bootstrap original theme. Also, Skeleton, one of the frameworks we are going to use in this book, has been extended to the WordPress theme (`http://themes.simplethemes.com/skeleton/`) and to Drupal (`http://demo.drupalizing.com/?theme=skeleton`).

◆ **Cross browser compatibility**: This task of assuring how the web page is displayed on different browsers is a really painful one. With a framework, we can minimize this hurdle, since the developers, most likely, have done this job before the framework is released publicly. Foundation is a good example in this case. It has been tested in the iOS, Android, and Windows Phone 7 browsers (`http://foundation.zurb.com/docs/support.html`).

◆ **Documentation**: A good framework also comes with documentation. The documentation will be very helpful when we are working with a team, to get members on the same page and make them follow the standard code-writing convention. Bootstrap (`http://twitter.github.com/bootstrap/getting-started.html`) and Foundation (`http://foundation.zurb.com/docs/index.php`), for example, have provided detailed documentation on how to use the framework.

There are actually many responsive frameworks to choose from, but as we mentioned, the ones that we are going to use in this book are Skeleton, Bootstrap, and Foundation. Let's take a look.

Skeleton

Skeleton (`http://www.getskeleton.com/`) is a minimal responsive framework; if you have been working with the 960.gs framework (`http://960.gs/`), Skeleton should immediately look familiar. Skeleton is 960 pixels wide with 16 columns in its basic grid; the only difference is that the grid is now responsive by integrating the CSS3 media queries.

> In case this is the first time you have heard about 960.gs or Grid System, you can follow the screencast tutorial by Jeffrey Way available at `http://learncss.tutsplus.com/lesson/css-frameworks/`. In this screencast, he shows how Grid System works and also guides you to create a website with 960.gs. It is a good place to start with Grid System.

Bootstrap

Bootstrap (`http://twitter.github.com/bootstrap/`) was originally built by Mark Otto (`http://markdotto.com`) and only intended for internal use in Twitter. Short story: Bootstrap was then launched as a free software for public. In it's early development, the responsive feature was not yet included; it was then added in Version 2 in response to the increasing demand for RWD.

Bootstrap has a lot more added features as compared to Skeleton. It is packed with styled user interface components of commonly-used interfaces on a website, such as buttons, navigation, pagination, and forms. Beyond that, Bootstrap is also powered with some custom jQuery plugins, such as a tab, carousel, popover, and modal box.

To get started with Bootstrap, you can follow the tutorial series (`http://www.youtube.com/playlist?list=PLA615C8C2E86B555E`) by David Cochran (`https://twitter.com/davidcochran`). He has thoroughly explained from the basics to utilizing the plugins in this series.

 Bootstrap has been associated with Twitter so far, but since the author has departed from Twitter and Bootstrap itself has grown beyond expectation, Bootstrap is likely to get separated from the Twitter brand as well (`http://blog.getbootstrap.com/2012/09/29/onward/`).

Foundation

Foundation (`http://foundation.zurb.com`) was built by a team at ZURB (`http://www.zurb.com/about/`), a product design agency based in California. Similar to Bootstrap, Foundation is beyond just a responsive CSS framework; it is equipped with predefined styles for a common web user interface, such as buttons (`http://foundation.zurb.com/docs/components/buttons.html`), navigation (`http://foundation.zurb.com/docs/components/top-bar.html`), and forms. In addition to this, it has also been powered up with some jQuery plugins. A few high-profile brands, such as Pixar (`http://projection.pixar.com/`) and National Geographic Channel (`http://globalcloset.education.nationalgeographic.com/`), have built their website on top of this framework.

Who is using these frameworks?

Now, apart from the two high-profile names we have mentioned in the preceding section, it will be nice to see what other brands and websites have been doing with these frameworks to get inspired. Let's take a look.

Hivemind

Hivemind is a design firm based in Wisconsin. Their website (`www.ourhivemind.com`) has been built using Skeleton. As befits the Skeleton framework, their website is very neat, simple, and well structured. The following screenshot shows how it responds in different viewport sizes:

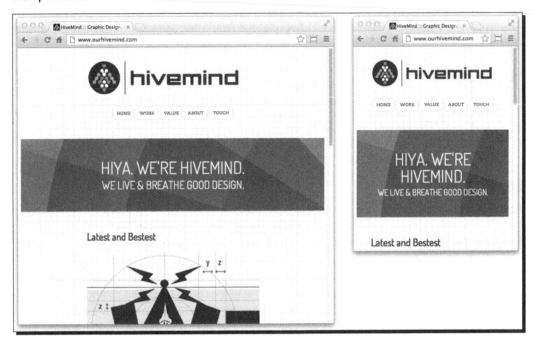

Living.is

Living.is (`http://living.is`) is a social sharing website for living room stuff, ideas, and inspiration, such as sofas, chairs, and shelves. Their website has been built using Bootstrap. If you have been examining the Bootstrap UI components yourself, you will immediately recognize this from the button styles. The following screenshot shows how the Living.is page is displayed in the large viewport size:

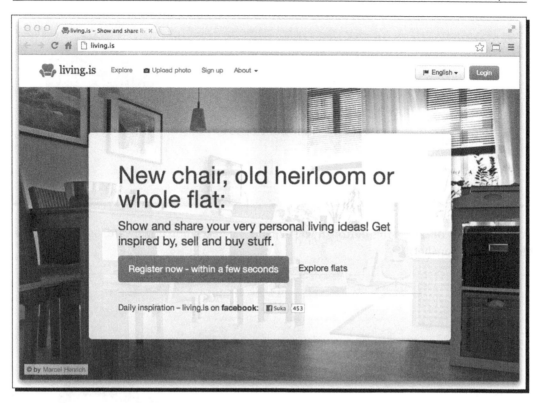

When viewed in a smaller viewport, the menu navigation is concatenated, turning into a navigation button with three stripes, as shown in the following screenshot. This approach now seems to be a popular practice, and this type of button is generally agreed to be a navigation button; the new Google Chrome website has also applied this button approach in their new release.

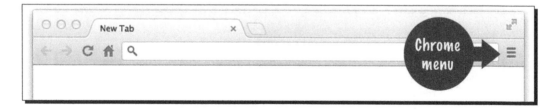

When we click or tap on this button, it will expand the navigation downward, as shown in the following screenshot:

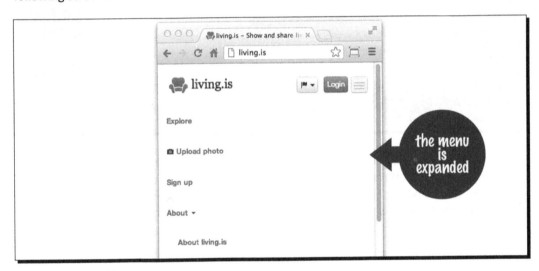

 To get more inspiration from websites that are built with Bootstrap, you can visit `http://builtwithbootstrap.com/`. However, the websites listed are not all responsive.

Swizzle

Swizzle (`www.getswizzle.com`) is an online service and design studio based in Canada. Their website is built on Foundation. The following screenshot shows how it is displayed in the large viewport size:

Swizzle used a different way to deliver their navigation in a smaller viewport. Rather than expanding the menu as Bootstrap does, Swizzle replaces the menu navigation with a **MENU** link that refers to the navigation at the footer.

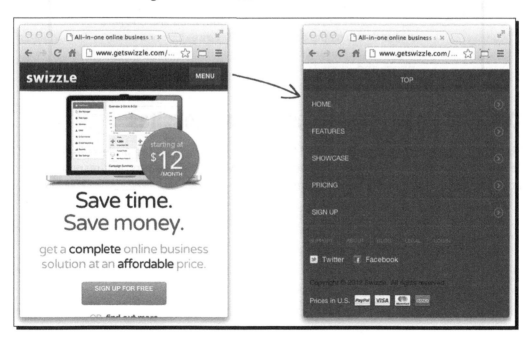

The cons

Using a framework also comes with its own problems. The most common problems found when adopting a framework are as follows:

- **Excessive codes**: Since a framework is likely to be used widely, it needs to cover every design scenario, and so it also comes with extra styles that you might not need for your website. Surely, you can sort out the styles and remove them, but this process, depending on the framework, could take a lot of time and could also be a painful task.

- **Learning curve**: The first time, it is likely that you will need to spend some time to learn how the framework works, including examining the CSS classes, the ID, and the names, and structuring HTML properly. But, this probably will only happen in your first try and won't be an issue once you are familiar with the framework.

- **Less flexibility**: A framework comes with almost everything set up, including the grid width, button styles, and border radius, and follows the standard of its developers. If things don't work the way we want them to, changing it could take a lot of time, and if it is not done properly, it could ruin all other code structure.

> Other designers may also have particular issues regarding using a framework; you can further follow the discussion on this matter at `http://stackoverflow.com/questions/203069/what-is-the-best-css-framework-and-are-they-worth-the-effort`. The *CSS Trick* forum has also opened a similar thread on this topic at `http://css-tricks.com/forums/discussion/11904/css-frameworks-the-pros-and-cons/p1`.

Tools required to build responsive websites

There are several tools that we will need to build our website from the projects in this book. To build a responsive website, we will need web browsers, code editors, and responsive bookmarklets for responsive design testing.

Web browsers

We will need a browser to develop and view the result of our responsive websites. I personally suggest using Firefox (`http://www.mozilla.org/firefox`) or Chrome (`www.google.com/chrome`) as the main browser for development. You can also install Opera (`http://www.opera.com/`), Safari (`http://www.apple.com/safari/`), and Internet Explorer (`http://windows.microsoft.com/en-US/internet-explorer/downloads/ie-9/worldwide-languages`) to make sure that the website is displayed properly in those browsers.

Code editors

A code editor is an indispensable equipment for developing a website. Technically, you can use any code editor as long as it can highlight the code properly.

My personal preference and the one that I have used in this book is Sublime Text 2. This editor is available for Windows, OS X, and Linux. It can be downloaded for free from `http://www.sublimetext.com/2` for the purpose of evaluating with an unlimited period of time. However, it sometimes bugs you to purchase the license.

If you are annoyed with this behavior, consider purchasing the license or using other options for code editors.

OS	Code editors
Windows	Notepad++ (`http://notepad-plus-plus.org/`)
	WebMatrix (`http://www.microsoft.com/web/webmatrix/`)
	TextPad (`http://www.textpad.com/`)
OS X	TextWrangler (`http://www.barebones.com/products/textwrangler/`)
	MacVim (`http://code.google.com/p/macvim/`)
	Brackets (`http://brackets.io/`)
Linux	Gedit (`http://projects.gnome.org/gedit/`)
	Geany (`http://www.geany.org/`)
	BlueFish (`http://bluefish.openoffice.nl/index.html`)

Responsive bookmarklets

It is better to test responsive websites on real mobile devices, such as iPhones and iPads, Android or Windows Phones, and Nokia devices. But if the budget doesn't allow, you can use a tool called a responsive bookmarklet.

It is a sort of emulator tool to test responsive design by resizing the dimension of the viewable area in the browsers. There are a lot of responsive bookmarklets available today. Here are some of them:

- RWD demonstration (`http://jamus.co.uk/demos/rwd-demonstrations/`)
- Screenqueri.es (`http://screenqueri.es/`)
- Responsinator (`http://www.responsinator.com/`)
- ResposnivePX (`http://responsivepx.com/`)
- Resizer (`http://codebomber.com/jquery/resizer/`)
- Screen Fly (`http://quirktools.com/screenfly/`)
- Adobe Edge Inspect (`http://html.adobe.com/edge/inspect/`)

If you are using Firefox 15 or higher (`http://www.mozilla.org/en-US/firefox/new/`), you can use its built-in feature called **Responsive Design View**. This can be accessed by navigating to **Tools | Web Developer | Responsive Design View**.

You can also have similar functionality in Chrome with an extension called **Window Resizer** (`https://chrome.google.com/webstore/detail/kkelicaakdanhinjdeammmilcgefonfh`). Safari users can use Resize Safari (`http://resizesafari.com/`).

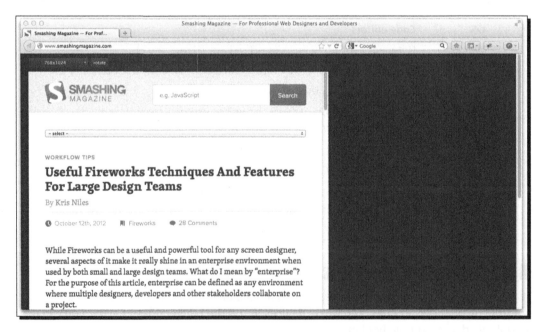

A brief introduction to CSS preprocessors

There is one more thing to be discussed before we begin work on the projects in this book, namely CSS preprocessors. What are they? Simply put, a CSS preprocessor extends CSS capabilities. By using CSS preprocessor, we can compose CSS in more dynamic ways. CSS preprocessors allow us to use variables and functions, as in programming languages such as JavaScript and PHP, to compose the styles.

There are several CSS preprocessors available today, such as LESS (`http://lesscss.org/`), Sass (`http://sass-lang.com/`), and Stylus (`http://learnboost.github.com/stylus/`). However, in this book we will limit our discussion to LESS and Sass. As these are some CSS preprocessors that have been adopted in the responsive frameworks, we are going to use them in this book. Bootstrap utilizes LESS as its style foundation, while Sass is adopted in Foundation.

CSS preprocessor compiler tool

CSS preprocessors, such as LESS and Sass, are written in a language that browsers do not recognize. So we have to compile it into standard CSS form, which browsers can read, and deliver the result with a compiler. There are several CSS preprocessor compilers available today; following is the list:

Tool	Supported languages	OS	Price
Less.js (`http://lesscss.org`) and Node.js (`http://nodejs.org/`)	LESS	Windows, OS X, and Linux	Free
WinLESS (`http://winless.org/`)	LESS	Windows	Free
LESS.app (`http://incident57.com/less/`)	LESS	OS X	Free
Simpless (`http://wearekiss.com/simpless`)	LESS	Windows and OS X	Free
ScoutApp (`http://mhs.github.com/scout-app/`)	Sass	Windows and OS X	Free
ChrunchApp (`http://crunchapp.net`)	LESS	Windows, OS X, and Linux	Free
Terminal or Command Prompt	LESS and Sass	Windows, OS X, and Linux	Free

Tool	Supported languages	OS	Price
CompassApp (`http://compass.handlino.com`)	Sass	Windows, OS X, and Lunix	$ 10
Codekit (`http://incident57.com/codekit/`)	LESS, Sass, and Stylus	OS X	$ 25

The tools listed in the preceding table, particularly with **GUI (graphical user interface)**, are sufficiently easy to use. However, we will discuss this matter further when we are about to work on the projects. For now, let's see how we write styles in the LESS and Sass languages.

LESS

LESS is a JavaScript-based CSS preprocessor created by Alexis Sellier (`http://alexissellier.com/`). As mentioned, LESS is used by Bootstrap, one of the frameworks we will explore in this book. LESS allows us to compose styles with some programming features. The following are the ones that we may use frequently in the projects in this book:

- Nesting rules
- Variables
- Mixins
- Parametric mixins
- Operation

Nesting rules

Traditionally in CSS, when we need to apply styles for the elements, let's say, under the `nav` element with `class` set to `nav-primary`, we may write the styles in the following way:

```
.nav-primary {
  background-color: #000;
  width: 100%;
}
.nav-primary ul {
  padding: 0;
  margin: 0;
}
```

```
.nav-primary li {
  display: inline;
}
.nav-primary li a {
  text-decoration: none;
  color: #fff;
}
.nav-primary li a:hover {
  color: #ccc;
}
```

As you can see, we repeat the parent class selector, `.nav-primary`, each time we apply styles to the elements under it. With LESS, we can eliminate this repetition and slightly simplify this code by nesting the CSS rules, as shown in the following example:

```
.nav-primary {
  background-color: #000;
  width: 100%;
  ul {
    padding: 0;
    margin: 0;
  }
  li {
    display: inline;
    a {
      text-decoration: none;
      color: #fff;
      &:hover {
        color: #ccc;
      }
    }
  }
}
```

There is nothing fancy in this code; we have just written it in a different way by nesting the style rules.

Variables

Variables in LESS, as in all programming languages, are useful to store a constant or fixed value; this value can later be assigned to the entire stylesheet. In LESS, a variable is defined with the @ sign and followed by the variable name. The variable name can be a combination of numbers and letters. In the following example, we will create some LESS variables to store colors and assign the variables to the style rules to pass the value.

```
@primaryColor: #234fb4;
@secondaryColor: #ffb400;
a {
  color: @primaryColor;
}
button {
  background-color: @secondaryColor;
}
```

In regular CSS, the preceding code will be compiled into the following code snippet:

```
a {
  color: #234fb4;
}
button {
  background-color: #ffb400;
}
```

Using variables, however, is not limited to storing colors, as we demonstrated in the preceding example. We can use variables for any other types of values, such as the radius size, for example:

```
@smallRadius: 3px;
```

One of the advantages of using variables is that in case we need to make changes, we don't have to search through the entire stylesheet; we can simply change the variable. This certainly is a time saver.

Mixins

Mixins are like variables; however, rather than storing a single value, we are able to store a set of CSS properties. These properties can later be inherited by other CSS rulesets. Let's say we have the following CSS rules in the stylesheet:

```
.links {
  -webkit-border-radius: 3px;
  -mox-border-radius: 3px;
  border-radius: 3px;
  text-decoration: none;
```

```
    font-weight: bold;
}
.box {
  -webkit-border-radius: 3px;
  -mox-border-radius: 3px;
  border-radius: 3px;
  position: absolute;
  top: 0;
  left: 0;
}
.button {
  -webkit-border-radius: 3px;
  -mox-border-radius: 3px;
  border-radius: 3px;

}
```

In the preceding example, we declared `border-radius` in three different CSS rules. Each time we declare it in other CSS rules, we need to include the prefixes to cover earlier browsers. In LESS, we are able to concatenate this border radius and have it inherited by other CSS rules in the stylesheet using mixins. A mixin in LESS is simply defined with a class selector; in this example, we will create a mixin called `.border-radius`:

```
.border-radius {
  -webkit-border-radius: 3px;
  -moz-border-radius: 3px;
  border-radius: 3px;
}
```

Then, we can insert `.border-radius` to the other CSS rules to pass the same properties, as follows:

```
.links {
  .border-radius;
  text-decoration: none;
  font-weight: bold;
}
.box {
  .border-radius;
  position: absolute;
  top: 0;
  left: 0;
}
.button {
  .border-radius;
}
```

Parametric mixins

Furthermore, we can also extend mixins into a function, or in this case it is officially called **parametric mixins**. This method allows us to add an argument or variables and make the mixins configurable. Let's see the example discussed here.

We are still using our previous example. But this time, we will not assign a fixed value; instead we will replace it with a variable, as follows:

```less
.border-radius(@radius) {
  -webkit-border-radius: @radius;
  -moz-border-radius: @radius;
  border-radius: @radius;
}
```

Now, we can insert this mixin into other CSS rulesets and assign a different value for each.

```less
a {
  .border-radius(3px);
  text-decoration: none;
  font-weight: bold;
}
div {
  .border-radius(10px);
  position: absolute;
  top: 0;
  left: 0;
}
button {
  .border-radius(12px);
}
```

When we compile it into a regular CSS, the preceding LESS code will be converted into the following:

```css
a {
  -webkit-border-radius: 3px;
  -moz-border-radius: 3px;
  border-radius: 3px;
  text-decoration: none;
  font-weight: bold;
}
div {
  -webkit-border-radius: 10px;
  -moz-border-radius: 10px;
```

```
    border-radius: 10px;
    position: absolute;
    top: 0;
    left: 0;
}
button {
    -webkit-border-radius: 12px;
    -moz-border-radius: 12px;
    border-radius: 12px;
}
```

As you can see from the examples, this practice could be very helpful when we are working with the CSS3 properties, eliminating the requirement to write the vendor prefixes repeatedly.

> There is a LESS extension called LESS Elements (http://lesselements.com/) that contains a number of very useful CSS3 mixins. If you plan to work with LESS, you can simply use this extension to cut your workload. Furthermore, SitePoint has also covered the use of LESS mixins in depth in a post available at http://www.sitepoint.com/a-comprehensive-introduction-to-less-mixins/.

Operations

We can also perform simple Math operations with LESS, such as addition, subtraction, division, and multiplication. Operations could be pretty useful in certain circumstances. In this example, we are going to calculate the proper width of the box by subtracting the padding from it so that it can fit in the parent container.

First, we will define the variable for the padding with the @padding variable:

```
@padding: 10px;
```

Then, we specify the box width and subtract the @padding variable from it:

```
.box {
    padding: @padding;
    width: 500px - (@padding * 2);
}
```

Remember that padding takes any two sides of the box, either the right and left or top and bottom, so as you can see that is why we multiply the @padding variable in the width property by 2. Finally when we compile this LESS operation into regular CSS, the example code will look like the following:

```
.box {
  padding: 10px;
  width: 480px;
}
```

In other cases, we can do the same to the height property, as follows:

```
.box {
  padding: @padding;
  width: 500px - (@padding * 2);
  height: 500px - (@padding * 2);
}
```

Sass (Syntactically Awesome Stylesheets)

Sass is a Ruby-based CSS preprocessor created by Hampton Catlin (http://www.hamptoncatlin.com/), Nathan Weizenbaum (http://nex-3.com/), and Chris Eppstein (http://chriseppstein.github.com/). Like LESS, Sass has the ability to add variables, mixins, and nesting rules, albeit with a few differences. Let's take a look at each of these.

Variables

In Sass, a variable is defined with the $ sign. Similar to our example with LESS, here we define the primary color in the Sass variable with $primaryColor and assign it to the style rules, as follows:

```
$primaryColor: #234fb4;
a {
  color: $primary;
}
button {
  background-color: $primaryColor;
}
```

Similar to LESS, when we compile this code into a regular CSS, it gets converted into the following:

```
a {
  color: #234fb4;
}
button {
  background-color: #234fb4;
}
```

Mixins

In Sass, a mixin is defined a bit differently than a mixin in LESS. The mixin in Sass is defined with the @mixin directive. Similar to our previous example in the LESS section, here we define a mixin for the border radius and then assign it to other rulesets with the @include directive, as follows:

```
@mixin border-radius {
  -webkit-border-radius: 3px;
  -moz-border-radius: 3px;
  border-radius: 3px;
}
a {
  @include border-radius;
  text-decoration: none;
  font-weight: bold;
}
div {
  @include border-radius;
  position: absolute;
  top: 0;
  left: 0;
}
button {
  @include border-radius;
}
```

Furthermore, we can also add an argument to a Sass mixin like we did in LESS, as follows:

```
@mixin border-radius($radius) {
  -webkit-border-radius: $radius;
  -moz-border-radius: $radius;
  border-radius: $radius;
}
```

Nested rules

Sass also allows us to nest rules, but it takes this method a step further. In Sass, we are able to nest individual property. Let me show you how to do it. First of all, in regular CSS, we sometimes define styles with their individual properties, as follows:

```
div {
    border-color: #ccc;
    border-style: solid;
    border-width: 5px;
}
```

In Sass, we can nest this rule in the following way:

```
div {
    border: {
        color: #ccc;
        style: solid;
        width: 5px;
    }
}
```

Selector inheritance

Selector inheritance sounds like a mixin, but it actually acts in a different way. While a mixin will inherit the styles to the other assigned selectors, selector inheritance will eventually group the selectors that share certain styles.

In the following example, we have the .button class, which defines the general styles of a button:

```
.button {
    padding: 5px 15px;
    border-radius: 3px;
    color: #fff;
    border: 1px solid #000;
}
```

We also have two types of buttons, namely *Submit* and *Reset*, and each will be defined with the .submit and .reset classes respectively. These buttons will have the general styles, except the background color, to convey their different purposes. In that case, we can utilize selector inheritance by assigning the .button class to other rulesets with the @extend directive, as shown in the following code snippet:

```
.submit {
    @extend .button;
    background-color: green;
}
```

```
.reset {
  @extend .button;
  background-color: red;
}
```

Unlike the mixin methods that simply duplicate the CSS properties to the assigned rulesets, selector inheritance, as mentioned, will group the selectors that share the same styles from the .button class. The preceding code will be converted into the following when compiled with regular CSS:

```
.button, .submit, .reset {
  padding: 5px 15px;
  border-radius: 3px;
  color: #fff;
  border: 1px solid #000;
}
.submit {
  background-color: green;
}
.reset {
  background-color: red;
}
```

Learning more on CSS preprocessors

Unfortunately, we are not going to dive further into the CSS preprocessor as it is actually beyond the scope of this book, and there are many other CSS preprocessor features that are yet to be covered. So if you are interested in the subject, I recommend you refer to the following sections.

Learning LESS

To learn more about LESS, refer to the documentations mentioned as follows:

◆ There is no better place to start learning about LESS than its official documentation (http://lesscss.org/#docs). It covers anything you'll need to know about LESS right from the basics. There are also some examples provided to implement the languages.

◆ Over at Webdesigntuts+, Daniel Pataki (http://danielpataki.com) has covered LESS in depth and even provided more useful examples (webdesign.tutsplus.com/tutorials/htmlcss-tutorials/get-into-less-the-programmable-stylesheet-language/).

- Oliver Caldwell has shared some tips in his post (`http://oli.me.uk/2012/02/25/getting-started-with-less.html`) on getting started with LESS. He has shown how to run the LESS compiler with Node.js (`http://nodejs.org/`) and NPM (`https://npmjs.org/`).

Learning Sass

To learn more about Saas, refer to the documentations mentioned as follows:

- The Sass documentation is immensely comprehensive, but for me it often works as a good sleep inducer. So, I would suggest *The Sass Way* (`thesassway.com`) for you to start with Sass from the beginning.

- If you prefer video rather than a text-based tutorial, you can follow the Youtube playlist (`www.youtube.com/playlist?list=PL2CB1F80266E986EA`) from LevelUpTuts that covers Sass thoroughly.

- Chris Coyier has shared a screencast on the introduction to Sass and Compass (`http://css-tricks.com/video-screencasts/88-intro-to-compass-sass/`) at CSS Tricks.

For further reference, Jonathan Verrecchia (`http://verekia.com`) has shared a good presentation slide about CSS preprocessors (`http://www.slideshare.net/verekia/deep-dive-into-css-preprocessors`). A few points that he has discussed in this presentation include CSS's limitations, a comparison between LESS, Sass, and Stylus, and also which CSS preprocessors you should use.

What are we going to create in this book?

Now that we have discussed the theoretical parts to equip us for our journey in this book, at this point you may be wondering exactly what are we going to create.

In this book, we are going to create three responsive websites with the frameworks that we have discussed earlier in this chapter, each with its own challenges. We most likely will also utilize the CSS preprocessor that comes with the frameworks, specifically with Bootstrap and Foundation.

Our first project in this book will be to create a responsive portfolio website with Skeleton. In the second project, we are going to create a responsive website for a product launch with Bootstrap. Lastly, we are going to build a responsive website with Foundation, for business purposes.

Summary

We discussed a lot of things in this first chapter. To sum up, we discussed the following:

- The basic elements for creating a responsive website, viewport meta tag, and CSS3 media queries, as well as seeing a few well-executed responsive websites
- The limitations of serving responsive images and also the current and future solution for this issue
- The frameworks that we are going to use to build websites in this book, namely Skeleton, Bootstrap, and Foundation
- CSS preprocessors to compose the styles for the websites LESS and Sass, as well as learning a few of their languages

In the next chapter, we will start our first project. We are going to create a responsive portfolio website using Skeleton.

2
Constructing a Responsive Portfolio Page with Skeleton

In our previous chapter, we discussed responsive web design and had a first look at the frameworks that make it possible for us to create a responsive website more quickly.

In this chapter, we will create a simple responsive portfolio website with Skeleton. So, if you are a creative person who wants to showcase your own work on your own website, this could be a perfect chapter to work through.

To sum it up, here is what we will focus on in this chapter:

- ◆ Digging into the Skeleton components
- ◆ Utilizing the Skeleton components
- ◆ Setting up a project with Skeleton
- ◆ Preparing the project assets
- ◆ Constructing a website with HTML5

So, let's get started.

Getting started with Skeleton

As mentioned in the previous chapter, one of the disadvantages of using a framework is the learning curve; we need to spend some time to learn how to use the framework, particularly if this is the first time using it. So, before we build our responsive portfolio website with Skeleton, it is a good idea to unpack and take a look at what is included in Skeleton.

Time for action – creating a working directory and getting Skeleton

Perform the following steps for creating a working directory and getting Skeleton:

1. First, create a folder named portfolio. This should be our working directory for the responsive portfolio website.

2. Under this portfolio folder, create two folders named html and psd.

3. Now it is time to get Skeleton. So, let's go to the Skeleton website (www. getskeleton.com).

4. Go to the **Download** section and download the Skeleton package. At the time of writing, the latest version of Skeleton is Version 1.2.

5. Save the downloaded file in the html folder.

6. This downloaded file is in the tar.gz format. Let's extract it to retrieve the files inside the downloaded file.

7. After extracting, you should find two new folders named stylesheet and images, and an HTML document named index.html. This is optional, but we can now safely remove the .tar.gz file.

8. Lastly, from the **Download** section on www.getskeleton.com, download the Skeleton PSD template, save it in the psd folder, and unpack it.

What just happened?

We have just created a working directory. We have also downloaded the Skeleton package as well as the PSD template, and placed it in the appropriate folder to work on this project.

What is included in Skeleton?

Compared to other frameworks that we have mentioned in this book, Skeleton is the simplest. It is not overstuffed with heavy styles or additional components, such as jQuery plugins, which we may not need for the website. Skeleton comes only with an `index.html` file, a few stylesheets containing the style rules, a few images, and a PSD template. Let's have a look at each of these.

Starter HTML document

Skeleton comes with a starter HTML template named `index.html`, so we don't have to worry about writing the basic HTML document. The author of Skeleton has added the essential elements in this template, including the parts discussed in the following sections.

The viewport meta tag

The viewport meta tag in this HTML starter template is set to `1` for both `initial-scale` and `maximum-scale`, as shown in the following code snippet:

```
<meta name="viewport" content="width=device-width, initial-scale=1,
maximum-scale=1">
```

As we mentioned in the first chapter, setting `initial-scale` to `1` will set the web page to be 100 percent of the viewport size, when we open the web page for the first time.

However, one thing that should be noted when setting `maximum-scale` to `1` is that it will prevent the zooming ability. Thus, it is suggested to ensure that the users, later on, can clearly see the content, text, or images, without zooming the web page.

HTML5 Shim

Since we will be using the HTML5 elements in our document, we need to include the HTML5 Shim JavaScript Library so that Internet Explorer 8 and its earlier versions recognize the new elements from HTML5.

HTML5 Shim, by default, has also been included in the Skeleton starter HTML document; you should find the following line inside the `<head>` section:

```
<!--[if lt IE 9]>
<script src="http://html5shim.googlecode.com/svn/trunk/html5.js"></
script>
<![endif]-->
```

The preceding HTML5 Shim script is wrapped within the conditional comment tag that is designated for Internet Explorer. The comment `<!--[if lt IE 9]>` stated "if less than Internet Explorer 9", which means the script within will only apply to Internet Explorer 8 and its earlier versions where new HTML5 elements are not recognized. Other browsers will simply ignore this comment tag.

 You can read a post by Paul Irish (`http://paulirish.com/2011/the-history-of-the-html5-shiv/`) for the history behind HTML5 Shim and about how it was invented and developed.

Responsive Grid

Skeleton is equipped with Responsive Grid to quickly build responsive layout. The Skeleton's grid system is 960 px wide and is made up from sixteen columns of grid that are defined in a very logical naming system.

The columns are defined with the `.columns` class coupled with the respective column numbers `.one`, `.two`, `.three`, `.four`, and so on, to define the column width. These classes can be found in the `skeleton.css` file. The following code snippet shows the definitions of the column numbers and column width in the stylesheet:

```
.container .one.column,
.container .one.columns { width: 40px; }
.container .two.columns { width: 100px; }
.container .three.columns { width: 160px; }
.container .four.columns { width: 220px; }
.container .five.columns { width: 280px; }
.container .six.columns { width: 340px; }
.container .seven.columns { width: 400px; }
.container .eight.columns { width: 460px; }
.container .nine.columns { width: 520px; }
.container .ten.columns { width: 580px; }
.container .eleven.columns { width: 640px; }
.container .twelve.columns { width: 700px; }
.container .thirteen.columns { width: 760px; }
.container .fourteen.columns { width: 820px; }
.container .fifteen.columns { width: 880px; }
.container .sixteen.columns { width: 940px; }
```

If you are not familiar with this practice or you don't know how it works, take a look at the following example.

In this example, we have three `div` elements; one of those is for the container. Inside this container, we will have a `div` element to contain a main area and an `aside` element to contain the sidebar area. The following code snippet shows how our markup looks in the code editor:

```
<div>
  <div>
    <h3>Main Content</h3>
    <p>Lorem ipsum dolor sit amet, consectetur adipiscing elit.
    Aenean consequat porttitor elementum. Mauris pulvinar semper
    lobortis. […]</p>
  </div>
  <aside>
    <h3>Sidebar</h3>
    <p>Lorem ipsum dolor sit amet, consectetur adipiscing elit.
    Aenean consequat porttitor elementum. Mauris pulvinar semper
    lobortis.[…]</p>
  </aside>
</div>
```

Since all the styling rules for the columns are predefined, we simply need to add the appropriate classes into these elements, as follows:

```
<div class="container">
  <div class="ten columns">
    <h3>Main Content</h3>
    <p>Lorem ipsum dolor sit amet, consectetur adipiscing elit.
    Aenean consequat porttitor elementum. Mauris pulvinar semper
    lobortis. […] </p>
  </div>
  <aside class="six columns">
    <h3>Sidebar</h3>
    <p>Lorem ipsum dolor sit amet, consectetur adipiscing elit.
    Aenean consequat porttitor elementum. Mauris pulvinar semper
    lobortis. […]</p>
  </aside>
</div>
```

Then, if we view the document in the browser, we will see something as shown in the following screenshot:

Yes, it's that simple. But just to remember, in Skeleton, the columns should be nested inside an element with the `.container` class, otherwise the column styles will not be applied.

Clearing styles

The column's elements are defined by using the CSS float property definition, which causes the column's parent element to collapse. To solve it, Skeleton provides special classes; we can use either the `.row` class or the `.clearfix` class to clear things around the columns. The following code snippet shows the clearing styles' definitions, which can be found in `skeleton.css`:

```
.container:after { content: "\0020"; display: block; height: 0; clear:
both; visibility: hidden; }
.clearfix:before, .clearfix:after,
.row:before,
.row:after { content: '\0020'; display: block; overflow: hidden;
visibility: hidden; width: 0; height: 0; }
.row:after,
.clearfix:after { clear: both; }
.row, .clearfix { zoom: 1; }
.clear { clear: both; display: block; overflow: hidden; visibility:
hidden; width: 0; height: 0; }
```

On the Smashing Magazine website, Louis Lazaris has thoroughly discussed the CSS float property and how it affects the elements around it in the post available at `http://coding.smashingmagazine.com/2009/10/19/the-mystery-of-css-float-property/`.

Media queries

Skeleton has provided CSS3 media queries to apply specific style rules for standard viewport size and also making the grid responsive. For example, the following media query will specify the styles for 959 px viewport size and less:

```
@media only screen and (max-width: 959px) {
    …
}
```

Remember that Skeleton is a 960 grid-based framework, which means the maximum width of the web page would only be 960 px. So when the viewport is 959 px wide or less, in other words, smaller than the base size, the styles under this media query will be applied. The same idea also applies to the other defined media queries for example:

```
/* Tablet Portrait size to standard 960 (devices and browsers) */
@media only screen and (min-width: 768px) and (max-width: 959px) { }
/* All Mobile Sizes (devices and browser) */
@media only screen and (max-width: 767px) { }
/* Mobile Landscape Size to Tablet Portrait (devices and browsers) */
@media only screen and (min-width: 480px) and (max-width: 767px) { }
/* Mobile Portrait Size to Mobile Landscape Size (devices and browsers) */
@media only screen and (max-width: 479px) { }
```

These media query definitions can be found in the `skeleton.css` and `layout.css` stylesheet.

Referring to our previous example, the web page is already responsive, as the column classes and the styles are predefined under the media queries in the `skeleton.css` stylesheet.

Thus, when we view it in a much smaller viewport with—in this example it as 320 px—we will get the result as shown in the following screenshot:

Typography styles

Typography styles have a key role in making a website readable. While the browsers have default styles for typography, Skeleton provides an improvement in this area for some elements, including headings, paragraphs, and pull-quotes. In Skeleton, these typography styles are available in the `base.css` stylesheet.

Button styles

Skeleton provides basic styles for buttons, which are applied by adding the `.button` class to some elements, such as the `<button>` or `<a>` elements, as shown in the following code snippet:

```
<button class="button" type="submit">Button Element</button>
<a href="#" class="button">Anchor Tag</a>
```

The result of the preceding code snippet is rendered, as shown in the following screenshot:

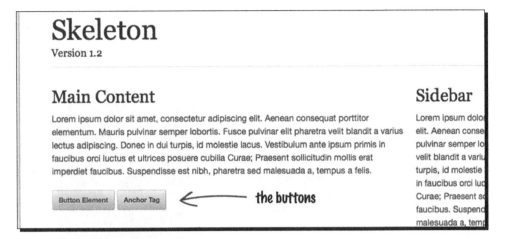

Form styles

Styling form elements can be complicated. But, Skeleton simplifies the process with its default styles. We simply need to structure the markup properly, without adding any special classes, as shown in the following code snippet:

```html
<form>
  <label for="name">Name</label>
  <input type="text" id="name">
  <label for="message">Message</label>
  <textarea id="message"></textarea>
  <button type="submit">Submit Form</button>
</form>
```

In the browsers, we will get the result as shown in the following screenshot:

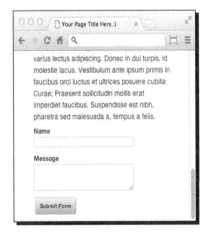

Apple icon devices

Skeleton comes with favicon and iOS icons, which we can easily replace with our own custom icons, if needed. The following screenshot shows these images in different sizes for different devices and resolutions:

The first one, which is the smallest, is the icon for iPhone. The second one, which is bigger than the first one, is to serve the iPad, while the biggest one will be displayed for Apple devices with higher resolution Retina Display.

 You can read the documentation available at Apple Dev Center (`http://developer.apple.com/library/safari/` `#documentation/AppleApplications/Reference/` `SafariWebContent/ConfiguringWebApplications/` `ConfiguringWebApplications.html#//apple_ref/doc/` `uid/TP40002051-CH3-SW3`) for more details on the use of these icons.

Photoshop template

We have downloaded a PSD template earlier in this chapter. This template contains only one extra layer. **Layer** is a semi-transparent overlay showing the 16 columns of the grid, as shown in the following screenshot:

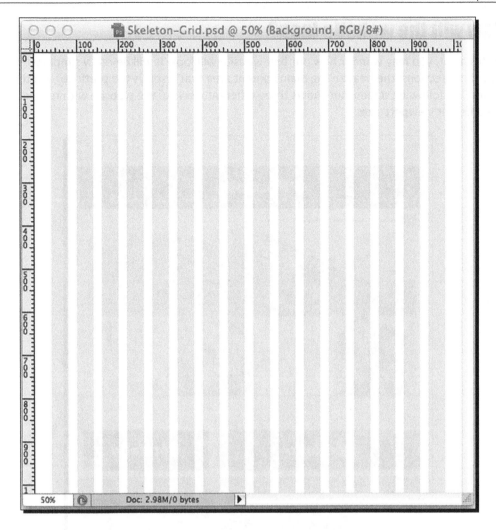

This grid is useful as a visual helper to design the website. So later on, when we translate the design into a web document, we will know the appropriate grid number for the translated elements.

How will the website look?

At this point, you may wonder how our first website will look. It will be really simple with only three sections: the header, the main content area that displays the portfolio, and the footer. The following screenshot shows three different views of the website with respect to the different viewport sizes:

Website navigation

Our website's navigation will be somewhat unusual; rather than being used to move between pages, it will be used to sort the portfolio. We have several categories of portfolios: they are **Illustration**, **Poster Design**, **Typography**, and **Packaging**. The following screenshot shows the result of selecting the **Illustration** category:

Thumbnail hover effect

We will also add a fancy effect to make our website more attractive. When we hover over one of the portfolio thumbnails, the description of that portfolio will be revealed. The following screenshot shows this effect:

Setting up the Skeleton document

Now, it is time to set up the Skeleton document. It is important to note that when we are working on a framework, it is best not to alter the codes in the core files, which are the original files from the downloaded package. If we change these files, it may make our website less maintainable, and our changes may be overwritten if the framework is upgraded later. Thus we need to add a CSS file for our own.

Time for action – adding an extra CSS file

Perform the following steps for adding an extra CSS file:

1. Go to our working directory, `portfolio`.

2. Then go to the `stylesheets` folder and create a new file.

3. Rename this new file as `styles.css`.

4. Open the `index.html` file.

5. Add the following lines inside the `<head>` tag, right after the default Skeleton styles `base.css`, `skeleton.css`, and `layout.css`:

```
<link rel="stylesheet" href="stylesheets/base.css">
<link rel="stylesheet" href="stylesheets/skeleton.css">
<link rel="stylesheet" href="stylesheets/layout.css">
<link rel="stylesheet" href="stylesheets/styles.css">
```

What just happened?

We have just created a new stylesheet named `styles.css`, which we will be using for our own styles apart from the default Skeleton styles. Then, we called this stylesheet in our HTML document so that the styles within this stylesheet show their effect.

The reason we added this stylesheet after the other stylesheet links is because we want our styles to take place over the other style definitions.

 You can read about CSS Specificity at
`http://coding.smashingmagazine.com/2007/07/27/`
`css-specificity-things-you-should-know/`.

Adding custom fonts

Earlier we were limited to fonts that were installed on a given user's machine, which meant that the only practical fonts were those with a broad installed base, such as Arial, Times, and Georgia. Today, we are able to embed font families for websites apart from the ones in the user's machine.

If you look at our design's header section, you can see that the main Porfolio heading uses an uncommon font—in this case, Alfa Slab One.

There are several options for embedding fonts. For this website we will use Google Web Fonts. In Google Web Fonts, we can find various font types that are allowed to be embedded on websites for free.

Time for action – embedding Google Web Fonts

Perform the following steps for embedding Google Web Fonts:

1. First, go to the Google Web Font website (`http://www.google.com/webfonts`).

2. Find a **Search** box and type `Alfa Slab One`; this is the name of the font that we are going to use for the website logo.

3. Click on the **Quick-use** link, as shown in the following screenshot:

This will direct you to a page that contains some additional information about this font, including how to embed it on a web page.

4. There are three ways to embed a Google font: using the standard way, using the @ import rule, or using JavaScript.

For this website, we will use the standard way. So, let's copy the following line:

```
<link href='http://fonts.googleapis.com/css?family=Alfa+Slab+One'
rel='stylesheet' type='text/css'>
```

5. Open index.html and paste the preceding line inside the <head> section directly above the links to other stylesheets, as follows:

```
<link href='http://fonts.googleapis.com/css?family=Alfa+Slab+One'
rel='stylesheet' type='text/css'>
<link rel="stylesheet" href="stylesheets/base.css">
<link rel="stylesheet" href="stylesheets/skeleton.css">
<link rel="stylesheet" href="stylesheets/layout.css">
<link rel="stylesheet" href="stylesheets/styles.css">
```

What just happened?

We have just embedded a new font family in our HTML document from Google Web Fonts.

 Alternatively, you can use the @font-face rule to embed the font. Font Squirrel provides a handy tool to generate the @font-face rule (http://www.fontsquirrel.com/fontface/generator). Before embedding the fonts, be sure you agree to the End-users License Agreement of the fonts.

Preparing the images

Since we will be working on a portfolio website, we obviously need some portfolio images to display. I would like to thank two of my artist friends, Ferina Berliani (http://nantokaa.tumblr.com/) and Arif Bahari (http://www.ariefbahari.com) for letting me use their artwork, and the following images show some of their works that we will be using in this book.

You can use your own images as long as they are sized to a 480 px by 480 px square; you can either use Photoshop or any other image editor of your choice to do so. Then put your images inside the `images` folder under the working directory and name them using this convention: `image-1.jpg`, `image-2.jpg`, `image-3.jpg`, and so on. We have a total of 12 image thumbnails:

Social media icons

In addition, we will place three social media icons in our footer area: one each for Facebook, Twitter, and Dribbble, as shown in the following screenshot:

In the default state, the icons are displayed in grey and then when we hover over these icons, the platform's main brand color will be displayed, such as Facebook's blue and Dribbble's pink. These icons have been provided along with this book.

However, you can substitute with any social media icons that are available on the Internet for free. Just make sure that it is also available in 48 px by 48 px size. These social icons usually come separately. Thus, we will need to concatenate them into one sprite file.

Time for action – sprite images

In the following steps, we will turn these icons into sprite images with a free CSS Sprite Generator Tool (`http://spritegen.website-performance.org/`):

1. Given the icons proper names, such as `twitter.png` and `twitter-hover.png`, as shown in the following screenshot:

   This naming convention also applies to other icons. You don't have to limit yourself to our example; you can provide more than three icons. After all the images are prepared, add these icons to a ZIP file.

2. Go to the CSS Generator Tool website (`http://spritegen.website-performance.org/`).

3. Upload the ZIP file that we created in Step 2.

4. Under the **Sprite Output Options** section, enter `10` in the **Horizontal Offset** and **Vertical Offset** fields to set them to 10 px:

5. Then, click on the **Create Sprite Image & CSS** button, as shown in the following screenshot:

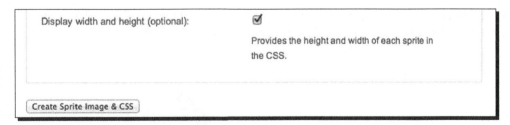

   This will generate the sprite image as well as the CSS rule to display it.

6. Download the image and save it under the `images` folder in our working directory.

7. Copy the CSS snippet into our `style.css` file. It should resemble the following code snippet:

```
.sprite-dribbble-hover{ background-position: 0 0; width: 48px;
height: 48px; }
.sprite-dribbble{ background-position: 0 -58px; width: 48px;
height: 48px; }
.sprite-facebook-hover{ background-position: 0 -116px; width:
48px; height: 48px; }
.sprite-facebook{ background-position: 0 -174px; width: 48px;
height: 48px; }
.sprite-twitter-hover{ background-position: 0 -232px; width: 48px;
height: 48px; }
.sprite-twitter{ background-position: 0 -290px; width: 48px;
height: 48px; }
```

What just happened?

We concatenated the social media icons into one file. We will display these icons on our website using the CSS rule that we have generated. This practice is known as **CSS Sprite**.

Alternatively, you can also follow a screencast by Chris Coyier available at CSS Tricks to create a sprite image in Photoshop (`http://css-tricks.com/video-screencasts/43-how-to-use-css-sprites/`), and as an addition, you can also follow a screencast by Lynda on how to create a sprite grid to help you in positioning sprite images (`http://www.youtube.com/watch?v=Gq7XCMofxcQ`).

Or else, if you are not familiar with CSS Sprites, Dave Shea has discussed this method thoroughly at A List Apart (`http://www.alistapart.com/articles/sprites`).

Contact icons

Our footer will include contact information, such as name, phone number, and e-mail address, each with its own icon as illustrated in the following screenshot:

These icons have been provided along with the code files available with this book, but you can use other icons in 24 px by 24 px size, which are available on the Internet. Similarly, if the icons come separately, you need to concatenate them in one file and generate the CSS rules, as we have demonstrated in the preceding section.

HTML5 elements

HTML5 introduces many new elements and we will use some of them for this website, such as `<header>`, `<section>`, `<figure>`, `<figcaption>`, and `<footer>`.

Element	Discussion
`<header>`	This is used for defining the head of a section. The `<header>` element can be used for the website's header and also the head of other sections where it is reasonable to add it, such as the article's header.
`<footer>`	The `<footer>` element defines the end or the lowest part of a section. Like the `<header>` element, `<footer>` can also be used for the website's footer or the footer part of other sections.
`<section>`	`<section>` can somehow be confusing. But according to the specifications (`http://www.w3.org/html/wg/drafts/html/master/sections.html#the-section-element`), the `<section>` element represents a generic section of a document or application.
`<figure>`	The `<figure>` element is used to represent the document figure, such as an illustration or an image. It can be used with `<figcaption>` to add the caption, if needed.
`<figcaption>`	As mentioned, `<figcaption>` represents the caption of the document's figure. Thus, it should be used along with the `<figure>` element.

Now, let's add these elements to our document.

HTML5 custom data attributes

There are times when developers need to retrieve data within specific elements for further data processing. In the past, some developers used to rely on the `rel` or `class` attributes to store that data, but that way leads to breaking the validity of the document's structure.

To accommodate that situation, HTML5 introduced a new attribute called custom data attribute. We can use this attribute to embed custom data within an HTML element. This attribute is specified with `data-` and followed by the attribute name. For example, an online gaming website can list the top players and use data attributes to store their scores.

```
<ul id="top-players">
  <li class="player-name" data-score="98.9">John Doe</li>
  <li class="player-name" data-score="80.5">Someone Else</li>
  <li class="player-name" data-score="70.2">Friend Someone Else</li>
</ul>
```

It is worth noting that the custom data attribute should only be used when we do not find any applicable or more appropriate attribute for that data. Storing the scores in the `class` attribute as `class="98.9"` is definitely not an applicable approach.

For further reference on data attributes, you can head over to the following pages:

- A documentation on custom data attributes available at `http://www.w3.org/html/wg/drafts/html/master/elements.html`
- *All You Need to Know About the HTML5 Data Attribute* (`http://webdesign.tutsplus.com/tutorials/htmlcss-tutorials/all-you-need-to-know-about-the-html5-data-attribute/`)
- An article on HTML5 data attributes by John Resig (`http://ejohn.org/blog/html-5-data-attributes/`)

Time for action – structuring the HTML document

Perform the following steps for structuring the HTML document:

1. Open the `index.html` file in your working directory.

2. Remove anything present between the `<body>` and `</body>` tags and replace it with the following code snippet to establish the header section. Our website's header is wrapped within the HTML5 `<header>` element and it contains the site logo that is wrapped within a `<div>` element with a class of `logo`.

```
<header class="header">
  <div class="logo">
    <h1>Portfolio</h1>
  </div>
</header>
```

3. Then, put the following `<form>` element with a class of `container` and `clearfix` next to the `<header>` element that we just added. We use this `<div>` to contain the website content.

```
<form class="container clearfix"> </form>
```

The `<form>` element is essentially an element like a `<div>` element. We use `<form>` instead of `<div>` as we will use the HTML form elements `<input>` and `<label>` to construct the website navigation.

 You can head over to the article (`http://reference.sitepoint.com/html/elements-form`) from SitePoint to see the complete list of elements that are part of an HTML form.

4. Inside the `<form>` element for a container, we add the HTML structure for the website navigation. As we mentioned earlier, our website navigation is uncommon. We will use the radio button as an input type and each `<input>` element is assigned with a unique ID followed by their respective `<label>` element, as shown in the following code snippet:

```
<input class="nav-menu" id="all" type="radio" name="filter"
checked="checked"/>
<label for="all">All</label>

<input class="nav-menu" id="illustrations" type="radio"
name="filter"/>
<label for="illustrations">Illustration</label>

<input class="nav-menu" id="posters" type="radio" name="filter"/>
<label class="nav-menu" for="posters">Posters Design</label>

<input class="nav-menu" id="typography" type="radio"
name="filter"/>
<label for="typography">Typography</label>

<input class="nav-menu" id="packaging" type="radio"
name="filter"/>
<label for="packaging">Packaging</label>
```

5. Then add an HTML5 `<section>` element with a class of `portfolio` next to those `<input>` and `<label>` elements that we just added.

```
<section class="portfolio"></section>
```

This `<section>` element will be used to contain the portfolio, which includes the image thumbnails and the captions.

6. Inside this `<section>` element, we add the portfolio image thumbnails. Each image thumbnail is wrapped within the HTML5 `<figure>` element.

We have 12 image thumbnails and we will divide them into four columns. Skeleton has 16 columns of grid and 16 divided by four results in four columns. So, each `<figure>` element is assigned with classes of `four` and `columns` with two additional classes of `all` and its category name.

```
<figure class="four columns all poster">
  <img src="images/image-1.jpg" alt=
  "This is 1st portfolio thumbnail.">
</figure>
```

The classes of `four` and `columns` are assigned to apply the column styles from Skeleton, while the class of `all` will be used to select the `<figure>` element when we need to apply CSS rules to all `<figure>` elements. We will use the category name class to group the figures and also apply styles to the figures that share the same category.

We will also provide some text that describes the image with an `alt` attribute. This `alt` attribute is useful for the browser to show alternative information for the users, in case the image fails to load.

7. The image thumbnails are grouped into a category. We assign the category name with the `title` attribute in the `<figure>` element, as follows:

```
<figure class="four columns" title="poster">
  <img src="images/image-1.jpg">
</figure>
```

8. The image thumbnail will have a caption containing the portfolio's description. We will use the HTML5 `<figcaption>` element to contain the description text and place it inside the `<figure>` element, as follows:

```
<figure class="four columns all poster">
  <img src="images/image-1.jpg" alt=
  "This is 1st portfolio thumbnail.">
  <figcaption>
    <h4>Lorem Ipsum</h4>
    <p>Lorem ipsum dolor sit amet, consectetur adipiscing
    elit. Morbi molestie lobortis magna eget sagittis.</p>
  </figcaption>
</figure>
```

9. Then, we will add an HTML5 data attribute to `<figure>` to store the category name where the `<figure>` element is assigned and we simply name this attribute `data-category`.

```
<figure class="four columns all poster">
  <img src="images/image-1.jpg" alt=
  "This is 1st portfolio thumbnail.">
  <figcaption>
    <h4>Lorem Ipsum</h4>
    <p>Lorem ipsum dolor sit amet, consectetur adipiscing
    elit. Morbi molestie lobortis magna eget sagittis.</p>
  </figcaption>
</figure>
```

Now, let's add the rest of the image thumbnails, as follows.

```
<figure class="four columns all illustration" data-
category="illustration">
  <img src="images/image-2.jpg" alt=
  "This is 2nd portfolio thumbnail.">
  <figcaption>
    <h4>Lorem Ipsum</h4>
    <p>Lorem ipsum dolor sit amet, consectetur adipiscing
    elit. Morbi molestie lobortis magna eget sagittis.</p>
  </figcaption>
</figure>
<figure class="four columns all poster" data-category="poster">
  <img src="images/image-3.jpg" alt=
  "This is 3rd portfolio thumbnail.">
  <figcaption>
    <h4>Lorem Ipsum</h4>
    <p>Lorem ipsum dolor sit amet, consectetur adipiscing
    elit. Morbi molestie lobortis magna eget sagittis.</p>
  </figcaption>
</figure>
<figure class="four columns all typography" data-
category="typography">
  <img src="images/image-4.jpg" alt=
  "This is 4th portfolio thumbnail.">
  <figcaption>
    <h4>Lorem Ipsum</h4>
    <p>Lorem ipsum dolor sit amet, consectetur adipiscing
    elit. Morbi molestie lobortis magna eget sagittis.</p>
  </figcaption>
</figure>
<figure class="four columns all illustration" data-
category="illustration">
  <img src="images/image-5.jpg" alt=
  "This is 5th portfolio thumbnail.">
  <figcaption>
```

```
        <h4>Lorem Ipsum</h4>
        <p>Lorem ipsum dolor sit amet, consectetur adipiscing
        elit. Morbi molestie lobortis magna eget sagittis.</p>
      </figcaption>
    </figure>
    <figure class="four columns all poster" data-category="poster">
      <img src="images/image-6.jpg" alt=
      "This is 6th portfolio thumbnail.">
      <figcaption>
        <h4>Lorem Ipsum</h4>
        <p>Lorem ipsum dolor sit amet, consectetur adipiscing
        elit. Morbi molestie lobortis magna eget sagittis.</p>
      </figcaption>
    </figure>
    <figure class="four columns all illustration" data-
    category="illustration">
      <img src="images/image-7.jpg" alt=
      "This is 7th portfolio thumbnail.">
      <figcaption>
        <h4>Lorem Ipsum</h4>
        <p>Lorem ipsum dolor sit amet, consectetur adipiscing
        elit. Morbi molestie lobortis magna eget sagittis.</p>
      </figcaption>
    </figure>
    <figure class="four columns all typography " data-
    category="typography">
      <img src="images/image-8.jpg" alt=
      "This is 8th portfolio thumbnail.">
        <figcaption>
        <h4>Lorem Ipsum</h4>
        <p>Lorem ipsum dolor sit amet, consectetur adipiscing
        elit. Morbi molestie lobortis magna eget sagittis.</p>
      </figcaption>
    </figure>
    <figure class="four columns all package" data-category="package">
      <img src="images/image-9.jpg" alt=
      "This is 8th portfolio thumbnail.">
      <figcaption>
        <h4>Lorem Ipsum</h4>
        <p>Lorem ipsum dolor sit amet, consectetur adipiscing
        elit. Morbi molestie lobortis magna eget sagittis.</p>
      </figcaption>
    </figure>
    <figure class="four columns all poster" data-category="poster">
      <img src="images/image-10.jpg" alt=
      "This is 9th portfolio thumbnail.">
      <figcaption>
        <h4>Lorem Ipsum</h4>
        <p>Lorem ipsum dolor sit amet, consectetur adipiscing
        elit. Morbi molestie lobortis magna eget sagittis.</p>
```

```
        </figcaption>
    </figure>
    <figure class="four columns all package " data-category="package">
      <img src="images/image-11.jpg" alt=
      "This is 10th portfolio thumbnail.">
      <figcaption>
        <h4>Lorem Ipsum</h4>
        <p>Lorem ipsum dolor sit amet, consectetur adipiscing
        elit. Morbi molestie lobortis magna eget sagittis.</p>
      </figcaption>
    </figure>
    <figure class="four columns all illustration "
    title="illustration">
      <img src="images/image-12.jpg" alt=
      "This is 10th portfolio thumbnail.">
      <figcaption>
        <h4>Lorem Ipsum</h4>
        <p>Lorem ipsum dolor sit amet, consectetur adipiscing
        elit. Morbi molestie lobortis magna eget sagittis.</p>
      </figcaption>
    </figure>
```

10. Lastly, for the website footer area, add the following HTML5 `<footer>` element with the `container clearfix` class next to the `<div>` element defined for the container, which we just added in Step 3:

```
<footer class="container clearfix">
  <div class="contact">
    <ul>
      <li class="contact-name">John Doe</li>
      <li class="contact-phone">(+1) 1-234-5678-9</li>
      <li class="contact-email">me@johndoe.com</li>
    </ul>
  </div>
  <div class="social">
    <p class="copyright">Copyright John Doe 2012</p>
    <ul>
      <li class="social-dribbble">
      <a href="#">Dribbble</a></li>
      <li class="social-facebook">
      <a href="#">Facebook</a></li>
      <li class="social-twitter">
      <a href="#">Twitter</a></li>
    </ul>
  </div>
</footer>
```

What just happened?

We have just added the structure for the website to `index.html` using the HTML5 elements and establishing the website header, the image portfolio, and the website footer.

Summary

In this chapter, we started our first project and accomplished the following things:

- Unpacked the Skeleton package and walked through some of the components
- Learned how to use Skeleton responsive grid
- Set up a working directory as well as the project documents
- Prepared the project assets
- Structured the project document with HTML5 elements

Now that the project has been set up, we are going to make up and tweak the website's look with CSS3 in the next chapter.

3
Enhancing the Portfolio Website with CSS3

In the previous chapter, we wrote the HTML5 code for our portfolio website. In this chapter, we will start working on CSS3. We will start with some simple visual effects that have just been introduced in CSS3, such as drop shadows, text shadows, and rounded corners.

Then, we will also create a more advanced effect called the thumbnail hover effect, which was only achieved via JavaScript prior to the introduction of CSS3.

To sum up, here are the tasks we are going to perform in this chapter:

◆ Style the website, beginning from the header and navigation, then work through the content area, and finish with the footer with some new CSS3 properties

◆ Create a portfolio filter function with CSS3

◆ Create a thumbnail hover effect with CSS3 Transforms and Transitions

◆ Adjust website appearance for specific viewport sizes with CSS3 media queries

CSS box model

An HTML element that is categorized as a block-level element is essentially a box; it consists of the content, margin, padding, and borders that are specified through CSS, as illustrated in the following screenshot:

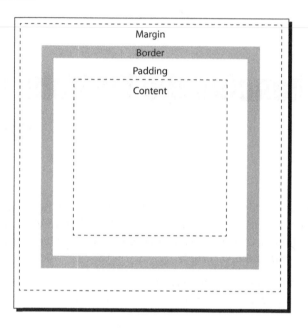

 You can further see the difference between block and inline elements as well as the list of the elements from the following references:

- *Block-level elements* (https://developer.mozilla.org/en-US/docs/HTML/Block-level_elements)
- *Inline elements* (https://developer.mozilla.org/en-US/docs/HTML/Inline_elements)

Prior to CSS3, we have been facing a constraint when specifying a box, for example, when we give an element a width and height of 100 pixels, as follows:

```
div {
  width: 100px;
  height: 100px;
}
```

The browser will simply translate it as a 100 pixel, square box.

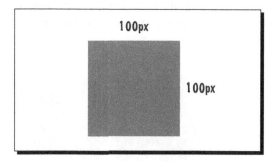

However, this is only true if the padding, margin, or border has not been added. Since the box has four sides, a padding of 10 pixels (`padding: 10px;`) will actually add 20 pixels to the width and height—10 pixels for each side.

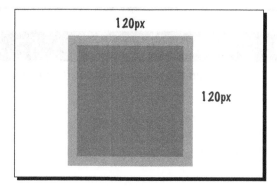

While it takes up space on the page, the element's margin is space reserved outside the element rather than part of the element itself; thus, if we give an element a background color, the margin area will not take on that color.

An introduction to the CSS3 box-sizing property

CSS3 offers additional options for controlling this box model with its `box-sizing` property.

Value	Description
content-box	This is the default value of the box model. This value specifies the padding and the border box's thickness outside the specified width and height of the content, as we have demonstrated in the preceding section.
border-box	This value does the opposite; it specifies the padding and the border box inside the specified width and height of the content.

Now let's get back to our example. This time we will set the `box-sizing` model to `border-box`. So the width and the height will remain 100 px, regardless of the padding and border length. The following illustration shows a comparison between the different outputs of the two values:

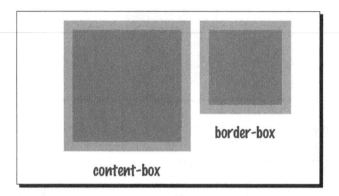

Time for action – specifying box-sizing

So, let's open up `style.css` and add the following rule at the beginning of the code:

```
* {
  -webkit-box-sizing: border-box;
  -moz-box-sizing: border-box;
  box-sizing: border-box;
}
```

What just happened?

We've used the CSS universal selector, the asterisk (*), to apply `border-box` sizing to all block-level elements so that we can easily set their final width and height.

 This simple tip was first promoted by Paul Irish, a lead developer of Modernizr and HTML5 Boilerplate. You can read his post (http://paulirish.com/2012/box-sizing-border-box-ftw/) for more details on this method.

CSS units of measurement

There are a number of units of measurement in CSS specification. In our website, we will mostly use the px, em, and percent units.

The pixel unit

px is an absolute length unit and probably the most popular unit used in web documents. px gives control of the exact length of an element. With reference to the documentation available at http://www.w3.org/TR/css3-values/#reference-pixel, a pixel in CSS refers to:

The visual angle of one pixel on a device with a pixel density of 96 DPI.

According to this explanation, 1 CSS pixel in a 96 DPI screen is equal to 1 device pixel. Thus, 10 px in CSS is simply equal to 10 px on the screen.

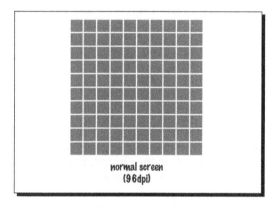

So for our project, we will use the px unit to measure box sizing.

The pixel unit in higher DPI screens

Today, with the increasing popularity of higher screen resolution, the preceding example is no longer relevant. The following screenshot is an example of a high-definition screen with a resolution of 192 DPI. An element that has a width and height of 10 px will actually take 20 device pixels.

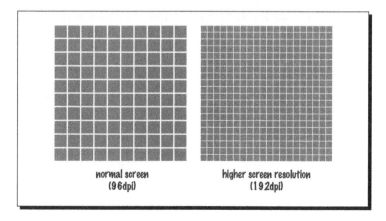

The element will still have the same physical size on the screen, only now there will be more device pixels embedded in the 1 CSS pixel.

> There are a lot of discussions regarding a pixel and its relation to screen resolution.
>
> ◆ Reda Lemeden, on his post, has covered the challenges and constraints on designing multiple device densities (`http://coding.smashingmagazine.com/2012/08/20/towards-retina-web/`)
> ◆ Scott Kellum, at A List Apart, has covered the pixel unit and its relevance towards multiple devices with different screen sizes and resolutions (`http://www.alistapart.com/articles/a-pixel-identity-crisis/`)

The em unit

em is a relative unit. It actually refers to the size of the capital alphabet "M" of the specified font. In CSS, `1em` technically refers to the device- or document-based font size. If there is a parent element with a specified font size in the em unit, the child elements nested within it will take the parent element's font size as the reference instead.

In our project, we will use em to specify the font size recommended by W3C (`http://www.w3.org/Style/Examples/007/units.en.html`).

Converting px to em

The default `body` font size in Skeleton is specified in `base.css` along with the default font family for `14px`, so this would be the base font size the em unit would refer to.

So, let's say we need to find the em number of `20px` with `14px` as the base font size. There is a tool to convert `px` to `em` (or vice versa) easily, called PXtoEM.com (`http://pxtoem.com/`). The following screenshot shows how we do the calculation with this tool:

Percent	Points		Pixels	EMs	Percent	Points		1. Enter a base pixel size
37.5%	5pt		6px	0.429em	42.9%	5pt		
43.8%	5pt		7px	0.500em	50.0%	5pt		**14** px
50.0%	6pt		8px	0.571em	57.1%	6pt		
56.3%	7pt		9px	0.643em	64.3%	7pt		**2. Convert**
62.5%	8pt		10px	0.714em	71.4%	8pt		PX to EM EM to PX
68.8%	8pt		11px	0.786em	78.6%	8pt		
75.0%	9pt		12px	0.857em	85.7%	9pt		**20** px or em
81.3%	10pt		13px	0.929em	92.9%	10pt		
87.5%	11pt		14px	1.000em	100.0%	11pt		Convert
93.8%	11pt		15px	1.071em	107.1%	11pt		
100.0%	12pt		16px	1.143em	114.3%	12pt		**3. Result**
106.3%	13pt		17px	1.214em	121.4%	13pt		1.429em
112.5%	14pt		18px	1.286em	128.6%	14pt		

As you can see from the preceding screenshot, with 14px as the base size, 20px is equal to 1.429em.

Calculating the em unit manually

Alternatively, we can convert px to em (and vice versa) using the formulas listed in the following table:

Unit conversion	Formula	Example
px to em	Size (px) / font size base (px)	20(px) / 14(px) = 1.429em (rounded)
em to px	Size (em) * font size base (px)	1.429(em) * 14(px) = 20px

Browser quirk for the em unit

Browsers translate the em unit a bit differently in some cases. In the example in the preceding section, 1.429em with 14px as the base size will turn into exactly 20px across all browsers (Google Chrome, Opera, Safari, and Firefox).

However, as we round up this number to be 1.4em by removing the last two numbers, the result will be slightly different. In Firefox and Opera, the resulting number will be 19.6px, while in Webkit browsers (Google Chrome and Safari), this number is rounded up to 20px.

You can inspect how the browsers translate em to px through **Developer Tool** under the the **Computed** panel.

```
► font-size: 20px;
► font-style: normal;
► font-variant: normal;
► font-weight: normal;
  height: 168px;
► line-height: 21px;
► margin-bottom: 20px;
► margin-left: 0px;
► margin-right: 0px;
► margin-top: 0px;
► padding-bottom: 0px;
► padding-left: 0px;
► padding-right: 0px;
► padding-top: 0px;
► vertical-align: baseline;
  width: 580px;
▼ Styles
element.style {

}
Matched CSS Rules
p {
    font-size: 1.4em;
}
```

```
▼ Text
  ► font-family          "HelveticaNeue","
  ► font-size            19.6px
  ► font-weight          400
  ► font-style           normal
  ► font-size-adjust     none
  ► color                #444444
  ► line-height          21px
  ► vertical-align       baseline
▼ Box Model
  ► margin-top           0px
  ► margin-right         0px
  ► margin-bottom        20px
p {
    font-size: 1.4em;
}
p {
```

The percent unit

Percent is a relative unit and works similarly to em; while em refers to font size, percent refers to the parent length regardless of the unit being used. For example, if the parent element has a height of 100px, 100% of its child element will be equal to 100px, 50% will be equal to 50px, and so on.

In our project, we will use the percent unit to measure box size, particularly when it is displayed in a smaller viewport size.

Setting font families

Skeleton sets Helvetica Neue and Helvetica as the default font in the body document; if these fonts are not available, it will apply Arial or the default sans-serif fonts to the user's machine.

We can find these fonts defined in the `base.css` stylesheet, as follows:

```css
body {
  background: #fff; font: 14px/21px "HelveticaNeue",
  "Helvetica Neue", Helvetica, Arial, sans-serif;
  color: #444;
  -webkit-font-smoothing: antialiased;
  -webkit-text-size-adjust: 100%;
}
```

The sans-serif fonts Georgia and Times New Roman are set for the Headings
(`h1`, `h2`, `h3`, and so on).

```css
h1, h2, h3, h4, h5, h6 {
  color: #181818; font-family: "Georgia", "Times New Roman", serif;
  font-weight: normal;
}
```

These fonts are well fitted to display paragraphs.

Lorem Ipsum

Lorem ipsum dolor sit amet, consectetur adipiscing elit. Aenean consequat porttitor
elementum. Mauris pulvinar semper lobortis. Fusce pulvinar elit pharetra velit blandit a
varius lectus adipiscing. Donec in dui turpis, id molestie lacus. Vestibulum ante ipsum
primis in faucibus orci luctus et ultrices posuere cubilia Curae; Praesent sollicitudin mollis
erat imperdiet faucibus. Suspendisse est nibh, pharetra sed malesuada a, tempus a felis.

Lorem ipsum dolor sit amet, consectetur adipiscing elit. Aenean consequat porttitor
elementum. Mauris pulvinar semper lobortis. Fusce pulvinar elit pharetra velit blandit a
varius lectus adipiscing.

Lorem ipsum dolor sit amet

Lorem ipsum dolor sit amet, consectetur adipiscing elit. Aenean consequat porttitor
elementum. Mauris pulvinar semper lobortis. Fusce pulvinar elit pharetra velit blandit a
varius lectus adipiscing. Donec in dui turpis, id molestie lacus. Vestibulum ante ipsum
primis in faucibus orci luctus et ultrices posuere cubilia Curae; Praesent sollicitudin mollis
erat imperdiet faucibus. Suspendisse est nibh, pharetra sed malesuada a, tempus a felis.

However, they don't quite work well in our example, as we will only have very less text on our website.

> ## Lorem Ipsum
>
> Lorem ipsum dolor sit amet, consectetur adipiscing elit. Morbi molestie lobortis magna eget sagittis.

So, we will set the Headings fonts in the same way we set the body fonts to maintain uniformity in the website.

Time for action – setting the Headings font family

Let's open `style.css` and place the following rule in the `box-sizing` declaration that we added in the *Time for action – specifying box-sizing* section:

```
h1, h2, h3, h4, h5, h6 {
    font-family: "HelveticaNeue", "Helvetica Neue", Helvetica, Arial,
    sans-serif;
    font-weight: bold;
}
```

What just happened?

We have just set the Headings font to be the same as the body fonts and set `font-weight` to `bold`.

 There is no exact definitive formula for pairing fonts; it is an art. But there are some general tips to follow to make it work. Ian Yates has shared a few tips on this subject over at Webdesigntuts+ (`http://webdesign.tutsplus.com/articles/typography-articles/a-beginners-guide-to-pairing-fonts/`).

Header styles

Now, it is time to add styles to the web sections. The header of our website is defined with the HTML5 `<header>` element and assigned with the `header` class. We also have a `<div>` element with the `logo` class that contains the website logo.

Time for action – adding the header styles

To add the header styles, perform the following steps:

1. In our `style.css` file, add the following CSS rule. This CSS rule will set the header's background color, padding, border, box shadow (we add it with the CSS3 `box-shadow` property), and margin bottom to set the distance between the header and the lower section.

```css
.header {
  padding: 22px 0;
  background-color: #3a3f43;
  margin-bottom: 14px;
  box-shadow: 0 1px 3px 0 rgba(0,0,0,0.3);
  border-bottom: 1px solid #181f25;
}
```

2. Then, add styles to the website logo's container. In the following CSS rule, add a CSS3 property `border-radius` to make the box's corners rounded:

```css
.logo {
  text-align: center;
  border-radius: 3px;
  background-color: #515558;
  width: 250px;
  padding: 5px 0;
  margin: 0 auto;
}
```

3. Now, add styles to the logo. Our website logo is simply text. We will assign a new font family "Alfa Slab One" to it, which we added with Google Web Font in *Chapter 2, Constructing a Responsive Portfolio Page with Skeleton*.

```css
.logo h1 {
  color: #fff;
  font-weight: normal;
  font-family: "Alfa Slab One", Arial, sans-serif;
  margin-bottom: 0;
}
```

What just happened?

We have just added styles to the header, including the background color, box shadow, and box styles (padding, margin, and border). We also assigned a new font family from Google Web Font, `"Alfa Slab One"`, to the website's logo. The following screenshot shows how our website will look at this point:

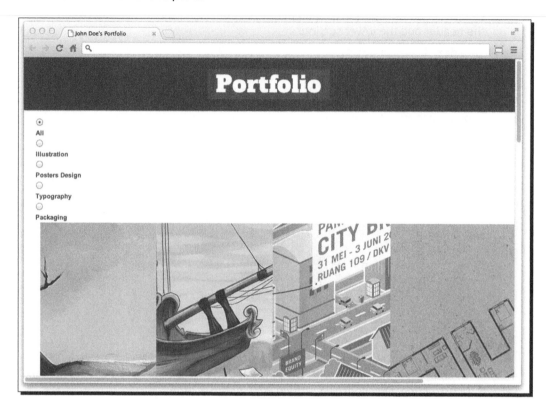

Using CSS selectors

In our project, we will use several CSS selectors to select an element within a particular structure. These selectors include the direct child selector, adjacent sibling selector, and general sibling selector. Let's have a look at these selectors one by one.

Direct child selector

CSS allows us to select the child elements nested inside a specific element (the parent element). You're probably familiar with how we select a child element through CSS; we firstly select the parent element (with its class, ID, or element type) followed by the child element we intend to select.

```css
.parent p {
  background-color: tomato;
}
```

The preceding code snippet selects every `<p>` element that is nested within an element with the class `parent`, without an exception.

But, there may be times when we only want to select the direct child of the parent. In other words, the grandchild elements of the parent shouldn't be affected. If that is the case, we can add a `>` notation in between to limit the selection to only the direct child of the parent, as follows:

```css
.parent > p {
  background-color: tomato;
}
```

Given the following HTML structure, the preceding CSS rule will only select the first and second paragraph.

```html
<div class="parent">
  <p> This is the 1st paragraph </p>
  <p> This is the 2st paragraph </p>
  <section>
    <h3>Section Title</h3>
    <p> This is the 3rd paragraph </p>
    <p> This is the 4th paragraph </p>
  </section>
</div>
```

This gives us the following result:

Adjacent sibling selector

The adjacent sibling selector is defined with a plus (+) notation. It selects the element that directly follows the previous element that was specified, for example, if we have a `<div>` element that is followed by a `<p>` element, as follows:

```
<div>This is the div element.</div>
<p>This is the 1st paragraph.</p>
<p>This is the 2nd paragraph.</p>
```

We target a `<p>` element that is directly after the `<div>` element and give it a background color of tomato, as follows:

```
div + p {
  background-color: tomato;
}
```

The previous example gives us the following result:

This is the div element.

This is the 1st paragraph.

This is the 2nd paragraph.

General sibling selector

The CSS general sibling selector is a new type of selector that's just been added in CSS3. This type of selector is declared with a ~ notation, as follows:

```
div ~ p {
  background-color: tomato;
}
```

And the result is the same as in the adjacent sibling selector, but instead of targeting only the first child, the general sibling selector will target every selected element that follows the previous element. So if we have the same HTML structure as in the adjacent sibling selector, the background color will affect all paragraph elements, as shown in the following screenshot:

This is the div element.

This is the 1st paragraph.

This is the 2nd paragraph.

Using CSS3 pseudo classes

We will discuss a few CSS3 pseudo classes. A pseudo class is used to select an element within a particular expression or condition. For example, `:hover` is a pseudo class; it applies CSS rules when we point the element with a mouse cursor.

In this project, we are going to use the following pseudo classes:

◆　`:checked`

◆　`:nth-child`

Let's have a look.

The CSS3 checked pseudo class

CSS3 has introduced a new pseudo class called `:checked`. This pseudo class selects an HTML element, either the checkbox or the radio input type, that is being checked or selected. In following code snippet, we select the radio input type with an ID of the type posters when it is checked.

```
#posters:checked {
/* style rules */
}
```

This pseudo class, `:checked`, is useful for selecting the selected radio input that we are using as website navigation. Similar to a traditional menu navigation that is built with an `<a>` element, we use `:hover` when the mouse cursor is over the element.

The CSS3 nth-child pseudo class

CSS3 has also introduced a new pseudo class named `:nth-child`. This pseudo class allows us to select elements in their specified sequence. To select the elements, `:nth-child` needs an argument. The argument can take either numbers or keywords (`odd` and `even`).

For example, the following code will select the third `<li>` element and set the background color:

```
li:nth-child(3) {
   background-color: tomato;
}
```

Given the following HTML structure, the preceding CSS rule will add background color to the `<li>` element in the middle:

```
<ul>
   <li>List 1</li>
   <li>List 2</li>
```

```
    <li>List 3</li>
    <li>List 4</li>
    <li>List 5</li>
</ul>
```

This is shown in the following screenshot:

- List 1
- List 2
- List 3
- List 4
- List 5

Using a keyword, either odd or even, is also allowed. Intuitively, the following code will apply background color to every <li> element that is in an odd sequence (first, third, fifth, and so on):

```
li:nth-child(odd) {
   background-color: tomato;
}
```

The :nth-child pseudo class also accepts a formula to select elements in a more specific sequence.

```
li:nth-child(2n+2) {
   background-color: tomato;
}
```

n in the formula is a variable, which takes numbers starting from 0, 1, 2, 3, and so on. So, the formula 2n+2 from the preceding example will select the <li> element in the order second, fourth, eighth, tenth, and so on.

To know further about how :nth-child works, you can refer to a post by Chris Coyier at CSS Tricks (http://css-tricks.com/how-nth-child-works/). He has also created a handy tool to test the formula with :nth-child (http://css-tricks.com/examples/nth-child-tester/).

Portfolio thumbnail and caption styles

Once we are done with the website header, we will start adding styles and laying out the portfolio images. We have 12 image thumbnails displaying the portfolio. Each image is wrapped within an HTML5 `<figure>` element and has a caption containing the thumbnail description that is wrapped within an HTML `<figcaption>` element.

Time for action – adding thumbnail and caption styles

To add a thumbnail and caption styles, perform the following steps:

1. Open `style.css`. First of all, we will provide a little distance at the top of the portfolio container by adding a margin:

    ```
    .portfolio {
      margin-top: 20px;
    }
    ```

2. We'll divide the images into four columns; each column will have `width` set to `240px`, which we got from the division *960px / 4 = 240px*. In addition to this, to make this number fit into the container, we also need to remove `margin-left` and `margin-right` that have been acquired from the `.columns` class in Skeleton.

    ```
    .portfolio .four.columns {
      width: 240px;
      margin-right: 0;
      margin-left: 0;
    }
    ```

3. Then we'll set the `position` mode for the `<figure>` element to `relative`, so the child element positions, such as `<img>` and `<figcaption>`, are positioned relative to this `<figure>` element. We also set the `overflow` area of the `<figure>` element to `hidden`.

    ```
    .portfolio > figure {
      position: relative;
      overflow: hidden;
    }
    ```

When setting `overflow` to `hidden` in the `<figure>` element, the element that flows over the `<figure>` element will be hidden. In our example, this area will be used to hide the `<figcaption>` element, as illustrated in the following screenshot:

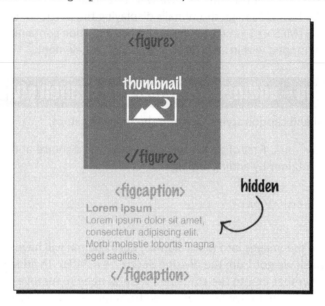

4. We will set the image's `max-width` to `100%` so the image fits inside its parent element (`figure`) regardless of how narrow it becomes.

```
.portoflio > figure img {
  max-width: 100%;
}
```

5. Furthermore, if we take a closer look at the image's thumbnail, we will find a little whitespace following the `<img>` element, which seems to be the nature of inline elements and, presumably, is also affected by its default vertical alignment (`http://www.impressivewebs.com/difference-block-inline-css/`).

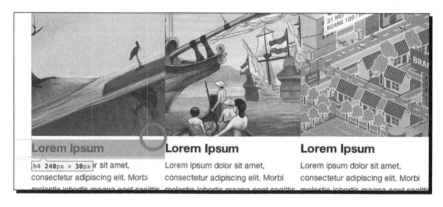

One of the solutions to remove this whitespace is to set `display` to `block`. So let's add `display: block` to the `<img>` element, as follows:

```
.portfolio > figure img {
  max-width: 100%;
  display: block;
}
```

Alternatively, to remove the whitespace, we can also set the `vertical-align` property to `top`.

6. Next, we will add styles for the thumbnail caption. The caption is wrapped within the HTML5 `<figcaption>` element. First, we will set the caption's `position` attribute to `absolute`.

```
.portfolio figcaption {
  position: absolute;
}
```

This will affect the parent's height and it will follow the child elements that are not set for the absolute position. At this point, the caption is hidden due to the position that is now overflowing from the `<figure>` area.

7. Then, we set the caption's height and width to `100%` so its dimensions (height and width) will always follow the parent, which in our case is the `<figure>` element.

```
.portfolio figcaption {
  position: absolute;
  width: 100%;
  height: 100%;
}
```

8. By setting the `<figcaption>` element's `position` attribute to `absolute`, we can freely reposition it to face any direction without affecting the surrounding elements. In this case, we set the caption's `left` and `top` position to `0`, as shown in the following code snippet:

```
.portfolio figcaption {
  position: absolute;
  width: 100%;
  height: 100%;

  left: 0;
  top: 0;
}
```

Since we have set the `<figure>` element's `position` attribute to `relative`, the caption's position is relative to the `<figure>` element (which is its parent), thereby resulting in the caption being on top of the image thumbnail, as shown in the following screenshot:

9. We then set the caption's background color. We set the background with the RGBA (Red, Green, Blue, and Alpha) color mode. Each color channel—Red, Green, and Blue—is specified with a number ranging from 0 to 255.

For example, setting 0 for each color channel (`rgba(0,0,0,1)`) will result in black color and is equal to `#000000` in the HEX color mode. Similarly, setting 255 for each color channel will result in white color; this is equal to `#ffffff` in the HEX color mode.

With RGBA, we can also adjust the color transparency through the Alpha channel. Values in the Alpha channel range from 0 to 1, where 0 is equal to 0% and 1 is equal to 100%. So in other words, 0.5 would be equal to 50%.

In the following rule, we set the background color to black and the transparency to 80%:

```
.portfolio figcaption {
  position: absolute;

  width: 100%;
  height: 100%;

  left: 0;
  top: 0;

  background-color: rgba(58,63,67,.8);
}
```

10. We add padding to set the distance between the caption text and the container's edge. In the following rule, we set `padding` to `10%`:

```
.portfolio figcaption {
  position: absolute;

  width: 100%;
  height: 100%;

  left: 0;
  top: 0;

  background-color: rgba(58,63,67,.8);

  padding: 10%;
}
```

As we have set the box sizing to `border-box` earlier, the caption size (height and width) remains `100%` regardless of the padding addition. The caption size still follows the parent size, which in our case is 240 px x 240 px.

11. Since the background color is dark, we need to set a lighter color for the caption text. In this case, we change the caption text color to white (`#fff`).

```
.portfolio figcaption h4 {
  color: #fff;
}
.portfolio figcaption p {
  color: #fff;
}
```

12. This is only a matter of preferences, but the text paragraph in the caption seems too big. So, we set the caption text paragraph to `1px` smaller than the base size. The base font size is `14px`, so `13px` is equal to `0.929em`.

```
.portfolio figcaption p {
  color: #fff;
  font-size: 0.87em;
}
```

What just happened?

We have just added style rules for the image thumbnail and the caption. At this stage, our portfolio section in the website appears as is shown in the following screenshot:

CSS3 2D Transformations

Over the last couple of years, several new CSS3 features have been released, including the CSS3 Transform (`http://www.w3.org/TR/css3-transforms/`). Using CSS3 Transform, we can translate, rotate, skew, and scale HTML elements.

The translate() function

The `translate()` function in CSS3 Transforms is used for moving elements relative to their original position. This function is declared with the following syntaxes:

- To move the element in the horizontal direction, we can write:

  ```
  transform: translateX(value);
  ```

- To move the element in the vertical direction, we can write:

  ```
  transform: translateY(value);
  ```

- Another way we can use the shorthand syntax is by combining the x and y values, as follows:

  ```
  transform: translate(x-value,y-value);
  ```

As you can see, the position of the element is specified with the x and y values, where x represents the horizontal coordinate and y represents the vertical coordinate. This principle relates to the Cartesian coordinate system (http://en.wikipedia.org/wiki/Cartesian_coordinate_system).

However, since the web page is read sequentially from top to bottom, the y coordinate is reversed; a negative y value specifies upward motion whereas a positive y value specifies downward motion.

Now let's say that we would like to move an element `100px` to the right. We can write this in the following way:

```
transform: translateX(100px)
```

Or we can specify it with the shorthand syntax, as follows:

```
transform: translate(100px,0)
```

Similarly, when we want to move it upward by `100px`, we can write this as follows:

```
transform: translateY(-100px)
```

Or we can also write this in the following way:

```
transform: translate(0,-100px)
```

In addition to this, to move the element diagonally, we'll specify both the x and the y coordinates, as follows:

```
transform: translate(100px,-100px)
```

The preceding declaration will move the element upward and to the right, as illustrated in the following screenshot:

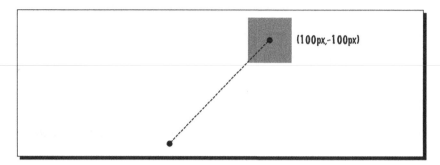

Vendor prefixes

The `translate()` function is supported in Google Chrome 4, Safari 3.1, Firefox 3.5, Internet Explorer 10, and Opera 10.5, though vendor prefixes are still required to make the transformations work on these browsers. So, the complete CSS rule to run a transformation is as follows:

```
-webkit-transform: translate(x,y); /* Webkit (eg. Chrome & Safari) */
-moz-transform: translate(x,y); /* Mozilla Firefox */
-ms-transform: translate(x,y); /* Internet Explorer */
-o-transform: translate(x,y); /* Opera */
transform: translate(x,y); /* Recommendation syntax from W3C */
```

The browsers will apply their specific prefix, for example, `-webkit-` will be implemented in WebKit-based browsers, such as Chrome and Safari, and ignore the other prefixes. Later, when the specification has been finalized and the browsers have fully applied it, the standard syntax from the W3C (`http://www.w3.org/`) is the one that will be applied.

So, it is a good idea to include all vendor prefixes for better browser compatibility.

In the above code snippet, we have to write five different lines that technically do the same thing to cover browser's capability. So if writing the vendor prefix manually seems to be a tedious task, there are several tools to help us deal with the vendor prefix.

Prefixr (`http://prefixr.com/index.php`) allows us to generate the vendor prefix quickly. If you are using Sublime Text 2, there is a package that allows you to run the prefix directly from the editor.

There is a JavaScript library called Prefix Free (`http://leaverou.github.com/prefixfree/`) that allows us to write the unprefixed syntax as it will append the needed vendor prefix on the fly.

CSS3 Transition

Another great addition in CSS3 is Transition. A CSS3 Transition allows us to change one CSS rule to another CSS rule gradually—rather than instantaneously—within a specific duration. A CSS3 Transition is defined with the following syntax (including the vendor prefix):

```
-webkit-transition: property duration timing-function delay; /* Webkit
(eg. Chrome & Safari) */
-moz-transition: property duration timing-function delay; /* Mozilla
Firefox */
-o-transition: property duration timing-function delay; /* Opera */
transition: property duration timing-function delay; /* Recommendation
syntax from W3C */
```

Currently, CSS3 Transition is supported in the Chrome 4, Firefox 4, Safari 3.1, Opera 10.5, and Internet Explorer 10.0 browsers (`http://caniuse.com/#feat=css-transitions`).

> Internet Explorer 9 does not support CSS3 Transition; this is why you do not see the `-ms-` prefix in the preceding syntax. But, Internet Explorer 10 will support CSS3 Transition without the prefix (`http://msdn.microsoft.com/en-us/library/ie/hh673535(v=vs.85).aspx`).

CSS3 Transition values

As you can see, four values have been specified in the syntax, namely `property`, `transition-duration`, `timing-function`, and `delay`. Let's peel them up one by one:

Value	Use
`property`	This value targets the CSS property to which the transition effect should be applied. The property could be `width`, `height`, `color`, `background`, and so on.
	But when this value is not explicitly specified, it will take `all` as the default value, which will apply the transition to all properties.
`transition-duration`	This value specifies the length of transition effect; this value is specified in milliseconds (ms) and seconds (s). For instance, `200ms` and `0.2s`.
`timing-function`	This value specifies the transition acceleration. There are five predefined acceleration types that we can use; they are `ease`, `ease-in`, `ease-out`, `ease-in-out`, and `linear`. You can see how these timing functions play in a post, at `http://www.css3.info/preview/css3-transitions/`.
`delay`	This value sets the delay time before the transition effect starts.

In the following code example, we have created a circle with a `div` element and we want to turn it into a rectangle when we hover over it.

```css
div {
  width: 200px;
 height: 200px;
  border-radius: 100px;
 border: 5px solid orange;
  background-color: tomato;
}
div:hover {
  border-radius: 0;
}
```

As mentioned earlier in the chapter, since we did not add the transition, the change will be instantaneous. Now, let's add the transition effect to `border-radius`, which is set to `200ms`, as follows:

```css
div {
/* the other rules, same as above*/

  -webkit-transition: border-radius 200ms;
  -moz-transition: border-radius 200ms;
  -o-transition: border-radius 200ms;
  transition: border-radius 200ms;
}
```

After that, the changes will take effect gradually and look more appealing, as illustrated in the following screenshot:

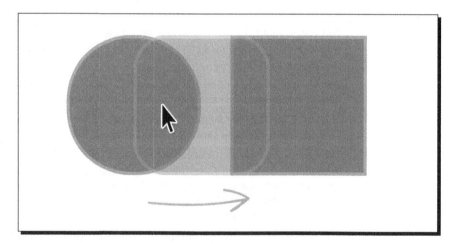

Time for action – creating a thumbnail hover effect

To create a thumbnail hover effect, perform the following steps:

1. Open `style.css`. Remember that we structure the caption with the HTML5 `<figcaption>` element. We have added several CSS rules in the previous steps, such as specifying the position, setting the width and height, setting the background color, changing the font color, and adding padding.

   This time, we will add CSS rules to create the hover effect. The idea here is that when we hover the thumbnail, the caption will gradually slide from a specific direction and cover the image.

   In the following CSS rule, we first move the caption to the right with CSS3 Transform:

   ```
   .portoflio figcaption {
     position: absolute;
     left: 0;
     top: 0;

   width: 100%;
     height: 100%;
     padding: 10%;

   background-color: rgba(58,63,67,.8);

     -webkit-transform: translateX(100%);
     -moz-transform: translateX(100%);
     -ms-transform: translateX(100%);
     -o-transform: translateX(100%);
     transform: translateX(100%);
   }
   ```

2. Then, we add the transition effect with CSS3 Transition. In the following rule, we set the transition for all the elements to `350ms`.

   ```
   .portoflio figcaption {
     position: absolute;
     left: 0;
     top: 0;

     width: 100%;
     height: 100%;
     padding: 10%;

     background-color: rgba(58,63,67,.8);
   ```

```
  -webkit-transform: translateX(100%);
  -moz-transform: translateX(100%);
  -ms-transform: translateX(100%);
  -o-transform: translateX(100%);
  transform: translateX(100%);

  -webkit-transition: all 350ms;
  -moz-transition: all 350ms;
  -o-transition: all 350ms;
  transition: all 350ms;
}
```

3. Lastly, we add the hover state. In the hover state, we set the caption to its original position by specifying 0 for translateX.

```
.container figure:hover figcaption {
  -webkit-transform: translateX(0);
  -moz-transform: translateX(0);
  -ms-transform: translateX(0);
  -o-transform: translateX(0);
  transform: translateX(0);
}
```

What just happened?

Well, there are several things that happen in this code. First, we reposition the caption with the transform property to 100% of the parent's width to the right, as follows:

```
  -webkit-transform: translateX(100%);
  -moz-transform: translateX(100%);
  -ms-transform: translateX(100%);
  -o-transform: translateX(100%);
  transform: translateX(100%);
```

At this point, the caption will not be visible because we have set the outer area of the figure element to be hidden. We have created a graphic to illustrate this.

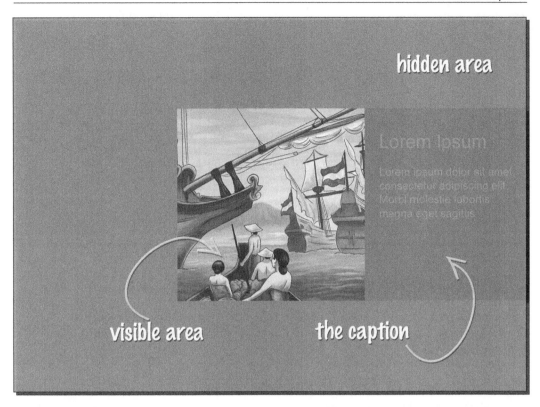

Then, we apply the transition effect to the caption and apply it to all the properties assigned with that caption:

```
-webkit-transition: all 350ms;
-moz-transition: all 350ms;
-o-transition: all 350ms;
transition: all 350ms;
```

Lastly, we add the styles to the hover state. The idea is that the caption will move from right to left and back to its original position. That is why we specified the translate coordinate as 0% in the hover state.

After adding all the CSS rules mentioned in this section, you should be able to see the hover effect:

Website navigation for filtering the portfolio

As we mentioned, website navigation is used to sort portfolios into their respective categories. Thus, our website navigation has been created with a radio input type followed by a label, as follows:

```
<input class="nav-menu" id="all" type="radio" name="filter"
checked="checked"/>
<label for="all">All</label>
<input class="nav-menu" id="illustrations" type="radio"
name="filter"/>
<label for="illustrations">Illustration</label>
<input class="nav-menu" id="posters" type="radio" name="filter"/>
<label for="posters">Posters Design</label>
<input class="nav-menu" id="typography" type="radio" name="filter"/>
<label for="typography">Typography</label>
<input class="nav-menu" id="packaging" type="radio" name="filter"/>
<label for="packaging">Packaging</label>
```

Time for action – creating a portfolio filter

To create a portfolio filter, perform the following steps:

1. Open `styles.css`. Our navigation is based on a radio input type that is assigned with the class `nav-menu`. First, we hide the radio button.

    ```css
    .nav-menu {
      display: none;
    }
    ```

2. Then, we add styles to the input `<label>`. In the following rule, we set the label's `display` property to `inline-block` so the labels will be displayed beside each other.

    ```css
    label {
      padding: 5px 10px;
      color: #3a3f43;
      cursor: pointer;
      display: inline-block;
    }
    ```

3. When the `<input>` radio button is selected, the `<label>` element's styles change. In this case, we set the background color to darker than it is to show that the menu is selected, so we also need to turn the text color to white.

    To select the `<label>` element next to the selected `<input>` radio, we use an adjacent selector.

    ```css
    .nav-menu:checked + label {
      color: #fff;
      background-color: #3a3f43;
      border-radius: 3px;
    }
    ```

4. Next, we define the filter function. First, we hide the portfolio thumbnail. We define the following CSS rule with `.nav-menu`, as follows:

    ```css
    .nav-menu,
    .portfolio > figure.columns {
      display: none;
    }
    ```

5. To achieve the filter functionality, we will combine several CSS selectors. First of all, we structure the website navigation with input radio type and each of them is assigned with a unique ID. These inputs have a label linked to them using the `for" [id] "` attribute. So when we click on the label, the input button is checked. Then, we can target these checked inputs using the `:checked` pseudo class from CSS3. In the following code, we first select the checked `<input>` radio that has an ID of `all`.

```
#all:checked
```

Coupled with the adjacent selector, we select the `portfolio` section:

```
#all:checked ~ .portfolio
```

After selecting the `portfolio` section, we can select the child elements inside it and apply the CSS rules. In this case, we will target elements that have the `all` class and set `display` to `block`.

```
#all:checked ~ .portfolio .all {
  display: block;
}
```

In this way, all portfolio thumbnails are visible when the `<input>` radio with an ID of `all` is checked.

6. Now, let's add the same thing for specific categories such as `poster`, `illustration`, `typography`, and `package`, as follows:

```
#all:checked ~ .portfolio .all,
#posters:checked ~ .portfolio .poster,
#illustrations:checked ~ .portfolio .illustration,
#typography:checked ~ .portfolio .typography,
#packaging:checked ~ .portfolio .package {
  display: block;
}
```

What just happened?

We've just added styles for the purpose of navigation and built the filter functionality with a combination of some CSS selectors.

> Despite being officially announced as part of CSS3 specification, the `:checked` pseudo class has actually been supported since as early as Firefox 1. To see how it works, you can view the demo from the W3C website that is available at `http://www.w3.org/Style/CSS/Test/CSS3/Selectors/current/html/full/flat/css3-modsel-25.html`.

At this point, you can sort the portfolios based on their categories with the navigation menu, as shown in the following screenshot:

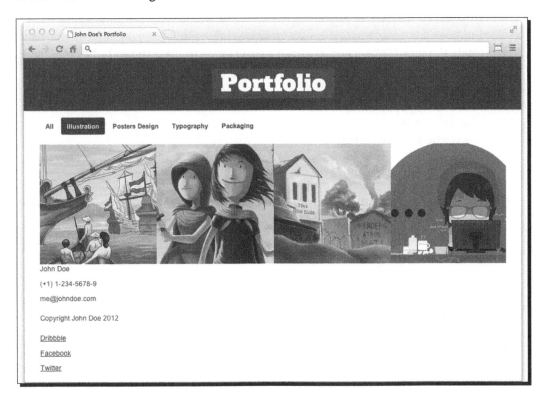

Footer section

In this section, we will add styles to the footer section. This section contains the link to our social presence and contact information, such as our phone number, e-mail, and name.

Time for action – styling the footer section

To style the footer section, perform the following steps:

1. We are still working within the `styles.css` file. Our website footer is defined with the HTML5 `<footer>` element and assigned to the class `footer`. First of all, we add some decorative styles, such as a margin, padding, and border line, as follows:

```
.footer {
  border-top: 1px solid #ccc;
  margin-top: 28px;
  padding: 28px 0;
}
```

2. Next, we place the social links' profiles on the left side of the page, as follows:

```
.social {
  float: left;
}
```

3. Inside the social link section, we have a small space to place the website's copyright text. We will change the color of this text to gray and add a small gap with margin-bottom.

```
.social .copyright {
  color: #ccc;
  margin-bottom: 10px;
  font-size: 1em;
}
```

4. The social links are structured with the `<li>` element. We need to display them side by side.

```
.social ul li {
  display: inline;
}
```

5. In this step, we will add styles for the links. First, in order to be able to set the width and height, we need to set the anchor element `display` to `inline-block`. Then, we set the `width` to `42px` and `height` to `36px`.

```
.social ul li a {
  display: inline-block;
  width: 36px;
  height: 42px;
}
```

6. We also add what's called CSS image replacement styles to hide the text inside the anchor element and replace it with an image later through the `background-image` property.

```
.social ul li a {
  display: inline-block;
  width: 48px;
  height: 48px;

/*below is the css image replacement styles*/
  text-indent: 100%;
  white-space: nowrap;
  overflow: hidden;
}
```

7. We add the social icons, which we have concatenated into a single sprite file in *Chapter 2, Constructing a Responsive Portfolio Page with Skeleton*, to the `<a>` element with the `background-image` property:

```css
.social-dribbble a,
.social-facebook a,
.social-twitter a {
  background-image: url('../images/social.png');
  background-repeat: no-repeat;
}
```

8. Next, we need to edit the CSS rules that were generated when we concatenated the social icon images. These CSS rules define the icon image's position:

```css
.social-dribbble-hover{
  background-position: 0 0;
  width: 48px;
  height: 48px;
}
.social-dribbble{
  background-position: 0 -58px;
  width: 48px;
  height: 48px;
}
.social-facebook-hover{
  background-position: 0 -116px;
  width: 48px;
  height: 48px;
}
.social-facebook{
  background-position: 0 -174px;
  width: 48px;
  height: 48px;
}
.social-twitter-hover{
  background-position: 0 -232px;
  width: 48px;
  height: 48px;
}
.social-twitter{
  background-position: 0 -290px;
  width: 48px;
  height: 48px;
}
```

First, we change the class name that defines the `hover` state (`.social-dribbble-hover`) with `:hover` and assign it to the link icons, as follows:

```css
.social-dribbble a:hover {
  background-position: 0 0;
```

```css
    width: 48px;
    height: 48px;
}
.social-dribbble{
    background-position: 0 -58px;
    width: 48px;
    height: 48px;
}
.social-facebook a:hover{
    background-position: 0 -116px;
    width: 48px;
    height: 48px;
}
.social-facebook{
    background-position: 0 -174px;
    width: 48px;
    height: 48px;
}
.social-twitter a:hover{
    background-position: 0 -232px;
    width: 48px;
    height: 48px;
}
.social-twitter{
    background-position: 0 -290px;
    width: 48px;
    height: 48px;
}
```

9. Since we have set the width and height in the previous step, we can remove the height and width definition from these CSS rules, as follows:

```css
.social-dribbble a:hover {
    background-position: 0 0;
}
.social-dribbble{
    background-position: 0 -58px;
}
.social-facebook a:hover{
    background-position: 0 -116px;
}
.social-facebook{
    background-position: 0 -174px;
}
.social-twitter a:hover{
    background-position: 0 -232px;
}
.social-twitter{
    background-position: 0 -290px;
}
```

10. ,We place the `contact` section to the right of the page:

```
.contact {
  float: right;
}
```

11. And change the color of the text and text link to gray.

```
.contact, .contact a {
  color: #ccc;
}
```

12. Then, we add the icons for the contacts, which we have concatenated into one sprite file in *Chapter 2*, *Constructing a Responsive Portfolio Page with Skeleton*, through the `background-image` property. But this time we will add them in the `:before` pseudo element.

The `:before` pseudo element adds the element before the content of the element that has been specified. It has a sibling named `:after`, which adds the element after the content of the specified element.

In an HTML structure, this can be illustrated as follows:

```
<div>
  <span> </span> <!-- :before -->
  Content
  <span> </span> <!-- :after -->
</div>
```

But, a pseudo element does not add an actual or physical element; that is why, it is called **pseudo**. When we add a pseudo element, it will be interpreted as if the element exists in the document (but it does not).

In CSS3, the pseudo element's syntax is revised. The syntax is defined with double colons (`::before` or `::after`) to differentiate it from a pseudo class, which uses the single-colon syntax (`:hover` or `:checked`).

In the following code snippet, we add the `:before` pseudo element to `<li>`. We change `display` to `inline-block` in order to be able to set `width` and `height`.

```
.contact ul li:before {
  content: '';
  display: inline-block;
  width: 24px;
  height: 24px;
  background-image: url('../images/contact.png');
  margin-right: 0.1em;
}
```

13. Lastly, we adjust the background position for the contact's icon image.

```
.contact-name:before {
  background-position: 0 -29px;
}
.contact-phone:before {
  background-position: 0 -63px;
}
.contact-email:before{
  background-position: 0 5px;
}
```

What just happened?

We just added styles to the footer section and included the social and contact sections inside it. The following screenshot shows how the footer section will appear:

Adjusting website styles in a smaller viewport

In this section, we are going to add styles for a specific viewport using CSS3 media queries.

Now, before we start adding styles, we need to copy all the media queries defined in Skeleton's `layout.css` into our `styles.css` file. The following code snippet shows how they appear in the file:

```
/* Smaller than standard 960 (devices and browsers) */
@media only screen and (max-width: 959px) {

}
/* Tablet Portrait size to standard 960 (devices and browsers) */
@media only screen and (min-width: 768px) and (max-width: 959px) {

}
```

```
/* All Mobile Sizes (devices and browser) */
@media only screen and (max-width: 767px) {

}
/* Mobile Landscape Size to Tablet Portrait (devices and browsers) */
@media only screen and (min-width: 480px) and (max-width: 767px) {

}
/* Mobile Portrait Size to Mobile Landscape Size (devices and
browsers) */
@media only screen and (max-width: 479px) {

}
```

Time for action – viewport size less than 960 px

We are about to add styles that are applicable to a viewport size that is less than 960 pixels:

1. First, we are going to put these styles inside the following media query. This media query specifies the styles for viewports that are smaller than 960 px.

    ```
    @media only screen and (max-width: 959px) {
    }
    ```

2. Since the device is getting smaller, we need to change the column and container widths to their relative units. In this case, the container width would be `100%` while the width of each column within the container would be `25%`, as the container is divided into four columns.

    ```
    .container {
      width: 100%;
    }
    .portfolio .four.columns {
      width: 25%;
    }
    ```

3. Then, we hide the navigation menu to let the users navigate by scrolling with their fingers:

    ```
    label {
      display: none;
    }
    ```

4. We add a little gap at the bottom of each row by adding `margin-bottom` to the figure element.

    ```
    .portfolio .all {
      margin-bottom: 15px;
    }
    ```

5. Since we have hidden the navigation, we need to shift the category information somewhere else.

In this case, we will place it at the top of the image. We can add it using the `:before` pseudo element and grab the category information from the HTML5 `data-*` attribute, as follows:

```css
.portofolio > figure:before {
  content: attr(data-category);
  font-size: 1em;
  padding: 8px;
  width: 100%;
  color: #fff;
  display: block;
  font-weight: bold;
  text-transform: capitalize;
  background-color: rgba(42,47,51,0.8);
  position: absolute;
}
```

6. In this smaller viewport, we will show the image caption instead of hiding it. So we'll set `position` to `relative` and the `translateX` to `0%`. We'll also set the default background color for the caption.

```css
.portfolio figcaption {
  position: relative;

  -webkit-transform: translateX(0%);
  -moz-transform: translateX(0%);
  -ms-transform: translateX(0%);
  -o-transform: translateX(0%);
  transform: translateX(0%);

  background-color: #3a3f43;
}
```

7. We use the `nth-child` pseudo element to select the `<figure>` element that is set with an odd order and set the background color darker than the default that we set in Step 6. In this way, each portfolio caption is distinguishable from the other.

```css
.portoflio figure:nth-child(odd) figcaption {
  background-color: #2a2f33;
}
```

8. Lastly, we need to adjust the margin of the footer section.

```css
.footer {
  border-top: 1px solid #ccc;
  margin-top: 42px;
  padding: 28px;
}
```

What just happened?

We just added styles for a viewport with a width less than 960 px. Here is the result:

Time for action – viewport size between 767 px and 480 px

This time we are going to add styles when the viewport size is between 767 px and 480 px. This size is most likely the size of mobile and tablet devices.

1. We will add styles inside the following media query:

```
@media only screen and (min-width: 480px) and (max-width: 767px) {

}
```

2. Since the viewport is getting smaller, we need to divide the columns into bigger sizes. In this case, we divide the `100%` width of the container by 2, so each column will have `width` set to `50%` of the viewport size.

```
.portfolio .four.columns {
  width: 50%;
}
```

What just happened?

We just added styles for a website that has a viewport size between 767 px and 480 px, and the following screenshot shows how it will appear:

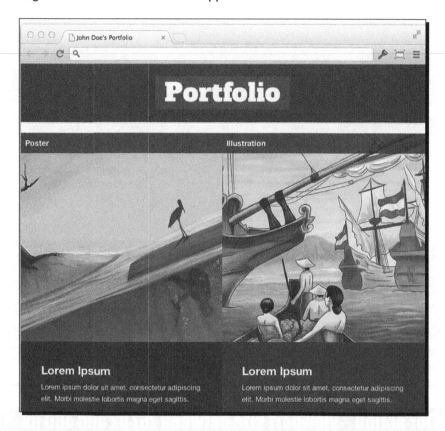

Time for action – viewport size less than 480 px

This time we are going to add styles for a viewport size that is less than 480 px:

1. The styles for a viewport with a size less than 480 px will be added inside the following media query:

    ```
    @media only screen and (max-width: 479px) {
    }
    ```

2. Since the viewport size is really small, we will set the column's `width` attribute to `100%` as well so the image is more visible.

    ```
    .portfolio .four.columns {
      width: 100%;
    }
    ```

3. In the footer section, we will remove the float definition and set `text-align` to center.

```
.footer {
  text-align: center;
}
.contact, .social {
  float: none;
  display: block;
}
```

What just happened?

We just added the styles for our website when it is viewed in a viewport size less than 480 px. The following screenshot shows how it appears:

Testing the website in a different viewport size

We are done with the website, and it is ready for testing. During this process, we test the website in a desktop browser and in a smaller viewport size only by minimizing the browser window. Alternatively, we can also test it with some other tools, such as the following:

- Firefox's built-in Responsive Tool (https://developer.mozilla.org/en-US/docs/Tools/Responsive_Design_View)
- Responsinator (http://www.responsinator.com/)
- Screenqueries (http://screenqueri.es/)

It is better to test the website in real devices—phones, tablets, or readers—to see how the website actually responds. The following screenshots shows how our website from this first project is displayed in iPhone and iPad.

The following screenshot shows our website when viewed in iPhone with the portrait screen orientation. In this screen orientation, where the viewport size is really small (320 px x 480 px), the navigation is hidden and replaced by the category name that is shown above each of the portfolio thumbnails. The image caption is also viewable next to each portfolio thumbnail.

The following screenshot shows how our website will appear when viewed in iPhone with the landscape screen orientation. Like in portrait orientation, the navigation is hidden. But since the viewport width is wider—480 px x 320 px—we can display two portfolio image thumbnails in a row, side by side.

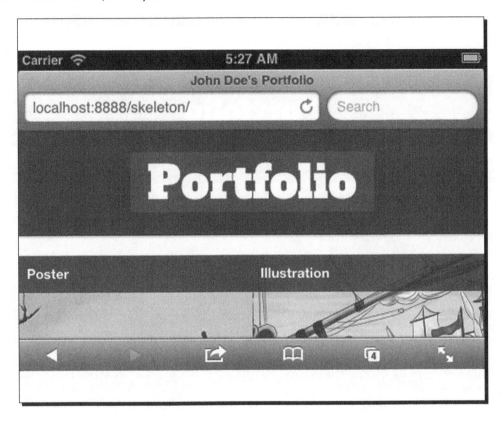

The following screenshot shows how our website will appear in iPad with the portrait screen orientation. As the viewport size is much wider than that of the iPhone (768 px x 1024 px), we are able to accommodate four portfolio image thumbnails in a row, and the caption is also visible below each thumbnail.

Now, we will see how our website appears in iPad with the landscape screen orientation. In this orientation, the viewport size is 1024 px x 768 px; this space is wide enough to accommodate four image thumbnails in one row. The navigation for this viewport size is visible; we can tap on the navigation menu to sort the portfolio.

Summary

We have just finalized our first responsive website with CSS3. In this chapter, we performed the following tasks:

- Polished our website with some new properties introduced in CSS3, such as `box-sizing`, `border-radius`, **and** `box-shadow`
- Created a fancy image hover effect with CSS3 Transforms and Transitions
- Created a portfolio filter function with a combination of CSS selectors
- Adjusted our website's styles in different viewport sizes with CSS3 media queries

Now that we are done with our first project with Skeleton, we are going to explore another framework to create a responsive website in the next chapter.

4

Developing a Product Launch Site with Bootstrap

We will start our second project in this chapter. In this project, we will build our responsive website with Bootstrap by using some of the provided components. Bootstrap is currently one of the most popular development frameworks. It comes with several stylesheets and jQuery plugins for establishing interactive websites or application user interfaces.

Unlike our first project in Chapter 2, Constructing a Responsive Portfolio Page with Skeleton, and Chapter 3, Enhancing the Portfolio Website with CSS3, in which we built only a single-page website, in this project we will build a responsive website with five pages. We will also learn how to use LESS, a CSS preprocessor, and to compose our website stylesheet.

To sum up, here are several things we are going to cover in this chapter:

- ◆ Introducing and examining Bootstrap components
- ◆ Setting up working directories
- ◆ Preparing website assets, including the images and JavaScript files
- ◆ Adding a new font family with `@font-face` rules
- ◆ Installing LESS applications for composing and compiling LESS into CSS
- ◆ Creating and structuring HTML documents

Getting started with Bootstrap

In *Chapter 1, Responsive Web Design*, we took a brief look at Bootstrap's features and saw a couple of examples of sites built on this framework. Now, we will start building our own website. However, before we start working on the code, we need to set up our working environment and get some essential files prepared.

Time for action – setting up Bootstrap

Perform the following steps to set up Bootstrap:

1. We have two options available for downloading the Bootstrap package. We can either download and customize the download page from the official site (http://getbootstrap.com/) or download it from the Github. Since we plan to use LESS (http://lesscss.org/), we will download the package directly from Github. So, let's head over to https://github.com/twitter/bootstrap and download the package. At the time of writing this book, Github is at version 2.2.1.

    The download button in Github is the one that is highlighted in blue, shown in the following screenshot:

    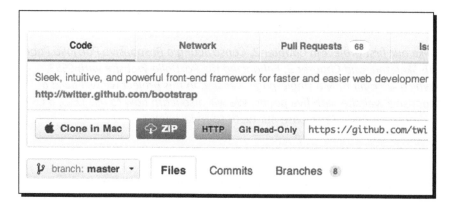

2. You should now have the Bootstrap package in a ZIP file, which at the time of writing this book is named bootstrap-master.zip. Extract this ZIP file to unpack the files inside it.

3. On extracting the ZIP file, by default, a folder named bootstrap-master is created, containing the Bootstrap core files. Rename this folder to bootstrap. This naming convention is optional; you can name it as you want to. Only note that this folder will be our working directory for this second project.

4. Now, let's go to the working directory. Inside the working directory, you should find the following items:

   - ❑ `docs`: The `docs` folder contains Bootstrap documentations, the very same documentations and pages that we find at http://twitter.github.com/bootstrap/.

   - ❑ `img`: The `img` folder, by default, contains glyph icons in the PNG format, and we will store our images for the website inside this folder.

   - ❑ `js`: The `js` folder contains the JavaScript files for the jQuery plugins Carousel, Modal, Dropdown, Scrollspy, Alert, and many more.

   - ❑ `less`: Bootstrap stylesheets are built on top of LESS, a CSS preprocessor. The `less` folder is used to store the LESS files, which are saved with the `.less` extension.

   - ❑ **The MarkDown files**: `README.md` and `CONTRIBUTING.md`.

   - ❑ **The JSON files**: `component.json`, `composer.json`, and `package.json`.

   Among all of these, the items such as the `docs` folder, `components.json`, `composer.json`, `package.json`, `CONTRIBUTING.md`, `README.md`, `LICENSE`, and `Makefile` are merely additional and will not be of much use in our project. This is an optional step, but let's remove them from the working directory.

5. Furthermore, let's go to the `js` folder, which contains the JavaScript files. Since we will use only `bootstrap-collapse.js` and `bootstrap-transition.js`, we can remove the other files. The two remaining files will be used to animate the menu navigation when the website is viewed in a small viewport size.

6. To run the plugin scripts, we will need jQuery, so let's go to http://jquery.com/.

7. Select **Production (32KB, Minified and Gzipped)** and click on **Download jQuery**.

8. Save it inside the `js` folder and name it `jquery.js`.

9. Inside the `js` folder, you will find a folder named `tests`. This folder contains scripts and documents for plugin testing. Since we don't use this on our website, we can remove them from the working directory.

10. Similarly, you will also find the `tests` folder inside the `less` folder, which contains some HTML documents and a stylesheet for testing the UI styles. We can also remove it from the working directory so our website will not rely on the HTML documents or stylesheets from this `tests` folder as well.

What just happened?

We have just downloaded and unpacked the Bootstrap package and given its main folder the name `bootstrap`, which will be the working directory for the project. We have also removed the files that we are not going to use in the project. So, at this stage, the remaining assets for the project include only those that are shown in the following screenshot:

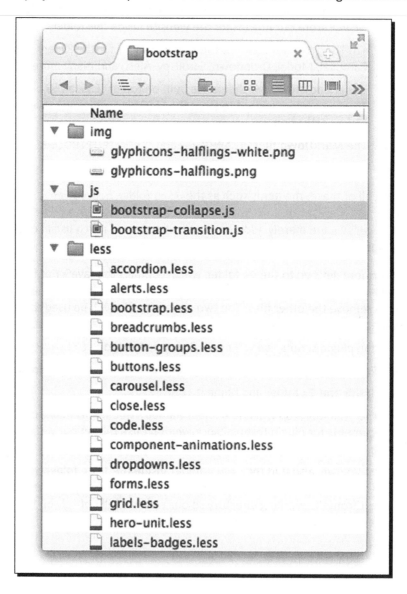

Preparing the website images

Similar to our first website, we will need some images to be displayed, such as the product images, the logo image, and the social media icons. We have a total of 16 product images, one image for the website logo, one "hello world" image, three images for the About page, and social media icons for Facebook, Dribbble, and Twitter. You can find all the images that we are going to use bundled along with this book, and the following screenshot shows the list of our images in the img folder:

The following screenshot shows a few of these images:

I would like to thank my friend, an artist at Kudos Plush (http://www.kudosplush.com), who allowed me to use their images for the project in this book. Alternatively, you can also use your own images. The important thing is that they should be stored in the working directory under the img folder.

Introducing LESS applications

Bootstrap stylesheets are built on top of LESS, a CSS preprocessor. You can find the LESS files, which are saved with the .less extension and stored within the less folder in the working directory.

In *Chapter 1*, *Responsive Web Design*, we took a brief look at a few LESS syntaxes; to process those syntaxes, we need a special application that is able to compose as well as compile LESS syntaxes into a standard CSS that browsers can recognize.

In this project, we are going to use a dedicated code editor for LESS, named CrunchApp (http://crunchapp.net).

Time for action – installing CrunchApp

Perform the following steps to install CrunchApp:

1. CrunchApp is an Adobe AIR application. If Adobe Air is already installed, we can skip directly to step 4; otherwise, we need to install it before we can install CrunchApp.

2. Go to the Adobe AIR website (http://get.adobe.com/air/).

3. Adobe.com will automatically detect your system and provide the proper file to be downloaded. Find and click on the **Download Now** button to download the file.

4. Launch the file and follow the installation instructions. Each OS will have a different method of installing the application.

 You can also read the tutorial available at `http://www.clickonf5.org/6268/how-to-install-adobe-air-windows-mac-ubuntu/` for more detailed instructions on Adobe AIR installation on each platform (Windows, OS X, and Linux).

5. After the Adobe AIR installation is complete, go to the CrunchApp website (`http://crunchapp.net/`) and download the CrunchApp installation file.

   At the time of writing this book, the installation file name is `Crunch.1.5.3.air`; this shows that the current version is 1.5.3.

6. Launch the CrunchApp installation file, `Crunch.1.5.3.air`.

7. The window shown in the following screenshot should appear. Click on the **Install** button to start the installation process.

8. The installer will prompt for installation location. Since the default location is fine, we can simply click on the **Continue** button.

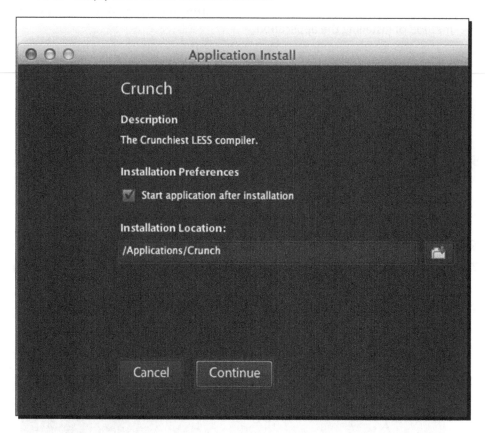

9. Wait until the installation is complete. After that, CrunchApp will automatically start running.

What just happened?

We have just installed CrunchApp, an application for composing and compiling files with the `.less` extension. You can actually use your current editor and set it up to be able to open and highlight LESS syntax.

But everyone has his/her own code editor of choice. Here, we decided to use CrunchApp, because it is a free application, is easy to use, and can be run on popular platforms such as Windows, OS X, and Linux.

Creating new LESS files

Similar to our first project, we will use some dedicated stylesheets to store our own style rules for the website. It is always a good idea to not interfere with the core files from Bootstrap so that when the framework core files are updated, our changes will not be overwritten with the new files, and thus the website is easily maintainable.

In the following steps, we will create a new `.less` file as we are going to compose the styles with LESS.

Time for action – creating a new LESS file with CrunchApp

To create a new LESS file with CrunchApp, perform the following steps:

1. Open CrunchApp.

2. Then, drag-and-drop the `less` folder from the working directory into the CrunchApp sidebar. CrunchApp will list all the `.less` files inside this folder, as shown in the following screenshot:

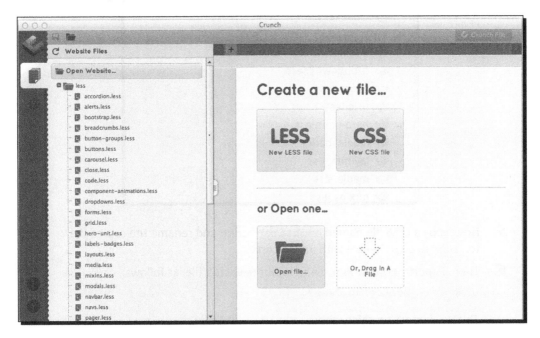

3. Create a new LESS file. There are several ways to do so, either by navigating to **File | New** or by pressing *Ctrl + N* (for Windows or Linux) or *Command + N* (for OS X).

4. Save the file in the working directory under the `less` folder and name it `_styles.less` with underscore. We initialize the file name with the underscore sign so that the file will be listed on top of other files, and thus our files are easily discoverable.

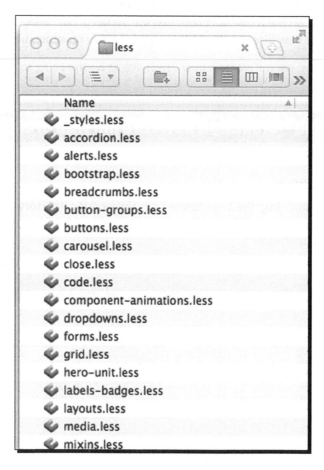

5. Now, copy a LESS file named `bootstrap.less` and rename the copied file to `_bootstrap.less`—with underscore.

6. Then, import `_bootstrap.less` to our new LESS file, as follows:

   ```
   @import "_bootstrap.less";
   ```

   This will import anything within `_bootstrap.less`.

7. Don't forget to save these changes in our new file.

What just happened?

We have just created a new LESS file named `_styles.less` to store our own styles. We also made a copy of `bootstrap.less`, renamed it to `_bootstrap.less`, and then imported it to the new LESS file. That way, we do not interfere with the core files from Bootstrap.

Compiling LESS syntax into standard CSS

LESS syntax is not the standard syntax that the browsers can understand. Thus, we need to compile LESS syntax into standard CSS rules before we can see the result in the browsers. CrunchApp, which we have just installed, is able to do so.

Time for action – adding LESS files to CrunchApp and compiling them into standard CSS

To add files to CrunchApp and compile them into standard CSS, perform the following steps:

1. First, create a new folder named `css` inside the working directory. In this folder, we will save all the CSS files generated from CrunchApp.

2. Then, open our `_styles.less` file. This file has imported `_bootstrap.less`, which contains `@import` rules for several LESS files within the `less` folder. So, everything that is defined or added within `_bootstrap.less` is compiled to `_styles.less`.

3. To compile it into CSS, you can press *Ctrl + Enter* (for Windows or Linux) or *Command + Enter* (for OS X).

4. After that, you will be prompted for a location in which to save the compiled file. Save it under the `css` folder that we have created in step 1.

What just happened?

We have just compiled `_styles.less` into CSS browser-compatible format. It imports all other `.less` files from `_bootstrap.less` and saves them to the CSS stylesheet named `_styles.css`. So, at this stage, this is the only stylesheet saved under the `css` folder in the working directory.

Alternative to CrunchApp

There are other options available for carrying out the same task too. Here, we have put together some resources where you can enable syntax highlighting for LESS syntax in some popular code editors and then use them along with a LESS compiler application, such as LESS.app for OS X or WinLESS for Windows.

Sublime Text 2 users can install the LESS syntax highlighter package (`https://github.com/danro/LESS-sublime`) through Package Control.

DreamWeaver users can install the extension available at Adobe.com (`http://www.adobe.com/cfusion/exchange/index.cfm?event=extensionDetail&extid=2756522`).

There is also a LESS highlighter bundle (`https://github.com/appden/less.tmbundle`) available for the TextMate code editor.

If you are a Windows user, you can use WebMatrix (`http://www.microsoft.com/web/`), a free web development tool provided and built by Microsoft. It already supports LESS; follow the instructions (at `http://www.microsoft.com/web/post/how-to-use-less-css-in-webmatrix`) on authoring LESS with WebMatrix as well as compiling it into CSS with its special extension, called OrangeBits.

Introducing the @font-face rule to add a custom font family

We are also going to add a new font family to make our website more appealing. If, you prefer to remain with Arial or Georgia, you can skip this section.

In our first project, we embedded the font with the Google Web Font service. When we embed the font with Google Web Font, the font is served from the Google server, which is a good way to save a little workload on our own server.

In this second project, we are going to take a look at another option: embedding the font with the `@font-face` rule. The `@font-face` rule allows us to host and serve the font ourselves.

One advantage of obtaining and hosting the fonts on our own is that we get more control over the font, for instance, subsetting the font, replacing or removing unnecessary characters, and adding new characters in the set.

Google Web Font also offers font the subsetting capability (`https://developers.google.com/webfonts/docs/getting_started#Subsets`). But the implementation is currently quite limited and not too flexible.

Finding free fonts for embedding on the web

One of the main concerns, however, when hosting and embedding fonts using `@font-face` is the font **EULA (End-user License Agreement)**. Some type foundries prohibit their font from being freely embedded on the web, with the exception of buying the license through some premium `@font-face` services, such as Typekit (`https://typekit.com`) or Fontdeck (`http://fontdeck.com`).

In 2009, Ethan Dunham started Font Squirrel (`http://www.fontsquirrel.com`) to bridge this license barrier and push the use of `@font-face` by collecting available fonts that are free for commercial use and are allowed to be embedded on the web.

At the time of writing this book, there are 819 font families with various typefaces in the Font Squirrel library from Serif, Sans serif, and Script to Calligraphic and Retro.

Writing the @font-face rule

Adding a new font family with the `@font-face` rule is relatively easy. We simply specify the new font family name with the `font-family` property along with the font file source. In the following example, we set a new font family named `MyFont` and use the `.ttf` font format within the source:

```
@font-face {
    font-family: "MyFont"; /* defining new font family name*/
    src: url(


    MyFont.ttf'); /* targeting the font source */
}
```

Then, we can add this new font family, `MyFont`, through the stylesheet with the `font-family` property, for example:

```
h1 {
    font-family: "MyFont";
}
```

Font formats for cross-browser compatibility

The `@font-face` rule was actually introduced since CSS2 specification, and thus, it has been supported in both earlier and latest browsers—Internet Explorer 5.5, Firefox 3.5, Chrome 4.0, Safari 3.2, Opera 10, iOS 3.2, Android 2.2, and so on.

Unfortunately, these browsers set their own rules that outline which font format to use for web embedding, as shown in the following table.

Browser	Compatible font format
Internet Explorer	`.eot` (`.woff` support added in Internet Explorer 9)
Firefox	`.ttf` and `.otf` (`.woff` support added in Firefox 3.6)
Chrome	`.ttf` and `.svg` (`.woff` support added in Chrome 5)
Safari	`.ttf`, `.otf`, and `.svg` (`.woff` support added in Safari 5.1)
Opera	`.ttf`, `.otf`, and `.svg`
iOS	`.svg`
Android	`.svg`

So, the line of codes for defining a new font family with `@font-face` turns out to be a bit longer as we need to provide four formats for the sake of, both earlier and latest, browser compatibility.

In the post at `http://paulirish.com/2009/bulletproof-font-face-implementation-syntax/`, Paul Irish has explained comprehensively about implementing the `@font-face` rule and has given a tip for the better `@font-face` syntax that works across all browsers, as follows:

```
@font-face {
    font-family: 'MyFont;
    src: url('MyFont.eot');
    src: local('?'),
    url('MyFont.woff') format('woff'),
    url('MyFont.ttf') format('truetype'),
    url('MyFont.svg#webfont') format('svg');
    font-weight: normal;
    font-style: normal;
}
```

In addition, if you prefer to not deal with the preceding syntax manually, you can achieve it easily with the free `@font-face` generator tool from Font Squirrel (`http://www.fontsquirrel.com/fontface/generator`).

Time for action – adding a new font with @font-face

To add a new font with `@font-face`, perform the following steps:

1. First, go to the `css` folder in the working directory.

2. Inside this `css` folder, create a new folder and name it `fonts`.

3. We will use a free font from Font Squirrel. So, let's head over to
   http://www.fontsquirrel.com/.

4. Browse the Font Squirrel library and download the `@font-face` kit for Droid Sans
   (http://www.fontsquirrel.com/fonts/Droid-Sans), this kit contains the
   font files with the `@font-face` rules in the stylesheet.

5. Extract the kit and place all the font files inside the `fonts` folder that we created
   in step 2.

6. You should also find a stylesheet named `stylesheet.css` in the extracted package.
   Open it in a code editor and copy the `@font-face` rules from `stylesheet.css`.
   Change the path in a `url` type to point to our `fonts` folder, as follows:

```
@font-face {
  font-family: 'DroidSansRegular';
  src: url('fonts/DroidSans-webfont.eot');
  src: url('fonts/DroidSans-webfont.eot?#iefix')
  format('embedded-opentype'),
  url('fonts/DroidSans-webfont.woff') format('woff'),
  url('fonts/DroidSans-webfont.ttf') format('truetype'),
  url('fonts/DroidSans-webfont.svg#DroidSansRegular')
  format('svg');
  font-weight: normal;
  font-style: normal;
}
@font-face {
  font-family: 'DroidSansBold';
  src: url('fonts/DroidSans-Bold-webfont.eot');
  src: url('fonts/DroidSans-Bold-webfont.eot?#iefix')
  format('embedded-opentype'),
  url('fonts/DroidSans-Bold-webfont.woff') format('woff'),
  url('fonts/DroidSans-Bold-webfont.ttf')
  format('truetype'),
  url('fonts/DroidSans-Bold-webfont.svg#DroidSansBold')
  format('svg');
  font-weight: normal;
  font-style: normal;

}
```

7. Go to CrunchApp, create a new LESS file, and name it `_fonts.less`. This file is
   dedicated to defining the `@font-face` rules.

What just happened?

We have just added a new font, Droid Sans, which will be our website's main font, and saved it within a new file named _fonts.less. We dedicate this new file to saving the @font-face rule in our project.

 You can also use other font families; just make sure that you do not violent the font license. As mentioned, some fonts are prohibited from being freely embedded on the web.

Responsive features in Bootstrap

Before we work on the HTML structure, we will first examine how Bootstrap applies its responsive features and see what classes are used to define the columns and other components so that we will be able to structure the HTML markup properly.

Bootstrap grid system

Bootstrap uses 12 columns of grid system. Each column is defined with classes ranging from span1 to span12. When we add several columns, the sum of our span classes should be equal to 12, and specifically in Bootstrap, the columns should be wrapped within a <div> element or other appropriate elements with the row class, as shown in the following code snippet:

```
<div class="row">
   <div class="span9"> This is the main content </div>
   <div class="span3"> and this is the sidebar... </div>
</div>
```

In the preceding example, we have two <div> elements wrapped within a <div> element that is assigned with the row class, while the two <div> elements within are respectively assigned with the span3 and span9 classes, which add up to 12.

Given the preceding example, we will get the following result in the browsers by adding a few decorative styles:

THIS IS THE MAIN CONTENT	AND SIDEBAR...

CSS3 media queries in Bootstrap

By default, Bootstrap does not include the responsive features. But those can easily be enabled by including the meta viewport tag and the stylesheet that contains the CSS3 media query definitions.

Bootstrap has provided several CSS3 media queries for supporting a wide range of viewport widths. See the following example:

```
@media (min-width: 1200px) {
  .container {
    width: 1170px;
    ...
  }
}
@media (min-width: 768px) and (max-width: 979px) { ... }
@media (max-width: 767px) { ... }
@media (max-width: 480px) { ... }
```

Referring to the preceding code snippet, when we enable the responsive feature by including these CSS3 media queries, Bootstrap extends the container width to `1170px` within the `1200px` viewport width.

However, the width of `1170px` would be too large for our website. So, in order for the styles to not be applied to the website, we need to remove the media query `@media (min-width: 1200px)` as well as the style rules from our stylesheet.

Time for action – creating a new LESS file to store CSS3 media queries

To add a new LESS file for storing CSS3 media queries, perform the following steps:

1. Open CrunchApp, create a new LESS file, and name it `_responsives.less`. This will be used to store our own definitions of CSS3 media queries.

2. Then, in the CrunchApp sidebar, find and open the LESS file named `responsive.less`. This is the default file where Bootstrap saves the CSS3 media queries.

3. Copy the following `@import` rules from `responsive.less`:
   ```
   @import "variables.less";
   @import "mixins.less";
   ```

4. These files, `variables.less` and `mixins.less`, store Bootstrap's core variables and mixins. The responsive style rules are dependent on these variables and mixins, so let's paste it into the `_responsive.less` file that we created in step 1.

5. Then, add the following line to import special class helpers for responsive design:
   ```
   @import "responsive-utilities.less";
   ```

6. Open a LESS file named `responsive-767px-max.less` from the CrunchApp sidebar.

7. Copy everything from `responsive-767px-max.less` and paste it into `_responsives.less` **after the line** `@import "responsive-utilities.less"`.

8. Then, add the following line to the `@import` styles for responsive navigation at the very bottom:

```
@import "responsive-navbar.less";
```

9. Save the file and compile it to CSS.

10. Save the compiled file in the `css` folder in the working directory.

What just happened?

We have just created a new file dedicated to saving our own styles within CSS3 media queries.

 To learn more about the Bootstrap grid system, you can visit the official documentation, which has accommodated everything you need to know on this matter (`http://twitter.github.com/bootstrap/scaffolding.html#gridSystem`).

Establishing navigation with Bootstrap

Bootstrap provides extensive classes to establish web navigations. The web navigation is basically formed with an element assigned to the class `navbar` as well as by nesting one more element inside it with the `navbar-inner` class to contain inner elements within the navigation, as follows.

```
<nav class="navbar">
  <div class="navbar-inner">
    ...
  </div>
</nav>
```

 The `navbar` class should be nested within the element with a class container that defines the width of the web page.

Then, we can add additional elements, such as the link menu. In Bootstrap, the link menu is structured with an unordered list element, `<ul>`, assigned to the class `nav`.

```
<nav class="navbar">
  <div class="navbar-inner">
    <ul class="nav">
      <li><a href="#">Home</a></li>
      <li><a href="#">About Us</a></li>
```

```
        <li><a href="#">Contact Us</a></li>
    </ul>
  </div>
</nav>
```

The preceding example will give us the following result, by default:

Furthermore, the navigation can be responsive. As we briefly discussed in *Chapter 1*, *Responsive Web Design*, when the website is viewed in a small viewport, the navigation will turn into a button, as shown in the following screenshot:

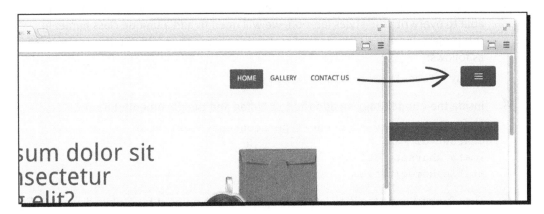

 For further reference, Bootstrap has provided a comprehensive documentation on forming web navigation at `http://twitter.github.com/bootstrap/components.html#navbar`.

Creating HTML documents

At this stage, we have done a few things from setting up the project's working directory as well as preparing the website assets to installing and creating new .less files with the LESS application, CrunchApp.

Now, we will start creating the HTML markup for our website. To create these documents, you can use any code editor of your choice.

Time for action – creating basic HTML5 documents

Perform the following steps to create basic HTML5 documents:

1. First, create a new file in code editor and save it as `index.html` in the working directory.

2. Add some essential stuff for an HTML document, including `doctype` and the `html`, `body`, and `head` tags as follows.

```
<!DOCTYPE html>
<html>
  <head> </head>
  <body> </body>
</html>
```

3. Some style rules in Bootstrap are defined with more specificity. So, in order to be able to overwrite the styles later on, we will need to add a unique class name. In this project, we add a class named `kudosplush` and then add it in the `<body>` tag as follows:

```
<body class="kudosplush"> </body>
```

4. Inside the `<head>` tag, we add the `title` tag and the document `charset`.

```
<meta http-equiv="Content-Type" content="text/html;
charset=UTF-8">
<meta charset="utf-8">
<title>Home</title>
```

5. The viewport meta tag is an important part of development for mobile devices. So, let's add it after the `title` tag:

```
<meta name="viewport" content="width=device-width,
initial-scale=1">
```

6. Then, link all the stylesheets that we have created by compiling the LESS files as follows:

```
<link href="css/_styles.css" rel="stylesheet">
<link href="css/_responsives.css" rel="stylesheet">
```

7. To allow old browsers to support HTML5 elements, we need to add HTML5 Shim.

```
<!--[if lt IE 9]>
<script src="http://html5shim.googlecode.com/svn/trunk/html5.js">
</script>
<![endif]-->
```

8. Afterwards, we add the website header with a `<header>` element, the content section with a `<div>` element, and footer with a `<footer>` element inside the `<body>` tag, as follows:

```
<body class="kudosplush">
  <header class="header"> </header>
  <div class="content"> </div>
  <footer class="header"> </footer>
</body>
```

We used the `<div>` element instead of using HTML5 `<section>` to define the content section because the section will not immediately be followed with a heading, as described in the documentation (`http://www.whatwg.org/specs/web-apps/current-work/multipage/sections.html#headings-and-sections`):

> *"The first element of heading content in an element of sectioning content represents the heading for that section. Subsequent headings of equal or higher rank start new (implied) sections, headings of lower rank start implied subsections that are part of the previous one. In both cases, the element represents the heading of the implied section."*

9. Inside the `<header>` element, we add a `<div>` element with the class container to contain the inner content of the header.

```
<div class="container"> </div>
```

10. Add a `<nav>` element with the class `navbar` to form the navigation.

```
<div class="container">
  <nav class="navbar"> </nav>
</div>
```

11. Inside the `<nav class="navbar">` definition, add a `<div>` element with the class `navbar-inner` to contain the inner elements within the navigation.

```
<div class="container">
  <nav class="navbar">
  <div class="navbar-inner"> </div>
  </nav>
</div>
```

12. Add an `<a>` element with the class brand inside the `<div class="navbar-inner">` definition to display the website logo later on.

```
<div class="container">
  <nav class="navbar">
    <div class="navbar-inner">
```

```
        <a class="brand" href="#">Kudos Plush</a>
      </div>
    </nav>
  </div>
```

13. Then, add the following code next to the `<a class="brand" href="#">` definition for the link menu.

```
<a class="brand" href="#">Kudos Plush</a>

<div class="nav-collapse collapse">
  <ul class="nav pull-right">
    <li class="active">
      <a href="index.html">Home</a>
    </li>
    <li><a href="gallery.html">Gallery</a></li>
    <li><a href="contact.html">Contact Us</a></li>
  </ul>
</div>
```

We wrapped the menu links within a `<div>` element with the `nav-collapse collapse` class in order for the navigation to collapse when it is viewed in a small viewport size.

14. Lastly, we add the button as the toggle key for the menu links. Define this button with the HTML5 `<button>` element and add the following code before the `<a class="brand" href="#">Kudos Plush</a>` definition as follows:

```
<button data-target=".nav-collapse" data-toggle="collapse"
class="btn btn-navbar collapsed" type="button">
    <span class="icon-bar"></span>
    <span class="icon-bar"></span>
    <span class="icon-bar"></span>
</button>
<a class="brand" href="#">Kudos Plush</a>
```

In Bootstrap, the three stripes icon is structured with three `<span>` elements, as explained in the documentation. But, we can replace them with an HTML character named *Trigram from Heaven*. This character is defined with HTML entity number `&#9776;` and gives us the following result in the browser:

We can then customize the look or the size with CSS rules.

15. While in the content section, for now, we will only add the div container to contain the future content.

```
<div class="container">  </div>
```

16. For the footer, we also need to add a `<div>` element that is assigned to the class container.

```
<footer class="footer">
  <div class="container"> </div>
</footer>
```

17. For the footer contents, we add two columns. So, let's add a `<div>` element assigned to the class row.

```
<footer class="footer">
  <div class="container">
    <div class="""row> </div>
  </div>
</footer>
```

18. Inside the `<div class="row">` definition, add two `<div>` elements for each column assigned to the class span6. So, they have equal width.

```
<footer class="footer">
  <div class="container">
    <div class="row">
      <div class="span6"> </div>
      <div class="span6"> </div>
    </div>
  </div>
</footer>
```

19. In the first column, we add the footer navigation structure as follows:

```
<div class="span6">
  <nav class="nav-footer">
    <ul>
      <li><a href="index.html">Home</a></li>
      <li><a href="gallery.html">Gallery</a></li>
      <li><a href="contact.html">Contact</a></li>
      <li><a href="about.html">About</a></li>
      <li><a href="policy.html">Policy</a></li>
    </ul>
  </nav>
</div>
```

20. In the second column, we add the copyright text and social media links.

```
<div class="span6">
  <small class="copyright">Copyright © 2012 John Doe - All
  rights reserved</small>
  <ul class="social-links">
   <li class="facebook"><a href="#">Facebook</a></li>
    <li class="twitter"><a href="#">Twitter</a></li>
    <li class="dribbble"><a href="">Dribbble</a></li>
  </ul>
</div>
```

21. Save the document.

22. Then, copy the document `index.html` into five copies.

23. Apart from `index.html`, save the copies with the names `gallery.html`, `contact.html`, `about.html`, and `policy.html`.

What just happened?

We have just created an HTML document, which becomes the basic document for our web pages. Each web page will have the same header, navigation, and footer structure.

The only difference would be the content structure; that is why we added only the `div` container in the content section at the moment.

In the following steps, we will start adding HTML content structure for each page.

Pop quiz

What is the HTML entity number that is used for generating the "three stripes" icon?

1. `&#9776;`

2. `#&9776;`

The homepage content

We are about to start structuring the HTML for the homepage. In the homepage, we will have five sections: the "Hello World" (Hero), the order section, the gallery, the testimonial, and the e-mail subscription form.

Time for action – adding an HTML content structure for our homepage

To add an HTML content structure for homepage, perform the following steps:

1. Open the `index.html` file in your code editor.

2. Add the following lines within the `<header>` element below the navigation to establish the Hello World (Hero) or introductory section:

```
<div class="hero-unit row">
  <div class="hero-text span7">
    <h1>Hello World. Welcome to our website!</h1>
    <p>Lorem Ipsum! Only</p>
    <p class="price">USD50.0</p>
  </div>
  <div class="hero-image span5">
    <img src="img/hero-image.png" alt=
    "KudosPlush Hero image">
  </div>
</div>
```

3. Next, we add what we call the **call-to-action** (**CTA**) section within the `<div class="container">` definition in the content. This section contains some copy text (in reality, the text would be there to encourage visitors to order or buy the offered product) and a button.

   So, we will split this section into two columns. The first column with the `span9` call will contain the copy text, while the next column with the class `span3` will contain the button.

```
<div class="cta row">
  <div class="copy-text span9">
    <p>Brownie oat cake donut gummies carrot macaroon cake
    jelly-o. Cheesecake apple pie gummi bears.</p>
  </div>
  <div class="button span3">
    <a class="btn btn-primary btn-block btn-order"
    href="#">Order Now</a>
  </div>
</div>
```

   In its basic form, the button is applied with class `btn`. However, in this project, we added it with a custom class called `btn-order` to apply our own style rules.

 Bootstrap provides extensive classes for styling buttons.

4. Add an `<hr>` element next to the `<div class="cta row">` definition to separate it from the next section, the Gallery.

5. Add the following lines to establish the Gallery section. We have previewed four of our product images. Each image is wrapped within an HTML5 `<figure>` element, and we will display all these images side by side in a row. Since Bootstrap uses 12 columns of the grid, each `<figure>` element is assigned to the class `span3` (12 divided by 4 results in 3).

```
<div class="gallery row">
  <figure class="span3">
    <img class="img-polaroid" src="img/image-1.jpg
    alt="featured product no.1">
  </figure>
  <figure class="span3">
    <img class="img-polaroid" src="img/image-2.jpg"
    alt=" featured product no.2">
  </figure>
  <figure class="span3">
    <img class="img-polaroid" src="img/image-3.jpg"
    alt=" featured product no.3">
  </figure>
  <figure class="span3">
    <img class="img-polaroid" src="img/image-4.jpg"
    alt=" featured product no.4">
  </figure>
</div>
```

6. Add an `<hr>` element to a separate Gallery with the next section, Testimonial.

7. We add the Testimonial section next to the Gallery. This section contains only copy text. In reality, this would be the testimonial of satisfied customers.

```
<div class="testimonial row">
  <p>Oat cake jelly faworki. Tootsie roll powder faworki
  applicake. Marshmallow macaroon icing soufflé.</p>
</div>
```

8. Lastly, we add the form for e-mail subscription. We use the HTML input type, `email`, add placeholder text for the input field, and use the `<button>` element for the submit key.

```
<form action="index_submit" method="get" accept-charset="utf-8">
  <input type="email" name="email_subscribe"
  placeholder="Input your email address">
  <button class="btn btn-large"
  type="submit">Submit</button>
</form>
```

What just happened?

We have just added HTML structure for the homepage content, including the Hello World (Hero) section. The Hero section will only be available in the homepage.

Also, in step 8, we added the `<input>` element within the form subscription with the `placeholder` attribute and `email` type.

The following screenshot shows how the homepage looks at the moment.

The HTML5 placeholder attribute

HTML5 introduced a new attribute named `placeholder`. The spec described this attribute as:

> *"A short hint (a word or short phrase) intended to aid the user with data entry when the control has no value."*

See the code snippet from step 8:

```
<input type="email" name="email_subscribe" placeholder="Input your
email address">
```

This gives us the following result in the browser:

Earlier, we used to rely on JavaScript to achieve a similar effect. Today, with `placeholder`, the application gets much simpler.

New input types in HTML5

HTML5 also introduced a bunch of new input types, such as `email`, `url`, `number`, `range`, and `search`. In step 8, we added the `email` input type.

```
<input type="email" name="email_subscribe" placeholder="Input your
email address">
```

These new input types are special as they come with built-in validations. So, when the users enter an invalid e-mail format, for example, within our form subscription, it will return an error, as shown in the following screenshot:

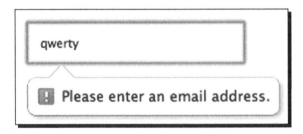

Furthermore, these new inputs give better experience in mobile devices. Given our example with the `email` input type, we will be provided with a special virtual keyboard for typing e-mail with the addition of the @ key to make typing e-mail addresses faster.

 You can head over to `http://diveintohtml5.info/ forms.html`, where *Mark Pilgrim* has discussed this topic in detail in the article *Dive Into HTML5* (`http://diveintohtml5.info/`).

The Gallery page content

We are going to add HTML content structure for the Gallery page. In this page, we will display all our product images. We have a total of 16 images, and we will display four images in a row—as we did it on the home page.

Time for action – adding HTML content structure for the Gallery page

To add HTML content structure for the Gallery page, perform the following steps:

1. Open `gallery.html` in your code editor.

2. First, we add page title with the `H1` element.

```
<h1>Plush Gallery <small>collection to our previous toys</small></
h1>
```

3. Then, add a `<div>` element assigned to the class `gallery` page to contain the gallery images.

```
<div class="gallery page"> </div>
```

4. As mentioned, the structure for the gallery is the same as in the homepage. Each `<figure>` element is assigned to the class `span3`. That way, it will divide these images into four images in a row.

We also add a special class from Bootstrap, `img-polaroid`, to apply image styles.

```
<div class="row">
  <figure class="span3">
    <img class="img-polaroid" src="img/image-1.jpg"
    alt="product image no.1">
  </figure>
  <figure class="span3">
    <img class="img-polaroid" src="img/image-2.jpg"
    alt="product image no.2">
  </figure>
  <figure class="span3">
    <img class="img-polaroid" src="img/image-3.jpg"
    alt="product image no.3">
  </figure>
  <figure class="span3">
    <img class="img-polaroid" src="img/image-4.jpg"
    alt="product image no.4">
  </figure>
  <figure class="span3">
    <img class="img-polaroid" src="img/image-5.jpg"
    alt="product image no.5">
  </figure>
  <figure class="span3">
    <img class="img-polaroid" src="img/image-6.jpg"
    alt="product image no.6">
  </figure>
```

```
  <figure class="span3">
    <img class="img-polaroid" src="img/image-7.jpg"
    alt="product image no.7">
  </figure>
  <figure class="span3">
    <img class="img-polaroid" src="img/image-8.jpg"
    alt="product image no.8">
  </figure>
  <figure class="span3">
    <img class="img-polaroid" src="img/image-9.jpg"
    alt="product image no.9">
  </figure>
  <figure class="span3">
    <img class="img-polaroid" src="img/image-10.jpg"
    alt="product image no.10">
  </figure>
  <figure class="span3">
    <img class="img-polaroid" src="img/image-11.jpg"
    alt="product image no.11">
  </figure>
  <figure class="span3">
    <img class="img-polaroid" src="img/image-12.jpg"
    alt="product image no.12">
  </figure>
  <figure class="span3">
    <img class="img-polaroid" src="img/image-13.jpg"
    alt="product image no.13">
  </figure>
  <figure class="span3">
    <img class="img-polaroid" src="img/image-14.jpg"
    alt="product image no.14">
  </figure>
  <figure class="span3">
    <img class="img-polaroid" src="img/image-15.jpg"
    alt="product image no.15">
  </figure>
  <figure class="span3">
    <img class="img-polaroid" src="img/image-16.jpg"
    alt="product image no.16">
  </figure>
</div>
```

What just happened?

We have just added the HTML content structure for the Gallery page. In this page, we added the page heading and all the product images. At this stage, our Gallery page looks as shown in the following screenshot:

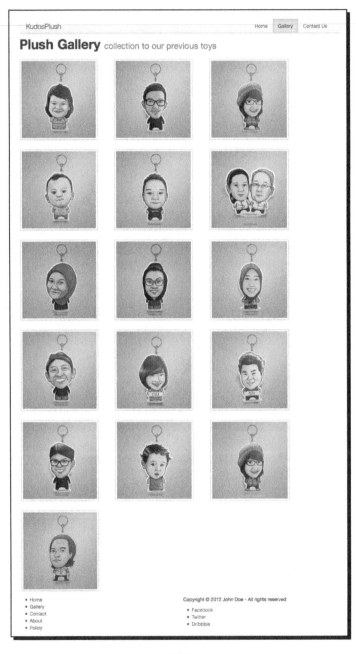

Contact page content

Next, we are going to work on the Contact page. In this page, we will add three sections: the map image (in a real case, this would show the store location), the address information, and the contact form for contacting the website owners online.

Time for action – adding HTML structure for the Contact page

To add HTML structure for the Contact page, perform the following steps:

1. First open up `contact.html` in your code editor.

2. Then, add the content title with `H1`, as we did in the Gallery page.

   ```
   <h1>Contact Us <small>we would like to hear from you</small></h1>
   ```

3. Then, we add the map image. This map section will be hidden when viewed in a very small viewport size, so we add a special class `hidden-phone` in the container, as follows:

   ```
   <div class="row hidden-phone">
     <div class="map span12">
       <img class="img-polaroid" src="img/map.jpg"
       alt="This is where we are">
     </div>
   </div>
   ```

4. Add an `<hr>` element next to the preceding map section to separate it from the next section.

5. Add the second row to wrap the section.

   ```
   <div class="row"> </div>
   ```

6. In the second row, we add the address and contact information as well as the contact form. So, we split this section into two columns. The first column will wrap the address.

   ```
   <div class="address span6">
   <h3>KudosPlush Toys</h3><br>
     <address>
       Street Anywhere In the World 123<br>
       The Country, NaN 123456<br>
       <abbr title="Phone">P.</abbr> (123) 987-654321 <br>
       <abbr title="Fax">F.</abbr> (123) 123-123456
     </address>

     <p>Cupcake ipsum dolor sit amet oat cake cotton candy
     carrot cake gummi bears. Chupa chups croissant powder
   ```

```
danish toffee pudding jujubes cupcake cotton candy.
Tootsie roll jelly beans macaroon sweet faworki
dragée.</p>

<p>Jelly danish danish chocolate cake gingerbread candy
fruitcake donut jelly beans. Dragée cheesecake tootsie
roll halvah carrot cake fruitcake sweet roll. Topping
dragée pudding. Candy oat cake candy canes.</p>
</div>
```

7. The second column will wrap the contact form. This form is quite simple; it consists of the `name`, `email`, and `message` input fields as well as the submit button.

```
<div class="form span6">
  <h4>Contact Form</h4>
  <form action="index_submit" method=
  "get" accept-charset="utf-8">
    <div class="row">
      <label class="span2" for="name">Your Name</label>

      <input class="span4" id="name"
      type="text" placeholder="e.g. John Doe">
    </div>

    <div class="row">
      <label class="span2" for="email">Email Adress</label>
      <input class="span4" id="email" type=
      "email" placeholder="eg. yourname@email.com">
    </div>

    <div class="row">
      <label class="span2" for="message">
      Your Message</label>
      <textarea class="span4" id="message"></textarea>
    </div>

    <button type="submit" class="btn btn btn-large
    btn-submit pull-right">Submit</button>
  </form>
</div>
```

What just happened?

We have just added HTML structure for the Contact page content. We first added the map (in a real case, this would show the business or store location), and then we also added the address information, including imaginary phone and fax numbers. Lastly, we added the contact form for visitors contacting online.

Here is how the Contact page looks at the moment:

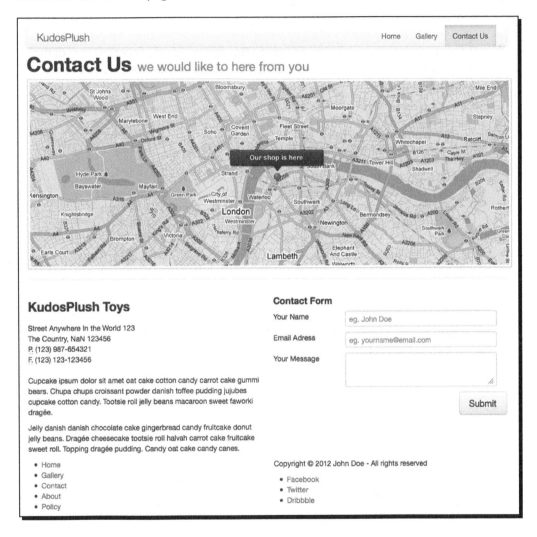

The About page content

Now, we are going to add HTML content structure for the About page. This page will have two sections, the business story and the founder profiles.

Time for action – adding HTML content structure for the About page

To add HTML content structure for the About page, perform the following steps:

1. First, open `contact.html` in your code editor.

2. As with previous pages, we will add the title of the page.

```
<h1>About <small>read the story</small></h1>
```

3. Then, we add the Business Story section. This section ideally tells the story of the business and the products. But, since we have many stories, we only add some random text in it.

```
<div class="row">

  <div class="img-story span6">
    <img class="img-polaroid" src="img/img-about.jpg">
  </div>
  <div class="story span6">
    <p>Donut pie brownie sweet lollipop. Lollipop wypas
    dessert sesame snaps chocolate cake chocolate bar
    croissant. Lollipop jelly jelly liquorice bonbon sweet.
    ... Chupa chups sugar plum powder gingerbread bonbon.
    Tiramisu tart cookie jelly beans.</p>
  </div>
</div>
<hr>
```

4. Lastly, add the founder's profile section. This section will be split up into two columns as our imaginary business has two founders.

```
<h3>Meet the Founders</h3>
  <div class="profile row">
    <div class="span6">
      <div class="row">
        <div class="span2">
          <img class="img-polaroid" src="img/salman.jpg">
        </div>
        <div class="span4">
          <h4>Salman Fariz Alutfi</h4>
          <p>Donut pie brownie sweet lollipop. Lollipop wypas
          dessert sesame snaps chocolate cake chocolate bar
          croissant...</p>
        </div>
      </div>
    </div>
    <div class="span6">
      <div class="row">
```

```
        <div class="span2">
          <img class="img-polaroid" src="img/arif.jpg">
        </div>
        <div class="span4">
          <h4>Arief Bahari</h4>
          <p>Donut pie brownie sweet lollipop. Lollipop wypas
          dessert sesame snaps chocolate cake chocolate bar
          croissant...</p>
        </div>
      </div>
    </div>
  </div>
```

What just happened?

We have just added HTML content structure for the About page. On this page, we added a map image; alternatively, you can replace it by embedding a real map from services such as Google Maps. We also added the profiles of the two founders of the business.

The following screenshot shows what this page currently looks like:

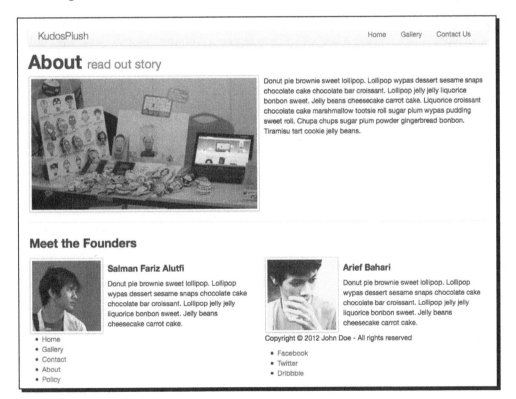

Now, we only have one more document to work on, the Policy page.

The Policy page

Typically, a website should have a Privacy and Policy page containing some agreements regarding the website. For example, information that the website collects when we visit the it, ads on the website that may also collect our information, or what policy is protecting the collected information.

In this project, we will also add this kind of page. This page is the simplest on our site. It will only consist of the page title and the text content, which is divided into two columns.

Time for action – adding HTML content structure for the Privacy and Policy page

To add HTML content structure for the Privacy and Policy page, perform the following steps:

1. Open `policy.html` in your code editor.

2. Then, add the title with the `<h1>` tag.

    ```
    <h1>Privacy &amp; Policy <small>sweet user agreement</small></h1>
    ```

3. Let's add the content. As we mentioned, this content will be divided into two columns. We will use a pair of `<div>` elements with the `.span6` class. The content of this page is extremely long, so in the following code snippet, we have cut it off to fit well in the page.

    ```
    <div class="span6">
      <h3>Donut pie brownie sweet lollipop.</h3>
      <p>Donut pie brownie sweet lollipop. Lollipop wypas
      dessert sesame snaps chocolate cake chocolate bar
      croissant. Lollipop jelly jelly liquorice bonbon sweet ..</p>
    </div>
    <div class="span6">
      <h3>Powder jelly toffee marshmallow cake</h3>
      <p>Cupcake ipsum dolor sit. Amet bear claw croissant.
      Pudding toffee jujubes topping ice cream icing chupa
      chups. Cotton candy cupcake sugar plum lemon drops. Pastry
      pudding croissant cupcake ...</p>
    </div>
    ```

What just happened?

We have just finished structuring the last page, the Privacy and Policy page. In this project, we added several paragraphs to fill the content and split it into two columns. At this stage, here is how the Privacy and Policy page appears:

KudosPlush   Home   Gallery   Contact Us

Privacy & Policy sweet user agreement

Donut pie brownie sweet lollipop.

Donut pie brownie sweet lollipop. Lollipop wypas dessert sesame snaps chocolate cake chocolate bar croissant. Lollipop jelly jelly liquorice bonbon sweet. Jelly beans cheesecake carrot cake. Liquorice croissant chocolate cake marshmallow tootsie roll sugar plum wypas pudding sweet roll. Chupa chups sugar plum powder gingerbread bonbon. Tiramisu tart cookie jelly beans. Lemon drops ice cream dessert. Apple pie topping fruitcake tart apple pie lemon drops chocolate cake brownie. Caramels icing toffee marshmallow jujubes donut pastry jelly-o icing. Wafer sesame snaps liquorice sweet. Dragée danish apple pie candy chocolate bar wypas. Gummi bears macaroon powder bear claw. Chocolate cake jelly pastry jujubes chocolate apple pie.

Chocolate cake liquorice topping

Chocolate cake liquorice topping gingerbread wypas toffee dessert. Pie powder wafer oat cake liquo rice gummies. Lemon drops chupa chups danish muffin pastry faworki halvah. Jujubes sweet danish gummies jelly-o donut biscuit. Toffee sesame snaps wypas jelly-o jelly-o ice cream jelly.

Soufflé chocolate bar pastry dragée. Cake soufflé lemon drops tiramisu halvah pie apple pie. Candy canes sweet roll jujubes oat cake gingerbread. Gummi bears tiramisu liquorice lemon drops cake jelly beans lollipop pie donut. Liquorice brownie brownie muffin halvah wypas. Gummi bears applicake cotton candy chocolate cake donut. Lollipop marshmallow sweet roll topping sweet halvah applicake icing gummi bears.

Tiramisu candy canes lollipop.

Cheesecake chocolate bar donut. Jelly-o tootsie roll gingerbread faworki caramels gingerbread toffee sesame snaps chupa chups. Tootsie roll wafer sesame snaps sweet roll biscuit bear claw. Candy canes carrot cake sweet cake chocolate bar gummies. Pudding candy canes cookie applicake cotton candy. Jujubes icing jelly beans pie gummies.

- Home
- Gallery
- Contact
- About
- Policy

Powder jelly toffee marshmallow cake

Cupcake ipsum dolor sit. Amet bear claw croissant. Pudding toffee jujubes topping ice cream icing chupa chups. Cotton candy cupcake sugar plum lemon drops. Pastry pudding croissant cupcake. Croissant macaroon chocolate cake. Muffin cotton candy jelly beans chocolate candy canes. Sesame snaps oat cake candy pudding chocolate cookie.

Powder candy canes gummies sweet roll

Powder candy canes gummies sweet roll. Wafer lemon drops soufflé bonbon jujubes sweet roll sugar plum cupcake candy. Powder jujubes topping liquorice halvah dragée. Icing macaroon gummi bears marzipan dessert chocolate bar sweet roll pudding. Fruitcake jelly-o halvah. Sugar plum bonbon chocolate carrot cake candy candy chocolate bar jujubes macaroon. Pie gingerbread chocolate bonbon gingerbread.

Sweet roll jelly-o bonbon carrot cake caramels lemon drops muffin. Toffee lemon drops applicake tootsie roll sesame snaps oat cake. Marzipan topping chocolate sesame snaps chocolate. Pudding liquorice cookie danish liquorice. Pastry apple pie bear claw macaroon apple pie. Topping croissant carrot cake gummies sesame snaps.

Marshmallow cupcake gummi bears muffin sesame snaps.

Marshmallow cupcake gummi bears muffin sesame snaps. Sweet cotton candy carrot cake brownie cookie cupcake. Wypas candy caramels oat cake lollipop cotton candy icing. Bonbon pastry cookie jelly beans chocolate bar jelly beans. Cupcake toffee cake marshmallow. Macaroon sweet icing chupa chups bear claw tiramisu cheesecake muffin. Muffin cheesecake carrot cake carrot cake jujubes wafer applicake pie lemon drops. Cotton candy wafer chocolate marshmallow dessert candy pastry.

Copyright © 2012 John Doe - All rights reserved

- Facebook
- Twitter
- Dribbble

Summary

In this chapter we have done many things to construct the website, including:

- Setting up Bootstrap and Project working directories
- Preparing the website images and the JavaScript
- Adding a new font family with the `@font-face` rule
- Installing and using an application to edit and compile LESS files
- Structuring the HTML documents

We are about halfway through our project. In the next chapter we will start styling our website's presentation using CSS3 with LESS syntax.

5
Enhancing the Product Launch Site with CSS3 and LESS

In the previous chapter we laid the foundation of our product launch site with Bootstrap, including setting up the Bootstrap, creating the working directory, and preparing website assets, such as images and JavaScript libraries. We also installed a LESS application, called CrunchApp, to later compose and compile LESS into CSS. Lastly, we structured the HTML markup for the website.

In this chapter we are going to focus on enhancing the look of our website, thus we are mostly going to work with CSS3, which will be compiled using LESS.

In this chapter, we will execute the process in the following order:

◆ We will first work on the website's header and footer styles, since all the pages will have the same styles

◆ We will add styles for the content section on each page

◆ We will add styles for a specific viewport width with CSS3 Media Queries

◆ We will examine and sort out the styles that are not necessary and test our website in different viewport sizes

Let's get started!

Custom LESS variables

In the previous chapter, we imported the built-in variables from Bootstrap. However, we need to define our own variables to meet the special requirement for our website.

In *Chapter 1, Responsive Web Design*, we discussed how to define a variable in LESS. But just in case you are not willing to flip back to the previous chapter, the variable in LESS is simply defined with the @ symbol.

For example, the following code snippet defines the white color with the @color variable:

```
@color: #fff;
```

This is just a small tip. You can name the variable as desired, but make sure that the name is logical to the variable purpose, descriptive, easy to memorize, and also easy to write.

Time for action – defining custom variables

For defining custom variables, perform the following steps:

1. Let's open CrunchApp.

2. Create a new LESS file and name it as _variables.less. This file is dedicated to store our own variables. Also, make sure that this file is stored within the less folder in our working directory.

3. We will define our new font family that we added in the previous chapter with the @font-face rule. Thus, we need to import _fonts.less into the _variables. less file.

    ```
    @import "_fonts.less";
    ```

4. The new font family, Droid Sans, is set as the primary font of our website with the @ primaryFont variable.

    ```
    @primaryFont: "DroidSansRegular", Arial, sans-serif;
    ```

You can name this variable in accordance with the font family name, let's say, @droidSans. But if you decide to change the font family, you will most likely need to change the variable name too.

For example, if I change the font family to Open Sans, I have to change the variable name from @droidSans to @openSans and the names of the variables that I have added through the stylesheet to represent that change. This certainly is not a very pleasant task.

For further tips on naming conventions, you can read the post available at CSS Wizardry (http://csswizardry.com/2010/08/ semantics-and-sensibility/).

5. In this project, we set the basic font size to `1em`. We save the font size value into a variable named `@baseFontSize` as follows:

```
@baseFontSize: 1em;
```

6. We set the line height to twice that of the basic font size. We can achieve it by using the following code:

```
@lineHeight: @baseFontSize * 2;
```

7. We set the basic length for measuring CSS properties, such as the padding and the margin. In this project, we set the basic length to `10px`.

```
@baseLength: 10px;
```

8. We also need to define our website color scheme with variables. If you take a look at the images shown in the following screenshot, you will notice that we have three unique colors: green, brown, and cream. These colors will be the brand colors of our website.

First, we set green as the primary color of the website. We save the color with a variable named `@primaryColor`.

```
@primaryColor: #3e6b6d;
```

Brown is the secondary color saved within `@secondaryColor`.

```
@secondaryColor: ##cd9a62;
```

Cream is set as the tertiary color and we save it in a variable named `@tertiaryColor`.

```
@tertiaryColor: ##fff7b6;
```

9. Open `_styles.less`.

10. Import our `_variables.less` file to `_styles.less`.

   ```
   @import "_variables.less";
   ```

   So, we can reuse these variables in `_styles.less`.

What just happened?

We just defined the custom variables for our site in a new LESS file named `_variables.less` and we then imported this file to `_styles.less`. At this stage, our `_styles.less` file contains the following two import rules:

```
@import "_bootstrap.less";
@import "_variables.less";
```

Now, we can use our custom variables along with the LESS variables that come from the Bootstrap.

Custom LESS mixins

In addition, we also need to define our own mixins for the same reasons that we created the custom variables in the preceding section.

Time for action – defining custom LESS mixins

Perform the following steps to define the custom LESS mixins:

1. Let's open CrunchApp.

2. Create a new LESS file and name it as `_mixins.less`. Save it in the `less` folder. We will use `_mixins.less` to store our own mixins' definitions.

3. **Image replacement** is a technique of hiding text and then replacing it with an image through the `background-image` property. In our project, we will apply this method to display the website's logo image and social media icons. We will define the style rules for image replacement in `.ir`, as follows:

   ```
   .ir {
       text-indent: 100%;
       white-space: nowrap;
       overflow: hidden;
   }
   ```

4. Next, we define a mixin for the text shadow. But this time we will also add some parameters to it. As discussed in *Chapter 1*, *Responsive Web Design*, these are also called as parametric mixins.

   Let's add the following line to define the text shadow mixin:

   ```
   .text-shadow(@h: 1px, @v: 1px, @b: 1px, @txtshadowcolor: @black) {
     text-shadow: @h @v @b @txtshadowcolor;
   }
   ```

5. Open `_styles.less`.

6. Import our `_mixins.less` file with the `@import` rule as follows:

   ```
   @import "_mixins.less";
   ```

   So, we can use these mixins within `_styles.less`.

What just happened?

We just defined two new mixins, one for applying the image replacement technique and one for applying the text shadow. We had a glimpse of LESS mixins in *Chapter 1*, *Responsive Web Design*. Using mixins in LESS allows us to pass particular styles by simply declaring the class selector as part of another definition, so we don't have to write all the style rules again.

We can add some parameters to the mixin for the text shadow so that we can customize the values.

The CSS3 `text-shadow` property requires four parameters: the horizontal offset, the vertical offset, the shadow blur, and lastly, the shadow color.

In step 4, these text shadow parameters are represented with the following variables: `@h` for the horizontal offset, `@v` for the vertical offset, `@b` for the shadow blur, and `@txtShadowColor` for the shadow color.

These parameters also have their own default values: `1px` for `@h`, `@v`, and `@b` and black for the default text shadow. Bootstrap provides a variable to add the black color with the `@black` variable.

There are a number of image replacement methods; the one that has been the most popular over the years is called **FIR** or **Fahrner Image Replacement**. It utilizes the `text-indent` property with the extreme negative value, `-9999px`.

The image replacement method that we just added in the preceding steps is popularized by Scott Kellum (http://www.zeldman.com/2012/03/01/replacing-the-9999px-hack-new-image-replacement/).

LESS color functions

LESS provides a few functions for adjusting colors and the following table shows some of the color functions that we are going to use frequently in this project:

Function	Use	Example
`lighten(@color, n%);`	Makes the color lighter than its initial value	`@black: #000000` `lighten(@black, 10%);` In this example, we make the black color lighter by 10 percent and turn it to #1a1a1a
`darken(@color, n%);`	Makes the color darker than its initial values	`@white: #ffffff` `darken(@color, 10%);` In this example, we make the white color darker by 10 percent and turn it to #e6e6e6
`fade(@color, n%);`	Lowers the color density	`@black: #000000` `fade(@black, 10%);` In this example, we lower the black color density to 10% and it turns into the RGBA color format with 10% on the Alpha channel, for example, `rgba(0,0,0,0.1)`

Introducing the Scope concept

If you are familiar with other programming languages, such as JavaScript, you will find a programming concept called Scope, where the local functions or variables are initially applied. In this case, LESS also follows the same concept.

In the following example, we have two `@color` variables. These variables store different values, one stores #000000 and the other one stores #ffffff, and one of these is nested within the particular selector as follows:

```
@color: #000000

.nav {
  a {
    @color: #ffffff;
    color: @color;
  }
}
.content {
  p {
    color: @color;
  }
}
```

In the preceding example, the `.nav` class will take the variable that is defined within its brackets, and the color will turn into `#ffffff` when compiled to CSS. But the `@color` variable nested inside the `a` class will not be applied to `p`, which is nested in `.content`. Instead, the `p` class takes the global `@color` variable, which stores the color number `#000000`.

General style rules

Before we go into the specifics, we will define some general style rules that apply to particular elements in our HTML document, such as the headings, horizontal lines, inputs, and textarea elements.

Time for action – adding general style rules

To add general style rules perform the following steps:

1. Let's open our `_styles.less` file.

2. First, we specify the `box-sizing` model for the HTML elements to `border-box`. Bootstrap has a special mixin to specify the box model with `.box-sizing`.

   ```
   * {
       .box-sizing(border-box);
   }
   ```

   The `.box-sizing` mixin includes the vendor prefix. If we open the `mixins.less` file, where Bootstrap stores its mixins' definitions, we can find the `.box-sizing` mixin defined as follows:

   ```
   .box-sizing(@boxmodel) {
     -webkit-box-sizing: @boxmodel;
        -moz-box-sizing: @boxmodel;
             box-sizing: @boxmodel;
   }
   ```

   This eliminates the requirement to write the vendor prefixes ourselves, which is quite a time saver.

3. Then, we specify the document's font family, font size, and line height.

   ```
   body {
       font-family: @primaryFont;
       font-size: @baseFontSize;
       line-height: @lineHeight;
   }
   ```

4. Turn the color of headings to brown.

```
h1, h2, h3, h4, h5, h6 {
    color: @secondaryColor;
}
```

5. Next, we add styles for the horizontal line with the `<hr>` element. We first remove the default `<hr>` element from the borderline by setting the `border` property to `0`.

```
hr {
    border: 0;
}
```

6. We replace the border style with `1px` of height and CSS3 Gradient. In this case, Bootstrap does not provide a mixin for creating a gradient that meets our specification. So, we have to write it ourselves as follows:

```
hr {
    border: 0;
    height: 1px;
    background-image: -webkit-linear-gradient(left,
    fade(@black, 0%), fade(@black, 15%), fade(@black, 0%));
    background-image:    -moz-linear-gradient(left,
    fade(@black, 0%), fade(@black, 15%), fade(@black, 0%));
    background-image:     -ms-linear-gradient(left,
    fade(@black, 0%), fade(@black, 15%), fade(@black, 0%));
    background-image:      -o-linear-gradient(left,
    fade(@black, 0%), fade(@black, 15%), fade(@black, 0%));
    background-image:         linear-gradient(left,
    fade(@black, 0%), fade(@black, 15%), fade(@black, 0%));
}
```

In the preceding code, we added three color stops in the gradient and used the `@fade` function to specify the color.

- ❑ In the first and last color stops, we faded the color to `0`; the color will not be visible in the browser

- ❑ In the second color stop, we faded the color to `15%`; the color is faded, but still visible

Lastly, we add margins at the top and bottom to add some whitespaces between the horizontal line and the sections it separates.

```
margin: (@baseLength * 4) 0;
```

When we view this in the browser, we will get the following result:

Thanks to Chris Coyier for the tip on the style rules: you can head over to the following post at CSS-Tricks.com (`http://css-tricks.com/simple-styles-for-horizontal-rules/`) to find additional tips for styling the `<hr>` element.

Additionally, you can head over to the post at Hongkiat.com for further discussion on creating gradient with CSS3 (`http://www.hongkiat.com/blog/css3-linear-gradient/`).

7. We will overwrite the default border color and shadow color of the `<input>` and `<textarea>` elements when they are in the `focus` state with our brand colors. We will define the style rules for these elements together, nested under the kudosplush class, as follows:

```
.kudosplush {
    input, textarea {
        &:focus {

        }
    }
}
```

Within the `&:focus` curly brackets, we define the border color with the `@borderColor` variable.

```
.kudosplush {
    input, textarea {
        &:focus {
            @borderColor: darken(@secondaryColor, 10%);
        }
    }
}
```

Referring to the Scope concept, this variable will be applied only within the `&:focus` curly brackets and the nested selectors.

Next, we also define the shadow color and styles with the `@inputShadow` variable. In this case, we add two shadows: the inner and outer shadows.

```
.kudosplush {
    input, textarea {
        &:focus {
            @borderColor: darken(@secondaryColor, 10%);
            @inputShadow: inset 0 1px 1px fade(@black,    7%),
            0 0 8px fade(@borderColor, 50%);
        }
    }
}
```

Now we can apply the `@borderColor` variable to set the `<input>` and `<textarea>` border colors.

```
.kudosplush {
    input, textarea {
        &:focus {
        @borderColor: darken(@secondaryColor, 10%);
        @inputShadow: inset 0 1px 1px fade(@black,    7%),
        0 0 8px fade(@borderColor, 50%);
        border-color: @borderColor;
        }
    }
}
```

Then, we use the `.box-shadow` mixin from Bootstrap along with the `@inputShadow` variable (as the value) to set the CSS3 box shadow as follows:

```
.kudosplush {
    input, textarea {
        &:focus {
        @borderColor: darken(@secondaryColor, 10%);
        @inputShadow: inset 0 1px 1px fade(@black,    7%),
        0 0 8px fade(@borderColor, 50%);
        border-color: @borderColor;
        .box-shadow(@inputShadow);
        }
    }
}
```

8. Lastly, we use a mixin from Bootstrap that defines the input placeholder text styles. In this case, we make the placeholder text color a little softer using the LESS color function, `darken()`.

```
input {
    .placeholder(darken(@white, 10%));
}
```

9. Save the `_styles.less` file. Then, press *Ctrl + Enter* (for Windows and Linux) or *Command + Enter* (for OS X) to convert all these codes into regular CSS. Save the result in the `_styles.css` file within the `css` folder.

What just happened?

We just added general style rules for particular elements, such as the headings, horizontal line, and inputs, and then compiled them into a regular CSS. When you view them in the browser, you should get the following result if you focus on the `<input>` and `<textarea>` elements:

Eliminating vendor prefixes

Some of the styles discussed in the preceding section are built with mixins that come with Bootstrap. One of the advantages of using these mixins is that we don't have to worry about the vendor prefixes that are required to ensure cross-browser compatibility.

If we take a look at one of the mixins, let's say `.box-shadow`, you will find that the vendor prefixes have been properly defined as follows:

```
.box-shadow(@shadow) {
  -webkit-box-shadow: @shadow;
     -moz-box-shadow: @shadow;
          box-shadow: @shadow;
}
```

Thus, when we compile it into a regular CSS, all these vendor prefixes will be automatically passed over to the assigned CSS ruleset. For example, in the preceding steps, we have assigned `.box-shadow` to the `input` and `textarea` focus states as follows:

```
input, textarea {
  &:focus {
    @borderColor: darken(@brown, 10%);
    @inputShadow: inset 0 1px 1px fade(@black, 7%),
    0 0 8px fade(@borderColor, 50%);

    border-color: @borderColor;
    .box-shadow(@inputshadow);
  }
}
```

When we compile this code into a regular CSS, it will turn into the following:

```
input:focus,
textarea:focus {
  border-color: #bf813d;
  -webkit-box-shadow: inset 0 1px 1px rgba(0, 0, 0, 0.07),
  0 0 8px rgba(191, 129, 61, 0.5);
  -moz-box-shadow: inset 0 1px 1px rgba(0, 0, 0, 0.07),
  0 0 8px rgba(191, 129, 61, 0.5);
  box-shadow: inset 0 1px 1px rgba(0, 0, 0, 0.07),
  0 0 8px rgba(191, 129, 61, 0.5);
}
```

The other mixins that store CSS3 properties and the vendor prefixes act in the same way. You can see all the mixins more thoroughly in `mixins.less`, which you can find in the `less` folder in our working directory.

The button styles

Bootstrap has its own default button styles. At the time of writing this book, Bootstrap sets the color for the basic button to gray, while the primary button is set to the blue color, as shown in the following screenshot:

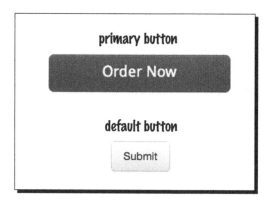

Unfortunately, these colors don't fit our design. So, we need to overwrite them with our own brand colors.

Time for action – overwriting the Bootstrap button styles

For overwriting the Bootstrap button styles, perform the following steps:

1. Open `_styles.less`.

2. First, we overwrite the default button styles, including the button's background color, border radius, and text shadow. We nest the style rules for buttons under the `.kudosplush` class to overwrite the default style from Bootstrap as follows:

```
.kudosplush {
    .btn {
        .buttonBackground(@secondaryColor,
        darken(@secondaryColor, 10%), @white,
        0 1px 1px fade(@white, 75%));
        .border-radius(@borderRadiusSmall);
        .text-shadow(1px,1px,0,fade(@black, 30%)) ;
    }
}
```

In the preceding code snippet, we changed the background color and border radius with Bootstrap's `.buttonBackground` and `.border-radius` mixins respectively. We also set the button's border radius to be a bit smaller using Bootstrap's `@borderRadiusSmall` variable, which is set to 3px.

We used the `.text-shadow` mixin that we have defined on our own to change the text shadow color.

3. Then, we overwrite the primary button styles. In this ruleset, we will overwrite the background color in the same way as in the default button. We also increase the font size and the padding a bit and transform the entire text to uppercase.

```
.btn-primary {
    .buttonBackground(@green, darken(@green, 10%),
    @white, 0 1px 1px rgba(255,255,255,.75));
    font-size: @fontsize * 1.2;
    padding: (@length * 2) (@length * 4);
    text-transform: uppercase;
}
```

4. Save the file and compile it into a regular CSS.

What just happened?

We just added styles to override the default button styles from Bootstrap. The following screenshot shows how the button styles have been changed from the default to the one of our choice.

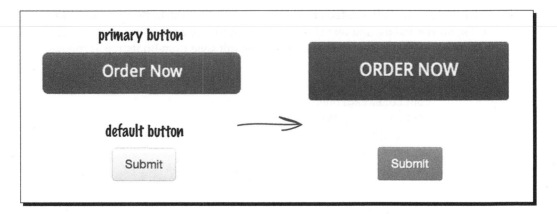

If you inspect further in the _styles.css file, you will see that it has also compiled the button hover styles, active styles, and disabled styles. It has even provided support for the gradient color in Internet Explorer with a filter, as shown in the following code snippet:

```
.kudosplush .btn-primary {
  font-size: 1.2em;
  padding: 20px 40px;
  text-transform: uppercase;
  color: #ffffff;
  text-shadow: 0 1px 1px rgba(255, 255, 255, 0.75);
  background-color: #375e60;
  background-image: -moz-linear-gradient(top, #3e6b6d, #2c4b4c);
  background-image: -webkit-gradient(linear, 0 0, 0 100%,
  from(#3e6b6d), to(#2c4b4c));
  background-image: -webkit-linear-gradient(top, #3e6b6d, #2c4b4c);
  background-image: -o-linear-gradient(top, #3e6b6d, #2c4b4c);
  background-image: linear-gradient(to bottom, #3e6b6d, #2c4b4c);
  background-repeat: repeat-x;
  filter: progid:DXImageTransform.Microsoft.gradient
  (startColorstr='#ff3e6b6d', endColorstr=
  '#ff2c4b4c', GradientType=0);
  border-color: #2c4b4c #2c4b4c #101b1c;
  border-color: rgba(0, 0, 0, 0.1) rgba(0, 0, 0, 0.1)
  rgba(0, 0, 0, 0.25);
```

```
*background-color: #2c4b4c;
/* Darken IE7 buttons by default so they stand out more given they
won't have borders */

filter: progid:DXImageTransform.Microsoft.gradient
(enabled = false);
}
```

Why are the buttons that large?

As you can see in the preceding screenshots, our buttons are quite large. You are probably wondering, why are they that large?

In *Chapter 1*, *Responsive Web Design*, we have mentioned that more people are accessing websites from mobile devices, and most of them are featured with multitouch screens. People use their fingers instead of a mouse or a physical keyboard to interact with websites, which includes clicking on the links, scrolling on the page, and pressing the buttons. So, we need to provide a convenient target space that comfortably fits the user's finger.

A study from Microsoft, *Target Size Study for One-Handed Thumb Use on Small Touchscreen Devices* (http://research.microsoft.com/pubs/75812/parhi-mobileHCI06.pdf), shows that by providing a wider target size for the user interface--such as the buttons--users are able to interact easier and faster with lesser errors, which eventually serves a better user experience.

On the contrary, specifying very minimal target size will, in fact, irritate the users; users tend to make tap errors when the target size is too small for their fingers.

Further on this discussion, you can follow:

- *Touch Target Sizes* (http://www.lukew.com/ff/entry.asp?1085)
- *Finger-Friendly Design: Ideal Mobile Touchscreen Target Sizes By Anthony T* (http://uxdesign.smashingmagazine.com/2012/02/21/finger-friendly-design-ideal-mobile-touchscreen-target-sizes/)
- *Mobile UX - the intricacies of designing for mobile devices* (http://www.slideshare.net/ribot/mobile-ux-the-intricacies-of-designing-for-mobile-devices-presentation)
- *Why Whitespace matters* (http://boagworld.com/design/why-whitespace-matters/)

Referring to these studies, we will specify the length on our website—for the parameters such as the whitespace, width, height, and font size—wider for user convenience.

The header styles

In this section, we will start off by adding styles for the website header. Our website header contains the logo and the site navigation. Except on the homepage, we also add the *Hero* section (`http://twitter.github.com/bootstrap/examples/hero.html`).

Time for action – adding website header styles

For adding website header styles, perform the following steps:

1. Open `_styles.less`.

2. First, we change the header's background color with the LESS color function, `darken()`, as well as by specifying the padding for top and bottom, as follows:

```
.header {
    background-color: darken(@white, 2%);
    padding: (@length * 2) 0;
}
```

3. We will display the website's logo in the header. To display the image logo, we need to specify the size as well as hide the text by including the image replacement mixin, `.ir`. The logo in Bootstrap is added within `.brand` and we will nest `.ir` under the `.brand` class as follows:

```
.header {
background-color: darken(@white, 2%);
padding: (@length * 2) 0;
    .brand {
        .ir;
            width: 188px;
            height: 100px;
            padding: 0;
    }
}
```

Then, we add the logo image through the `background` property.

```
.header {
    background-color: darken(@white, 2%);
    padding: (@baseLength * 2) 0;
    .brand {
        .ir;
        width: 188px;
        height: 100px;
        background: url('../img/plush-logo.png') no-repeat;
    }
}
```

4. By default, the navigation bar, or `navbar`, has a number of decorative styles as shown in the following screenshot:

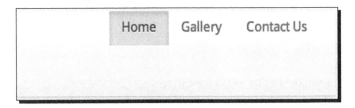

As we can see in the preceding screenshot, it has a gradient background, box shadow, and borderline. In this project, we will overwrite these with our own styles. So, let's nest all these styles under the `.header` class.

```
.header {
/* existing styles */
    .navbar {
        .navbar-inner {
            @navShadow: inset 0 0 0 fade(@black, 0%),
            0 0 0 fade(@black, 0%);
            .box-shadow(@navShadow);
            #gradient > .vertical(fade(@white,0%),
            fade(@white,0%));
            border: 0;
        }
    }
}
```

Bootstrap provides several mixins to add CSS3 gradients, which you can find nested under `#gradient` in `mixins.less`.

Given the preceding code snippet, we have just added a vertical gradient using the `#gradient > .vertical` setting to change the default vertical gradient in `navbar`, as follows:

```
#gradient > .vertical(fade(@white,0%),fade(@white,0%));
```

It requires two color stops, and we specified these colors using the `fade()` function and setting it to `0%` to make this gradient invisible.

Additionally, you can use the following selectors:

- `#gradient > .horizontal` to add the horizontal gradient
- `#gradient > .directional` to add the diagonal gradient
- `#gradient > .radial` to add the radial gradient

5. We also need to overwrite the default styles for the link menu in the navigation, including changing the text color and adding the background color and some whitespaces (with margin and padding). So, let's nest these styles under the `.header` class as well.

```less
.nav {
    margin-top: @baseLength * 3;
    li {
        margin-left: @baseLength;
    }
    a {
        .text-shadow(0,0,0,@white);
        text-transform: uppercase;
        color: @primaryColor;
        padding: 0 (@baseLength * 1.5);
        height: @baseLength * 4;
        line-height: @baseLength * 4.3;
        &:hover {
            .box-shadow(inset 0 0 0 fade(@black, 0%));
            .border-radius(@borderRadiusSmall);
            background-color: @primaryColor;
            color: @tertiaryColor;
        }
    }
    .active {
        > a {
            .box-shadow(inset 0 0 0 fade(@black, 0%));
            .border-radius(@borderRadiusSmall);
            .text-shadow(0,0,0,fade(@white, 0%));
            background-color: @primaryColor;
            color: @tertiaryColor;
        }
    }
}
```

6. Save the file and compile it into a regular CSS.

What just happened?

We just styled the header section. In this section, we added the logo image with the image replacement technique, which was introduced by Scott Kellum (http://scottkellum. com/). We have used this technique in our first project, but here is a little detail on how the technique hides the text.

The image replacement technique is specified with the following style declaration:

```
text-indent: 100%;
white-space: nowrap;
overflow: hidden;
```

The text is moved to the right of its container by `100%`. Thus, we actually have to first specify the width of the text container in order for this code to work properly. As the text is overflowing from the container, the `overflow` property is set to `hidden` to hide the text.

We also have overwritten the Bootstrap `navbar` default styles with our own, and the following screenshot shows how our website's header and navigation appear at this stage:

The footer styles

As mentioned earlier in this chapter, after working on the header section, we will work on the footer section. Our footer is rather simple. In the footer, we have menu navigation, social media icons, and a small copyright text, quite similar to the footer from our previous project. So, let's get started!

Time for action – adding footer styles

To add the footer styles, perform the following steps:

1. Open `_styles.less` in CrunchApp.
2. First, let's add a few basic styles to the footer, such as the background color, text color, and some whitespaces.

    ```
    .footer {
        color: lighten(@black, 70%);
        background-color: darken(@white, 2%);
        padding: (@baseLength * 5) 0;
        margin-top: @baseLength * 3;
    }
    ```

3. We remove the margin of the `<ul>` elements and display the `<li>` elements side by side, with `display:inline`, as well as provide a little gap on its right with `margin-right`, as follows:

```less
.footer {
    color: lighten(@black, 70%);
    background-color: darken(@white, 2%);
    padding: (@baseLength * 5) 0;
    margin-top: @baseLength * 3;
    ul {
        margin: 0;
    }
    li {
        display: inline;
        margin-right: @baseLength;
    }
}
```

4. Next, we set the color of the links in the footer, as well as the color of the links when they are being hovered over. Nest these styles under the `.footer` class.

```less
.footer {
    /* existing styles */
    a {
        color: lighten(@black, 70%);
        &:hover {
            color: lighten(@black, 30%);
            text-decoration: none;
        }
    }
}
```

5. As we have mentioned before, the social media icons are similar to our previous projects, in fact, we are using the same images. Nest all these styles under the `.footer` class as well.

```less
.footer {
/* existing styles */
    .social-links {
        text-align: right;
        li {
            margin-right: 0;
        }
        a {
            display: inline-block;
            width: 36px;
            height: 42px;
            .ir;
```

```
    }
.dribbble a, .facebook a, .twitter a {
    background-image: url('../img/social.png');
    background-repeat: no-repeat;
}
.dribbble a {
    background-position: -7px -58px;
    &:hover {
        background-position: -7px 0;
    }
}
.facebook a {
    background-position: -7px -174px;
    &:hover {
        background-position: -7px -116px;
    }
}
.twitter a {
    background-position: -7px -290px;
    &:hover {
        background-position: -7px -232px;
    }
}
}
}
```

6. Lastly, we align the copyright text to the right as follows:

```
.copyright {
        text-align: right;
        display: block;
    }
```

7. Save it and compile it into CSS.

What just happened?

We have just added the styles for the footer section, such as the background color, links' color at the navigation, and also added the social media icons with sprite images. At this stage, here is how the footer looks:

Home Gallery Contact About Policy   Copyright © 2012 John Doe - All rights reserved

Working on the homepage

We will be working on the specific styles for each page and we will start off with the homepage. We have a few sections on the homepage, such as the Hero (Hello World), Call-to-action, Gallery, Testimonial, and Subscribe Form.

The Hero section

The Hero or Hello World section is simply the section where we add content such as text, image, or perhaps a button as well to draw the visitor's attention to the website in the first place. In our case, this section is nested within the `<header>` element.

Time for action – adding styles for the Hello World section

To add styles for the Hello World section, perform the following steps:

1. Open `_styles.less` in CrunchApp.

2. First, we set the background color to inherit from the parent element, which is a `<header>` element, and then set the text with the primary color. In Boostrap, this section is specified with the `.hero-unit` class as follows:

```
.hero-unit {
    background-color: inherit;
    padding: (@baseLength * 3) 0;
    color: @primaryColor;
    margin-bottom: 0;
}
```

3. The text in the Hero section is wrapped within the paragraph elements and we will increase the font size just to make it standout a bit more. So nest these styles under the `.hello-unit` class.

```
.hero-unit {
    background-color: inherit;
    padding: (@baseLength * 3) 0;
    color: @primaryColor;
    margin-bottom: 0;
    p {
        font-size: @baseFontSize * 2.8;
        line-height: @lineHeight / 1.8;
    }
}
```

4. We have a paragraph with the `.price` class, which contains the product's price. In this case, we will make the price look distinct by applying a secondary color to it and making it bolder. So let's nest these styles under the `.hero-unit` class as well.

```
.hero-unit {
    background-color: inherit;
    padding: (@baseLength * 3) 0;
    color: @primaryColor;
    margin-bottom: 0;
    p {
        font-size: @baseFontSize * 2.8;
        line-height: @lineHeight / 1.8;
    }
    .price {
        font-weight: bold;
        color: @secondaryColor;
    }
}
```

5. Save the file and compile it to CSS.

What just happened?

We have just added the styles to the Hero section on the homepage by adjusting the background color to inherit from the parent element and adjusting the paragraph's font size so that it catches the user's eyes. At this stage, here is how it looks:

The Call-to-action section

The Call-to-action section is a common section in a product page or sales page, where we place some text, or perhaps also a button, with a prominent appearance to grab the visitors' attention in the hope that they perform an action in accordance to what we expect. In this project, we have placed some placeholder text with a button that says **Order Now**.

Time for action – adding styles for the Call-to-action section

To add styles for the Call-to-action section, perform the following steps:

1. Let's get back to `_styles.less`.

2. Unlike the Hero section, the Call-to-action section is part of the homepage content and is wrapped within a `<div>` element assigned with the `.cta` class. First, let's add `margin-top` to give some whitespaces between the Call-to-action section and the section preceding it.

```
.content {
  .cta {
    margin-top: @baseLength * 4;
  }
}
```

3. We change the color of the placeholder text to the secondary color and increase its font size.

```
.cta {
    margin-top: @baseLength * 4;
    .copy-text {
        color: @secondaryColor;
        font-size: @baseFontSize * 1.5;
    }
}
```

4. Save the file and compile it into CSS.

What just happened?

We have just added styles for the Call-to-action section. In the preceding steps we merely provided whitespaces and adjusted the placeholder font styles. We actually have the **Order Now** button, but we specified the button's color in the earlier section and Bootstrap has covered the complementary styles—the CSS3 rounded corners, gradients, shadows, and so on.

The following screenshot shows how it appears:

The Gallery section

On the homepage, we also have a Gallery section that features four images of the product. This Gallery section is positioned right after the Call-to-action section and is wrapped within a `<div>` element assigned with the `.gallery` class. As shown in *Chapter 4*, *Developing a Product Launch Site with Bootstrap*, each of the images in this Gallery section is wrapped within the new HTML5 `<figure>` element. This section is also a part of the homepage content, so we will nest the styles in the following steps under `.content`.

Time for action – adding styles for the Gallery section

For adding styles for the Gallery section, perform the following steps:

1. Open `_styles.less` in CrunchApp.

2. We can rely on Bootstrap's default styles for most of the gallery's needs, including the image styles. In *Chapter 4*, *Developing a Product Launch Site with Bootstrap*, we have added a Bootstrap special class `img-polaroid`, which gives us the following result:

So, in this step, we simply need to adjust the distance between these images, which flow over the place as shown in the following screenshot:

If we inspect it using Web Developer Tool (in Google Chrome) or Firebug (in Firefox), we will find out the cause. The `<figure>` element inherits `margin-right` for `40px` from the browser's default styles.

```
margin-bottom: 16px;
▶ margin-left: 20px;
margin-right: 40px;
margin-top: 16px;
marker-end: none;
marker-mid: none;
```

So let's set `margin-right` for the `<figure>` element to `0`, as follows:

```
.gallery {
  figure {
    margin-right: 0;
  }
}
```

3. Save the file and compile it to CSS.

What just happened?

Technically, we only removed `margin-right` from the `<figure>` element that is inherited from the default browser's stylesheet. The Gallery section now appears as shown in the following screenshot:

The Testimonial section

A website that offers a product or service commonly has a section for displaying customer testimonials or reviews, and as you can see, we also have one on our website. It is statistically said that providing customer testimonials or reviews on the website can help in increasing the sales (http://econsultancy.com/id/blog/9366-e-commerce-consumer-reviews-why-you-need-them-and-how-to-use-them).

The Testimonial section is also a part of the homepage section, so we will nest the styles under .content in the following steps.

Time for action – adding styles for the Testimonial section

Perform the following steps for adding styles to the Testimonial section:

1. Let's get back to _styles.less.

2. We will add styles to set the text alignment to the center, set the text color to be lighter with the LESS color function, and specify a larger size for the font.

```
.testimonial {
        font-size: @baseLength * 3;
        padding-bottom: @baseLength * 2;
        color: lighten(@black, 50%);
        text-align: center;
}
```

3. Save the file and compile it into CSS.

What just happened?

We have just added styles to the Testimonial section, which is quite simple. We simply changed the text color, font size, and alignment. Nothing too fancy in this section and the following screenshot shows how it appears:

Subscribe Form

We also have an e-mail subscription form, it consists of an <input> element with a new email type form and a submit button.

Time for action – adding styles for an input email

To add styles for an input e-mail, perform the following steps:

1. Let's get back to `_styles.less`.

2. This section is wrapped within a `<div>` element with the `.subscribe-form` class. We will first add a little distance between this section and the footer with `margin-bottom` and adjust the content alignment to the center.

```
.subscribe-form {
    margin-bottom: @baseLength * 2;
    text-align: center;
}
```

3. We will use most of Bootstrap's default input styles and change only a few details. In this case, we will expand the input width to be wider, as follows:

```
.subscribe-form {
    margin-bottom: @baseLength * 2;
    text-align: center;
    input {
        width: @baseLength * 28;
    }
}
```

4. Then, we set the height of the input and the submit button to be equal.

```
.subscribe-form {
    margin-bottom: @baseLength * 2;
    text-align: center;
    input {
        width: @baseLength * 28;
    }
    input, button {
        height: @baseLength * 5;
        padding: @baseLength (@baseLength * 2);
        margin-bottom: 0;
    }
}
```

5. Save the file and compile it into CSS.

What just happened?

We have just added styles to the `<input>` element and the submit button in the Subscription Form section. In the preceding steps, we aligned the form to the center, and then we specified the width and height of the `<input>` element.

Technically, we are done with the homepage, and the following screenshot shows how our website homepage appears:

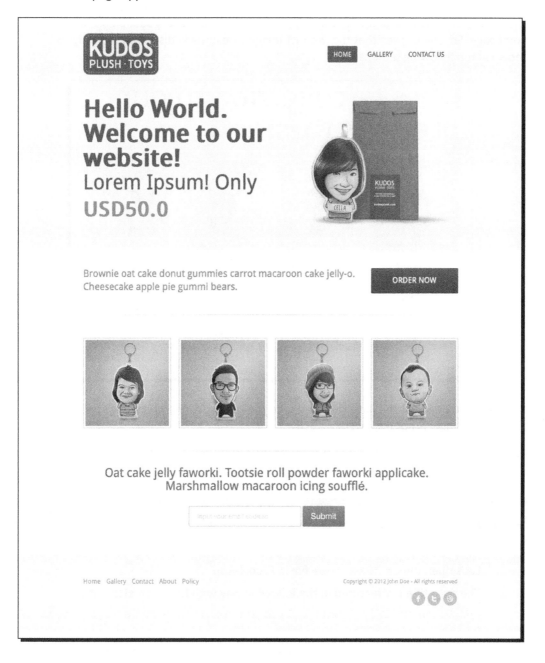

The Gallery page

Next, we are going to work on the Gallery page. This page features images of the product and, in fact, the HTML structure of this page is similar to the Gallery section on the homepage. So, you will see that the product images are already displayed properly, as shown in the following screenshot:

We only need to adjust the page title styles; as you can see in the preceding screenshot, the title, at this stage, is not displayed correctly.

The title and the images are part of the page content, so we will nest all the styles under .content.

Time for action – adjusting the page title styles

Perform the following steps for adjusting the page title styles:

1. Let's open the _styles.less file in CrunchApp.

2. The page title is structured in the following way with the `<h1>` element:

   ```
   <h1>Plush Gallery <small>collection to our previous toys</small></h1>
   ```

   We also have a `<small>` element for displaying a smaller title text. But it turns out that it is displayed with a bigger font.

If we inspect this element through Firebug, we will find out that the font size within the `<small>` element is set to `1.75em`. As we have discussed in *Chapter 3, Enhancing the Portfolio Website with CSS3*, the `em` unit relates to the base font size of the document or the parent element. In our case, `1.75em` turns out to be equal to `77px`, as shown in the following screenshot:

▶ **font-family**	"DroidSansRegular",Arial,sans–serif	
▼ **font-size**	**77px**	
h1 small	1.75em	_styles.css (line 581)
~~small~~	~~85%~~	_styles.css (line 496)
body	1em	_styles.css (line 5015)
h1	2.75em	_styles.css (line 563)
body	1em	_styles.css (line 146)
html	100%	_styles.css (line 33)

So let's decrease the font size; in this case, we decrease it to `0.75em` as follows:

```
h1 {
small {
     font-size: 0.75em;
     }
  }
```

3. Furthermore, if we view the result in the following screenshot:

We find that the whitespace between the title and the header is narrower than the one between the Gallery images, which makes this section imbalanced. So, let's add some more whitespaces at the top of the title with a margin as follows:

```
h1 {
    margin: (@baseLength * 4) 0 (@baseLength * 2);
    small {
        font-size: 0.75em;
    }
}
```

4. Save the file and compile it to CSS.

What just happened?

Technically, we did not add styles to the Gallery page as Bootstrap has predefined the styles for us, including the styles for image and layout. In the preceding steps, we only adjusted the page title styles.

The following screenshot shows how the Gallery page appears at this stage:

The Contact page

We are now going to work on the Contact page. On this page, we have three sections: the map image, the store contact and address, and the online contact form.

Similar to the other pages, most of the styles on this page are already defined between Bootstrap and some extra styles that we have added earlier in this chapter. So we only need to do a little adjustment to enhance its looks.

We will add these styles under the `.content` class.

Time for action – adding styles for the Contact page

For adding styles to the Contact page, perform the following steps:

1. Open `_styles.less` in CrunchApp.

2. If we take a look at the contact form on this page, we will see that the height of the `<input>` and `<textarea>` elements is short. It could be difficult for the users to tap the input correctly. So let's extend their height a little.

    ```less
    .contact {
        .contact-form {
            input {
                height: (@baseLength * 4);
            }
            textarea {
                min-height: (@baseLength * 8);
            }
        }
    }
    ```

3. We will also add a little more whitespace between the address and the contact form sections.

    ```less
    .contact {
        .contact-form {
            input {
                height: (@baseLength * 4);
            }
            textarea {
                min-height: (@baseLength * 8);
            }
        }
        .contact-form, .address {
            padding: (@baseLength * 2) (@baseLength * 1.5);
            margin-bottom: @baseLength * 2;
        }
    }
    ```

4. We will also add borderline in between, to separate these two sections.

```
.contact {
        .contact-form {
            input {
                height: (@baseLength * 4);
            }
            textarea {
                min-height: (@baseLength * 8);
            }
        }
        .contact-form, .address {
            padding: (@baseLength * 2) (@baseLength * 1.5);
            margin-bottom: @baseLength * 2;
        }
        .address {
            border-right: 1px solid darken(@white, 5%);
        }
    }
```

5. Save the file and compile it to a regular CSS.

What just happened?

We have just made some adjustments in the Contact page to make it look more appealing. Technically, we adjusted the `<input>` and `<textarea>` height to make the users tap on the input easily, particularly when they are accessing from mobile devices (with touch-screen support). We also separated the contact form and the address section by adding a thin borderline and added more whitespaces in between with padding and margin.

Why whitespace matters

Paul Boag in his post on `http://boagworld.com/design/why-whitespace-matters/` has explained thoroughly about whitespace and why it is important in web design.

At this stage, here's how the Contact page appears:

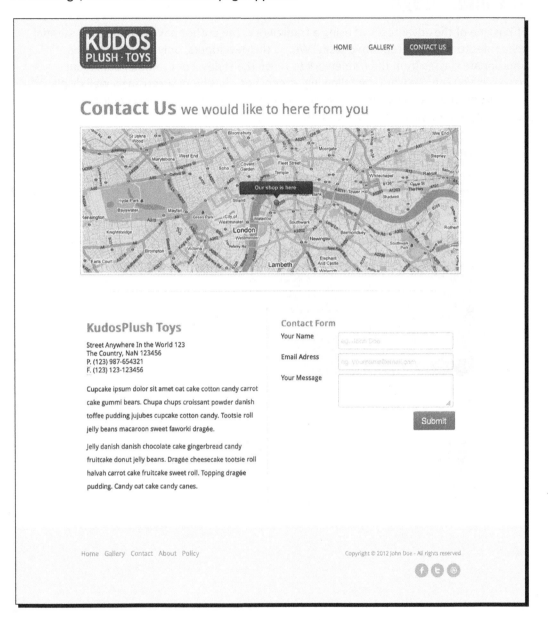

The About page

This is one of the advantages of using a framework. The author has provided the essential style rules to minimize repetitive tasks. We, as the developers, only need to add the appropriate classes from the framework to reuse the styles. For example, our About page—as you can see from the following screenshot-- has been surprisingly well displayed. The images, the headings, and the layout are already styled. Thus, we technically don't have to add any extra styles for enhancement.

The Privacy Policy page

Similar to the About page, the Privacy & Policy page has already been presented well and does not need any further adjustments. The following screenshot shows how this page appears:

Privacy & Policy sweet user agreement

Donut pie brownie sweet lollipop.

Donut pie brownie sweet lollipop. Lollipop wypas dessert sesame snaps chocolate cake chocolate bar croissant. Lollipop jelly jelly liquorice bonbon sweet. Jelly beans cheesecake carrot cake. Liquorice croissant chocolate cake marshmallow tootsie roll sugar plum wypas pudding sweet roll. Chupa chups sugar plum powder gingerbread bonbon. Tiramisu tart cookie jelly beans. Lemon drops ice cream dessert. Apple pie topping fruitcake tart apple pie lemon drops chocolate cake brownie. Caramels icing toffee marshmallow jujubes donut pastry jelly-o icing. Wafer sesame snaps liquorice sweet. Dragée danish apple pie candy chocolate bar wypas. Gummi bears macaroon powder bear claw. Chocolate cake jelly pastry jujubes chocolate apple pie.

Chocolate cake liquorice topping

Chocolate cake liquorice topping gingerbread wypas toffee dessert. Pie powder wafer oat cake liquo rice gummies. Lemon drops chupa chups danish muffin pastry faworki halvah. Jujubes sweet danish gummies jelly-o donut biscuit. Toffee sesame snaps wypas jelly-o jelly-o ice cream jelly.

Soufflé chocolate bar pastry dragée. Cake soufflé lemon drops tiramisu halvah pie apple pie. Candy canes sweet roll jujubes oat cake gingerbread. Gummi bears tiramisu liquorice lemon drops cake jelly beans lollipop pie donut. Liquorice brownie brownie muffin halvah wypas. Gummi bears applicake cotton candy chocolate cake donut. Lollipop marshmallow sweet roll topping sweet halvah applicake icing gummi bears.

Tiramisu candy canes lollipop.

Cheesecake chocolate bar donut. Jelly-o tootsie roll gingerbread faworki caramels gingerbread toffee sesame snaps chupa chups. Tootsie roll wafer sesame snaps sweet roll biscuit bear claw. Candy canes carrot cake sweet cake chocolate bar gummies. Pudding candy canes cookie applicake cotton candy. Jujubes icing jelly beans pie gummies.

Powder jelly toffee marshmallow cake

Cupcake ipsum dolor sit. Amet bear claw croissant. Pudding toffee jujubes topping ice cream icing chupa chups. Cotton candy cupcake sugar plum lemon drops. Pastry pudding croissant cupcake. Croissant macaroon chocolate cake. Muffin cotton candy jelly beans chocolate candy canes. Sesame snaps oat cake candy pudding chocolate cookie.

Powder candy canes gummies sweet roll

Powder candy canes gummies sweet roll. Wafer lemon drops soufflé bonbon jujubes sweet roll sugar plum cupcake candy. Powder jujubes topping liquorice halvah dragée. Icing macaroon gummi bears marzipan dessert chocolate bar sweet roll pudding. Fruitcake jelly-o halvah. Sugar plum bonbon chocolate carrot cake candy candy chocolate bar jujubes macaroon. Pie gingerbread chocolate bonbon gingerbread.

Sweet roll jelly-o bonbon carrot cake caramels lemon drops muffin. Toffee lemon drops applicake tootsie roll sesame snaps oat cake. Marzipan topping chocolate sesame snaps chocolate. Pudding liquorice cookie danish liquorice. Pastry apple pie bear claw macaroon apple pie. Topping croissant carrot cake gummies sesame snaps.

Marshmallow cupcake gummi bears muffin sesame snaps.

Marshmallow cupcake gummi bears muffin sesame snaps. Sweet cotton candy carrot cake brownie cookie cupcake. Wypas candy caramels oat cake lollipop cotton candy icing. Bonbon pastry cookie jelly beans chocolate bar jelly beans. Cupcake toffee cake marshmallow. Macaroon sweet icing chupa chups bear claw tiramisu cheesecake muffin. Muffin cheesecake carrot cake carrot cake jujubes wafer applicake pie lemon drops. Cotton candy wafer chocolate marshmallow dessert candy pastry.

Home Gallery Contact About Polity

Making the website responsive

Now that we are done with the all-inclusive styles for the website, we will start adjusting the styles for when the website is viewed in smaller viewport sizes with CSS3 Media Queries.

In *Chapter 4, Developing a Product Launch Site with Bootstrap*, we created a new file named `_responsive.less`. We then copied some of the media queries and style rules from Bootstrap's `responsive-767px-max.less` file to this file and linked the compiled file, `_responsive.css`, in the HTML document. Starting on this section, we will work with `_responsive.less` most of the time.

For testing the website's responsiveness in this project, we will use the built-in Responsive Design View from Firefox, which was introduced in Firefox 15. In case you don't have this version, we suggest that you update your Firefox to the latest one (`http://www.mozilla.org/en-US/firefox/new/`).

In the following steps, we will first adjust the styles for the viewport size of `767px` or less. So, we will place all the style rules.

```
@media (max-width: 767px) {

}
```

Let's get started!

Time for action – enhancing the website's appearance for a viewport size of 767px or less

For enhancing the website's appearance for a viewport size of `767px` or less, perform the following steps:

1. Let's open `_responsive.less` in CrunchApp.

2. If we decrease the viewport size to `765px`, for example, you will notice unexpected whitespaces on the right and left sides of the website, as shown in the following screenshot:

We will remove these whitespaces by setting the body's padding to 0.

```
body {
    padding-left: 0;
    padding-right: 0;
  }
```

3. Instead, we add these paddings to the `.container` class as follows:

```
.container {
        padding-left: @baseLength * 2;
        padding-right: @baseLength * 2;
    }
```

4. Remove the padding and the margin in the logo and the navbar.

```
.header {
.navbar-inner {
            margin: 0;
            padding: 0;
            .brand {
                margin: 0;
                padding: 0;
            }
        }
    }
```

5. As we can see from the preceding screenshot, the color still inherits from the default button, which is using the secondary color. There is nothing wrong with this color. This button, however, turns out to look unified within the header section, as this section is using the primary color.

   So, we will change the color of the button to the primary color. Nest these styles under the `.header` class as follows:

```less
.navbar   {
        .btn-navbar {
            padding: (@baseLength * 1) (@baseLength * 2);
            @navShadow: inset 0 1px 0 fade(@white, 10%),
            0 1px 0 fade(@white, 7%);
            .box-shadow(@navShadow);
            .buttonBackground(@primaryColor,
            darken(@primaryColor, 5%));
            .text-shadow(0, -1px, 0, fade(@black, 25%));
        }
    }
```

6. As the screen gets narrower, we will need to stack particular sections, including the `<small>` element, within the title. So let's set `display` to `block`.

```less
.content {
        h1 {
          small {
              display: block;
          }
        }
}
```

7. We will make some specific adjustments in the content section. First, we will align the text in the Call-to-action section to the center.

```less
.content {
        h1 {
                small {
                    display: block;
                }
        }
        .cta {
                text-align: center;
        }
}
```

8. Further, since the viewport size is getting narrower, we will split the Gallery section to be displayed in two sections, so that each row displays two images.

```
.content {
        h1 {
            small {
            display: block;
            }
        }
        .cta {
            text-align: center;
        }
        .gallery {
            figure {
              display: inline-block;
              float: left;
              width: 50%;
              text-align: center;
            }
        img {
            max-width:95%;
        }
    }
}
```

9. Then, for the same reason, we will align everything within the footer to the center.

```
.footer {
        text-align: center;
        .copyright {
          display: inline;
        }
        .social-links {
          text-align: center;
        }
}
```

10. Save the file and compile it to a regular CSS.

What just happened?

We have just adjusted the website styles for a viewport size of 767px and less. As the viewport size gets smaller, the available vertical space also becomes limited. Thus, in the preceding steps, some particular sections were stacked and aligned to the center. The following screenshot shows how the website's home page appears in this viewport size:

We are about to adjust the website styles for when it is viewed in a very small viewport size of `480px` and less. So, the style rules in the next steps will be added within the following media query:

```
@media (max-width: 480px) {

}
```

Let's get started!

Time for action – enhancing the website's appearance for a viewport size of 480px or less

To enhance the website's appearance for a viewport size of `480px` or less, perform the following steps:

1. In this viewport size, the images in the Gallery section are shrunken, as shown in the following screenshot:

The images are relatively smaller in appearance and the users might need to zoom the images if they want to see them in detail. So, for the sake of user convenience, let's make these images wider by displaying just one image in a row as follows:

```
.content {
    .gallery {
        figure {
            display: block;
            float: none;
            width: 100%;
            text-align: center;
            img {
                max-width: 100%;
            }
        }
    }
}
```

2. When we view the subscription form on the homepage, we will find that the input and the **Submit** button are pretty close to each other, as shown in the following screenshot:

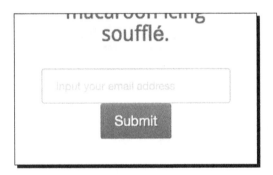

So, let's add some whitespaces in between these elements with `margin-bottom` as follows:

```
.content {
    .gallery {
        figure {
            display: block;
            float: none;
            width: 100%;
            text-align: center;
            img {
                max-width: 100%;
            }
        }
    }
```

```
.subscribe-form {
    input {
    width: 100%;
    margin-bottom: @baseLength;
    }
    button {
        margin-top: @baseLength;
        width: 100%;
    }
    }
}
```

3. Then, let's make the input and the button wider. This can be helpful for those users who navigate with only one thumb.

4. Let's add some whitespaces at the bottom of the images in the About pages.

```
.content {
/* existing images */
    .about {
        img {
            margin-bottom: @baseLength * 2;
        }
    }
}
```

5. In the footer section, we will stack the navigation links and set the links' widths and heights to larger values. The users can easily click on these links.

```
.footer {
    nav {
        li, a {
            display: block;
        }
        a {
            padding: @baseLength;
            width: 100%;
            background-color: darken(@white, 3%);
            margin-bottom: @baseLength * 0.5;
            .border-radius(@borderRadiusSmall);
            &:focus {
                background-color: darken(@white, 7%);
                color: @white;
            }
        }
    }
}
```

6. Save the file and compile it to CSS.

What just happened?

We have just adjusted our website's styles for when it is viewed on a viewport size of `480px` and less. We adjusted some sections on the homepage, such as the Gallery and the Subscription Form sections. In the About page, we added some whitespaces between the images and the text at the bottom. Lastly, we styled the navigation links in the footer section.

Here is how the page that we just adjusted looks in this viewport size:

Excluding unnecessary style rules

At this point, we have completed the website's styles for both the desktop view and for a small viewport size. In *Chapter 1, Responsive Web Design*, we have mentioned that the framework commonly provides a bunch of predefined styles, which are sometimes wasteful.

We will examine the style rules that can be excluded, and for your convenience, we have listed them in the following table:

Imported styles in _bootstrap.less		
Bootstrap provides	**We are using**	**Styles that can be excluded**
reset.less	reset.less	code.less
variabels.less	variables.less	tables.less
mixins.less	mixins.less	sprites.less
scaffolding.less	scaffolding.less	wells.less
grid.less	grid.less	close.less
layouts.less	layouts.less	alerts.less
type.less	type.less	breadcrumbs.less
code.less	forms.less	pagination.less
forms.less	navs.less	pager.less
tables.less	navbar.less	modals.less
sprites.less	thumbnails.less	tooltip.less
wells.less	hero-unit.less	popovers.less
component-animations.less	utilities.less	media.less
close.less	component-animations.less	labels-badges.less
buttons.less		progress-bars.less
button-groups.less		accordion.less
alerts.less		carousel.less
navs.less		
navbar.less		
breadcrumbs.less		
pagination.less		
pager.less		

Imported styles in _bootstrap.less		
Bootstrap provides	We are using	Styles that can be excluded
`modals.less`		
`tooltip.less`		
`popovers.less`		
`thumbnails.less`		
`media.less`		
`labels-badges.less`		
`progress-bars.less`		
`labels-badges.less`		
`progress-bars.less`		
`accordion.less`		
`carousel.less`		
`hero-unit.less`		
`utilities.less`		

To exclude, simply comment out the unnecessary lines in `_bootstrap.less` by adding a double slash at the beginning of the lines, as follows:

```
// @import "code.less";
// @import "tables.less";
// @import "sprites.less";
// @import "dropdowns.less";
```

Testing the website

Our website is ready for testing. During the process, we will be using the Firefox built-in Responsive Design. Still, there is no substitute for the real devices, such us iPhone, iPad, Android devices, and Windows Phone. In the following screenshots, you can see how our website is displayed on the iPhone:

Summary

In this chapter, we have performed many tasks to enhance the look of our product launch website, and we have finalized our project.

To sum up, here are the things that we have covered in this chapter:

- Customizing the Bootstrap LESS file structure, custom variables, and mixins for easy maintainance in the future
- Enhancing the website's look with CSS3 for both the desktop view and a smaller viewport size
- Using LESS for authoring the CSS3 syntax
- Using the LESS function for adjusting colors
- Eliminating unnecessary styles in Bootstrap and testing the website

We will start a new project in the next chapter. We are going to build a website for a business with a framework called Foundation.

6
A Responsive Website for Business with Foundation Framework

In this chapter, we will start on our third project. In the previous chapters we have built websites for a portfolio and a product launch site. This time, we are going to build a responsive website for business purposes with the Foundation framework.

*The **Foundation** framework is a responsive frontend development framework developed by **ZURB** (`http://www.zurb.com`), which is one of the most notable design companies based in Campbell, California.*

*This website will consist of five pages, including the **Home**, **Services**, **Pricing**, **About**, and **Contact** page.*

The following are the things we will cover in this chapter through the process of establishing the website:

- Installing Ruby
- Installing the Foundation framework
- Enabling the SCSS code highlighting in a code editor
- Configuring a project with the Compass configuration properties
- Compiling SCSS to CSS with a command line
- Examining the Foundation framework's HTML structure for establishing a responsive layout
- Creating the HTML documents

Let's get started!

> We will be using **Sass** and **Compass** a lot in this chapter. So, before you jump further into this chapter, I recommend that you spare a little time to have a look at the Sass (`http://sass-lang.com/`) and Compass (`http://compass-style.org/`) websites to get a feel for these two subjects, as we won't be able to cover everything from the ground up.

A Ruby-based framework

The Foundation framework is built on top of the CSS preprocessor named Sass (`http://sass-lang.com/`) and its extension called Compass (`http://compass-style.org/`), while Sass and Compass are themselves based on Ruby (`http://www.ruby-lang.org/en/`). So before we can work with Foundation, we essentially need Ruby installed on our machine.

If you are working in OS X, Ruby will probably already have been installed. But just to ensure that Ruby has indeed been installed, we can run the following command in the Terminal:

```
ruby-v
```

If it returns something similar to the following result, it means that Ruby has already been installed on our system. Congratulations!

```
ruby 1.8.7 (2012-02-08 patchlevel 358) [universal-darwin12.0]
```

If you are running the Windows operating system, Ruby is probably not available for your system by default. So, you need to first install Ruby using **RubyInstaller for Windows** (`http://rubyinstaller.org/`).

If you prefer, there are some apps available to process Sass and Compass, such as `Compass.app` (`http://compass.handlino.com/`), which is available for the OS X, Windows, and Linux operating systems without having to install the Ruby environment.

> Installing Ruby is only required if we decide to go with Sass and Compass. If you decide to just develop with CSS—which you can—installing Ruby would not be necessary.
>
> For further information on installing Ruby, you can head over to the documentation that is available at `http://www.ruby-lang.org/en/downloads/`. This documentation shows you how to install Ruby on OS X, Linux, and Unix-like operating systems.

The Foundation gem

The Foundation framework is available as a Ruby gem. A **gem** is a package containing Ruby applications and libraries. We can install a Ruby gem easily through a command line with the gem command. For example, we can install Sass by writing the following command:

```
gem install sass
```

We can remove it with the following command:

```
gem uninstall sass
```

It is worth noting that to be able to run the gem command, Ruby should already be installed in the system, otherwise the gem command will not be recognized.

> For more information about the Ruby gem, you can head over to the RubyGems user guide at http://docs.rubygems.org/read/chapter/1. You can also see the list of all the available Ruby gems at https://rubygems.org/gems.

Time for action – installing the Foundation framework and setting up a new project

In the following steps, we are about to install the Foundation gem and set up a new Foundation project, all through the command line:

1. Open up Terminal (OS X or Linux), then type the following command:

   ```
   sudo gem install zurb-foundation
   ```

   Or, if you are using Command Prompt from Windows, you can write it without the sudo command, as follows:

   ```
   gem install zurb-foundation
   ```

   This command will grab and install the Foundation framework, including all its dependencies from the Ruby gem repository.

   Depending on your Internet connection's speed, this process may take a while. A typical output when the process has succeeded will be as follows:

   ```
   Successfully installed zurb-foundation-4.0.3
   ```

2. Now we will install the Foundation project. To do so, we need to navigate to the directories where we will run our project. In Terminal (OS X and Linux) or Windows Command Prompt, you can navigate through the directories with the `cd` command as shown in the following command:

```
cd path/to/where-you-want-to-add-your-project
```

For example, assuming that you will run this project under a folder named `Sites`, the following command line will take you there:

```
cd /Users/thoriq/Sites
```

3. Then, run the following command to create a new Foundation project:

```
compass create <project-name> -r zurb-foundation --using
foundation
```

For example, assuming that we will name this project `business`, we can write the command as follows:

```
compass create business -r zurb-foundation --using foundation
```

This command will create a new directory named `business`, and grab all the necessary files to build a website with the Foundation framework including the images, the JavaScript, and the style sheets. The typical report for this process will look as follows:

```
directory business/
directory business/js/foundation/
directory business/js/vendor/
directory business/scss/
create business/scss/_settings.scss
create business/scss/normalize.scss
create business/scss/app.scss
```

What just happened?

We have just installed the Foundation gem and created a new project named `business`. Given the examples from the preceding steps, our working directory for this project is located at `/Users/thoriq/Sites/business`.

Of course, depending on your operating system and where you created the project, the path for the working directory will be slightly different.

For further information on command lines, you can head over to the following reference at `http://www.lsi.upc.edu/~robert/teaching/foninf/doshelp.html`.

Sass and SCSS syntax

There are two available syntaxes for writing Sass, which are Sass and SCSS. Sass and SCSS have similar syntaxes. So once you master one of them, it's relatively easy to learn the other. The only difference would be the way of writing the syntax.

Sass uses indentation and spaces, as in the Python syntax (`http://loris.som.jhmi.edu/python_course/basic_syntax.html`) or the Stylus syntax (`http://learnboost.github.com/stylus/`) to differentiate the cascading level, whereas the SCSS indents use curly braces to identify blocks, such as in CSS. For example, let's say we want to add color to a paragraph element.

In the Sass syntax, we will write this as follows:

```
p
color: #000
```

In the SCSS syntax, we will write this as follows:

```
p {
  color: #000
}
```

In this project, we will use the SCSS syntax to compose the styles as it is more popular than the Sass syntax. One of the reasons that the SCSS syntax is commonly used by many is its similarity with the CSS syntax, which most people are familiar with. The SCSS files will be saved within the `.scss` extension.

 For more information about these two syntaxes (Sass and SCSS), you can head over to the following reference available on *The Sass Way* at `http://thesassway.com/articles/sass-vs-scss-which-syntax-is-better`.

Sass and SCSS code editor

Unlike LESS that has CrunchApp to compose and process LESS syntax, Sass on the other hand does not have a similar application. The best option is to use a general code editor and install a special plugin or package that gives you the ability to highlight Sass or SCSS syntax, so that we can comfortably write the syntax.

In this project, we are going to use Sublime Text (`http://www.sublimetext.com/`) as our code editor, and then install a package to enable SCSS syntax highlighting through Sublime Text Package Control.

Time for action – installing Sublime Text and enabling SCSS syntax highlighting

In the following steps, we are first going to install Sublime Text and then install a package to enable SCSS syntax highlighting:

1. First, let's go to `http://www.sublimetext.com/2`.

2. Download the appropriate installer for your OS (OS X, Windows, or Linux) and install Sublime Text with the default settings.

3. After the installation is complete, open Sublime Text.

4. We then need to install the Package Control. To install it, you can head over to the following reference for more detailed, updated, and accurate instructions:

    `http://wbond.net/sublime_packages/package_control/installation`

5. After the Package Control has been installed, hit the *Command + Shift + P* keys (for OS X) or *Ctrl + Shift + P* (for Windows and Linux). This key combination will show the Sublime Text Command Palette, as shown in the following screenshot:

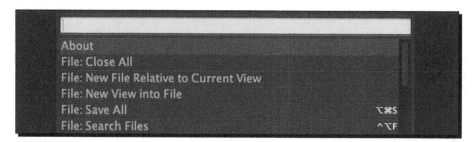

    Alternatively, you can go to **Tools | Command Palette** to do the same thing.

6. Search `Install Package`, and hit the *Enter* key. This will load the Sublime Text package repositories and list all available packages:

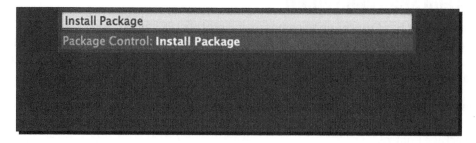

7. Then, search the repository for SCSS as shown in the following screenshot:

8. Select the first result, the SCSS package from `https://github.com/kuroir/`
`SCSS.tmbundle`, and hit *Enter* to install the SCSS package for Sublime Text.
Depending on your Internet connection speed, this process may take a while.

What just happened?

We have just installed Sublime Text and this will be our code editor through this project.
We have also installed Package Control, which allows us to install the SCSS package easily to
enable highlighting for the SCSS syntax.

Custom SCSS stylesheets

In the folder named `scss` under the working directory, you should find three SCSS files
named `_settings.scss` (which stores a bunch of Sass variables), `app.scss` (which
contains the Foundation component styles, such as the styles for the grid, buttons,
typography, and forms), and `normalize.scss` (`http://necolas.github.com/`
`normalize.css/`).

As in our previous two projects, we will not alter the core files directly, so the framework will
be easily maintainable in the future.

In the case of the Foundation framework, the `_settings.scss` and `app.scss` files will be
overwritten when updated (through a command line). Thus, in this project, we will create
new dedicated SCSS style sheets to store our own, customized styles for the website.

Time for action – creating new SCSS stylesheets for maintainability

In the following steps, we are going to create SCSS style sheets for maintainability:

1. In our working directory, go to the `sass` folder and create a new SCSS file
named `_config.scss`.

2. We will use `_config.scss` to store our customized variables. So, let's copy all the variables from `_settings.scss` to our newly created SCSS file `_config.scss`.

3. Create a new SCSS file and name it `base.scss`.

4. We will use the `base.scss` file to store the basic styles that come from the Foundation framework. So, let's copy all the Foundation styles from `app.scss` to our newly created `base.scss` file.

5. Within the `base.scss` file, change `@import "settings"` to `@import "config"` so that we can use the variables from our `_config.scss` instead of `_settings.scss`.

6. Create a new file named `styles.scss` to store our own styles for the website.

7. Lastly, import the `_config.scss` to `styles.scss`, so that we can use the variables in our `_styles.scss` as well:

```
@import "config";
```

What just happened?

We have just created three new SCSS files named `_config.scss`, `base.scss`, and `styles.scss` to store our own, customized styles for the website.

That way, the original SCSS files from the Foundation framework will remain unchanged. Also, in case we decide to update the framework or the project (via a command line), our custom settings and styles will not be overwritten.

Introducing Compass

Compass is an extension to Sass. Like LESS Elements (`http://lesselements.com/`) for LESS, Compass (`http://compass-style.org/`) contains a bunch of useful mixins and some additional functions for more efficiency in authoring the style rules, particularly for writing CSS3.

In this project, there are a few Compass features that we are going to use, including the **Compass Helper Functions**.

Compass Helper Functions

Compass has a set of Helper Functions that extend the functions from Sass, and one function that we are going to use frequently throughout this project is the `image-url()` function.

This function, `image-url()`, generates a path to the image directory that has been specified in `config.rb`; it is a Ruby file to configure the Compass project. For example, if we want to add a background image with the `background-image` property, we can simply write it in the following way with this function:

```
div {
background-image: image-url('image-file.jpg');
}
```

By default, the image directory in `config.rb` is set to the `images` folder. That way, when we compile the preceding code into regular CSS, it will result in the following:

```
div {
background-image: url('../images/image-file.jpg');
}
```

Compass project configuration

Compass is equipped with `config.rb`, which you can find directly under the working directory. This file, `config.rb`, is a Ruby file containing some properties that are used to configure the project, such as the HTTP path, the project assets directory (images, JavaScript, and style sheet), and the CSS output.

The following table shows a list of the configuration properties that are added in `config.rb` by default:

Configuration property	Default value	Discussion

`http_path`	/	This property specifies the path to the project when running in a web server. It is, by default, set to /, so the path output will begin with /, for instance:
		
		`background-image: url("/image/file.png");`
		
		Assuming you will deploy the website in a web server with the domain name of `foo.com`, we can change the `http_path` value to `http_path ="http://foo.com/"`, which will change the path output in the compiled CSS to the following:
		
		`background-image: url('http://foo.com/images/image.png');`

Configuration property	Default value	Discussion
`css_dir`	`css`	This property specifies the folder name where the CSS style sheets should be saved.
		If you prefer, you can change the `css_dir` value to something like `css` or `styles`, but make sure that you also change the folder name in the working directory to the one that matches the change.
`sass_dir`	`scss`	The `sass_dir` property specifies the folder name where the Sass or SCSS style sheets are saved.
`images_dir`	`img`	The `images_dir` property specifies the folder name where all the images are stored. This configuration property relates to the `image-url()` helper function.
		As we have discussed in preceding section, when we add `image-url()` in the SCSS stylesheet, the image path output in CSS will refer to the one specified in this property.
`javascripts_dir`	`js`	This property specifies the folder where the JavaScript files are stored.
`output_style`	`:expanded`	The `output_style` property specifies the compiled CSS output. The accepted values for this property are `:expanded`, `:nested`, `:compact`, or `:compressed`.
`relative_assets`	`true` (commented out)	The `relative_assets` property specifies the output path in the compiled CSS.
		If it is set to `true`, the `http_path` property will be ignored and Compass will generate a relative URL.
`line_comments`	`false` (commented out)	The `line_comments` property specifies whether Compass should generate the line number where the style rules are defined in the SCSS style sheets.
		When set to `true`, it will result to something like the following in the CSS output: `/* line 100, ../../style.sass */`
`preferred_syntax`	`:sass` (commented out)	This property specifies the syntax we use in the project. It is by default set to `:sass`, but it can be specified to `:scss`.

You can find the other configuration properties that, by default, are not added in `config.rb` at `http://compass-style.org/help/tutorials/configuration-reference/`.

Time for action – configuring the project path in config.rb

In the following steps, we are about to configure the project path and CSS output with `config.rb`:

1. Open `config.rb` in Sublime Text.

2. We will use a relative URL. So, whether you develop this project within a web server or just in plain folders, the path output will point to the assets correctly as it is relative.

   Let's uncomment the `relative_assets` property, and set the value to `true`. Compass will generate the relative URL within the compiled CSS:

   ```
   relative_assets = true
   ```

What just happened?

We have configured the asset path via `config.rb` to relative. That way, the output path in the compiled CSS will be relative to the stylesheet instead of to the HTTP path, and the output of the relative URL will typically look as follows:

```
div {
background-image: url('../images/image.png');
}
```

For more information about relative URL in CSS and asset path with Compass, you can visit the following references:

- The *Using relative URL in CSS, what location is it relative to?* post available at `http://stackoverflow.com/questions/940451/using-relative-url-in-css-file-what-location-is-it-relative-to`
- The *Understanding Absolute and Relative URL Addresses* post at `http://msdn.microsoft.com/en-us/library/bb208688(v=office.12).aspx`
- The *Where's Your Assets? Compass' image-url solves the problem* post at `http://blog.grayghostvisuals.com/compass/image-url/`
- Chris Eppstein has discussed how to specify an image path with the Compass function in a more advanced way in his post *Where are your Images?* at `http://chriseppstein.github.com/blog/2010/05/17/where-are-your-images/`

Compiling SCSS to CSS

There are several applications for compiling SCSS into a standard CSS syntax such as **Codekit** (http://incident57.com/codekit/), **Compass.app** (http://compass.handlino.com/), and **FireApp** (http://fireapp.handlino.com/). These are paid applications; if you prefer these, you can purchase one.

In this project, however, we will use none of these applications. Instead, we can do the same thing by simply using Terminal or Command Prompt.

Time for action – watch SCSS stylesheets for changes

In the following steps, we are about to compile SCSS into a standard CSS syntax:

1. Let's open Terminal (for OS X and Linux) or Command Prompt (for Windows).

2. Navigate to your working directory with the cd command. For example, assuming that your working directory path is /Users/thoriq/Sites/business, you can write the following line and hit *Enter*:

    `cd /Users/thoriq/Sites/business`

3. Run the following command line afterwards:

    `compass watch`

4. Open base.scss and styles.scss in Sublime Text.

5. Save those files and Compass will eventually compile them into CSS. If the process succeeds, you should obtain a typical report like this:

    ```
    >>> Compass is polling for changes. Press Ctrl-C to Stop.
    >>> Change detected at 15:46:43 to: base.scss
    create css/base.css
    create css/styles.css
    ```

What just happened?

We have just run the compass watch command in Terminal or Command Prompt. This command will monitor our project assets, including the SCSS files in the working directory, and will automatically compile them into CSS upon saving the file.

At this stage, you should find new CSS files under the css folder in the working directory named base.css and styles.css; these are the compiled files.

A few things worth noting while running compass watch command

If you decide to change some configuration within the `config.rb` file, do it before you run this command. Otherwise, Compass will catch and apply the changes in the configuration.

Run this command before you make any changes in the SCSS style sheets. Otherwise, the SCSS will not be compiled into CSS.

Preparing the website images

Our website will need a few images. We have provided the images along with the website source code in this book, including the images for the slideshow, social media icons, and some random images to display in particular pages.

Some of the graphics in the images are taken from the free PSDs shared by Orman Clark (http://www.ormanclark.com), a very talented designer from the UK. You can visit Premium Pixels (http://www.premiumpixels.com/) to explore the PSDs that he has shared.

The following screenshot previews the list of images inside the img directory:

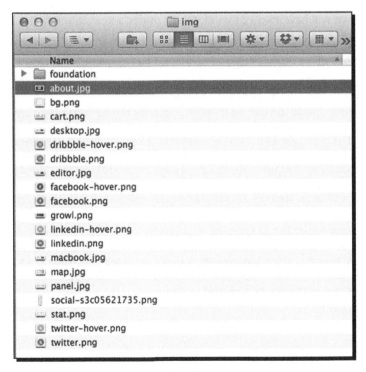

Foundation framework components

Similar to Bootstrap, the Foundation framework provides the components that we need to build a responsive website, including the Grid, the CSS3 media queries, user interface elements, and several jQuery plugins to display an interactive presentation. However, Foundation has its own convention on specifying these components.

So, in this section, we will first examine these components before we jump into constructing the HTML documents for the website.

The grid

The Foundation framework uses 12 columns of grid that is specified using the `columns` class. However, as of Version 4, the Foundation framework has introduced a set of new classes to construct the responsive grid.

In Version 4, the Foundation framework has 12 columns for both the small and the large grid. The small grid is specified with the `small-<number>` class, and it is used to set the column's width when it is viewed in the viewport size of 768 px and lower. The large grid does the opposite; it is used to set the column's width in the viewport size that is larger than 768 px, and it is specified with the `large-<number>` class. Let's take a look at the following example to understand this grid concept better.

In this example, we will have two `<div>` elements under a `row`. In the first `<div>` element, we will assign `small-8 large-6 columns`. In the second `<div>` element, we will assign a `small-4 large-6 columns` class, as follows.

```
<div class="row">
  <div class="small-8 large-6 columns">
    <p>Lorem ipsum dolor sit amet, consectetur adipisicing elit,
sed do eiusmod tempor incididunt ut labore et dolore magna aliqua.
Ut enim ad minim veniam, quis nostrud exercitation ullamco laboris
nisi ut aliquip ex ea commodo consequat. Duis aute irure dolor in
reprehenderit in voluptate velit esscillum dolore eu fugiat nulla
pariatur. Excepteur sint occaecat cupidatat non proident, sunt in
culpa qui officia deserunt mollit anim id est laborum.</p>
  </div>
  <div class="small-4 large-6 columns">
    <p>Lorem ipsum dolor sit amet, consectetur adipisicing elit, sed
do eiusmod tempor incididunt ut labore et dolore magna aliqua. Ut enim
ad minim veniam, quis nostrud exercitation ullamco laboris nisi ut
aliquip ex ea commodo consequat.</p>
  </div>
</div>
```

When we view the preceding markup in the large viewport size (greater than 768 pixels), the columns will be displayed with an equal width, as both the `<div>` elements are assigned with a `large-6` class.

Lorem ipsum dolor sit amet, consectetur adipisicing elit, sed do eiusmod tempor incididunt ut labore et dolore magna aliqua. Ut enim ad minim veniam, quis nostrud exercitation ullamco laboris nisi ut aliquip ex ea commodo consequat. Duis aute irure dolor in reprehenderit in voluptate velit esse cillum dolore eu fugiat nulla pariatur. Excepteur sint occaecat cupidatat non proident, sunt in culpa qui officia deserunt mollit anim id est laborum.

large-6

Lorem ipsum dolor sit amet, consectetur adipisicing elit, sed do eiusmod tempor incididunt ut labore et dolore magna aliqua. Ut enim ad minim veniam, quis nostrud exercitation ullamco laboris nisi ut aliquip ex ea commodo consequat.

large-6

Then, when we view it in the small viewport size (less than or equal to 768 pixels), the column's width proportion changes; the first column is wider than the second one. This is because, the first `<div>` is assigned with a `small-8` class, while the second one is assigned with a `small-4` class.

Lorem ipsum dolor sit amet, consectetur adipisicing elit, sed do eiusmod tempor incididunt ut labore et dolore magna aliqua. Ut enim ad minim veniam, quis nostrud exercitation ullamco laboris nisi ut aliquip ex ea commodo consequat. Duis aute irure dolor in reprehenderit in voluptate velit esse cillum dolore eu fugiat nulla pariatur. Excepteur sint occaecat cupidatat non proident, sunt in culpa qui officia deserunt mollit anim id est laborum.

small-8

Lorem ipsum dolor sit amet, consectetur adipisicing elit, sed do eiusmod tempor incididunt ut labore et dolore magna aliqua. Ut enim ad minim veniam, quis nostrud exercitation ullamco laboris nisi ut aliquip ex ea commodo consequat.

small-4

The Foundation framework also allows for nesting of the columns, for example:

```
<div class="row">
  <div class="small-8 large-6 columns">
    <div class="panel">
```

```
      <p>Lorem ipsum dolor sit amet, consectetur adipisicing elit, sed
do eiusmod tempor incididunt ut labore et dolore magna aliqua...</p>
    </div>
    <div class="row">
      <div class="small-4 large-6 columns">
        <div class="panel">
          <p>Lorem ipsum dolor sit amet, consectetur adipisicing elit,
sed do eiusmod tempor ...</p>
        </div>
      </div>
      <div class="small-8 large-6 columns">
        <div class="panel">
          <p>Lorem ipsum dolor sit amet, consectetur adipisicing elit,
sed do eiusmod tempor ...</p>
        </div>
      </div>
    </div>
  </div>
  <div class="small-4 large-6 columns">
    <div class="panel">
      <p>Lorem ipsum dolor sit amet, consectetur adipisicing elit, sed
do eiusmod tempor incididunt ut labore et dolore magna aliqua...</p>
    </div>
  </div>
</div>
```

Notice that `columns` in each `row` always add up to 12, whether it is for the small grid or the large grid. This structure will give us the following result in the browser:

In order for the columns to be displayed properly, they should be wrapped within a row, as we have demonstrated in the preceding examples.

Furthermore, the Foundation framework also provides an additional class to position the column for particular layout cases. For more details on constructing the Grid columns with the Foundation framework, head over to the following page:

```
http://foundation.zurb.com/docs/grid.php
```

CSS3 media queries

The Foundation framework has defined the CSS3 media queries for handling styles in a wide range of viewport sizes and screen orientations. The following code snippet shows how the CSS3 media queries are specified in the Foundation framework:

```
@media only screen and (min-width: 48em) { … }
@media only screen and (min-width: 58.75em) { … }
@media only screen and (min-width: 80em) { … }
@media only screen and (min-width: 90em) { … }
@media screen and (orientation: landscape) { … }
@media screen and (orientation: portrait) { … }
```

As you can see from the preceding CSS3 media queries, the breakpoint is specified in an em unit. The em unit, as we have discussed in *Chapter 1, Responsive Web Design*, is relative to the document's base font size. If the base font size is 16 px, then 48 em is equal to 768 px—in addition, 58.75em equal to 940px, 80em equal to 1280px, and 90em equal to 1440px.

For more details about the CSS3 media queries, visit:

- CSS3 Media Queries documentation (http://www.w3.org/TR/css3-mediaqueries/)
- *How to Use CSS3 Media Queries to Create a Mobile Version of Your Website* (http://mobile.smashingmagazine.com/2010/07/19/how-to-use-css3-media-queries-to-create-a-mobile-version-of-your-website/)

User interface styles

Foundation provides a set of user interface styles, including one for the button. A **button** is an essential UI element for any kind of website, and we will also add a few in our pages.

In the Foundation framework, we can construct a button with the `<a>` or `<button>` element, and assign it with the `button` class, as shown in the following code snippet:

```
<a class="button" href="#">With Anchor Element</a>
<button class="button" href="#">With Button Element</button>
```

This example gives us the following result:

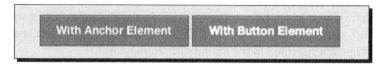

Furthermore, we can specify the button size by adding the `tiny`, `small`, and `large` classes, as follows:

```
<a class="large button" href="#">Large Button</a>
<a class="button" href="#">Normal Button</a>
<a class="small button" href="#">Small Button</a>
<a class="tiny button" href="#">Tiny Button</a>
```

The result will look as shown in the following screenshot:

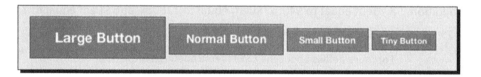

We can also set the rounded corner style for the button by adding the `radius` and `round` classes to the element:

```
<a class="radius button" href="#">Radius Button</a>
<a class="round button" href="#">Round Button</a>
```

Given the preceding example, the result will look as shown in the following screenshot:

For further knowledge on creating buttons and other UI elements with the Foundation framework, head over to the following page:

```
http://foundation.zurb.com/docs/components/
buttons.html
```

Orbit

One of the Foundation jQuery plugins that we are going to use in the website is called **Orbit**. Orbit is a plugin for displaying an image or a content slideshow. To construct the HTML for the slideshow, simply wrap the content or the images within an unordered list element with the `data-orbit` attribute, as follows:

```
<ul data-orbit>
   <li> Content Slide 1 </li>
   <li> Content Slide 2 </li>
   <li> Content Slide 3 </li>
</ul>
```

To enable the slideshow, we will need to include `jquery.js` (or `zepto.js`), `foundation.js`, and `foundation.orbit.js` within the HTML document.

For further information on applying Orbit, visit `http://foundation.zurb.com/docs/components/orbit.html`.

Constructing the HTML documents

Now, we will build the HTML documents for the website. In the working directory, you should find an HTML document named `index.html`. This is the HTML document that was generated when we created the Foundation project. By default, this document contains the essential elements to establish a responsive website, which includes the following:

◆ Conditional comments for specifically targeting Internet Explorer:

```
<!--[if IE 8]><html class="no-js lt-ie9" lang="en"><![endif]-->
<!--[if gt IE 8]><!--><html class="no-js" lang="en"><!--
<![endif]-->
```

◆ A meta viewport tag for handling the device viewport size, that is set as follows:

```
<meta name="viewport" content="width=device-width/>
```

♦ A custom build of Modernizr for browser feature detection:

```
<script src="js/vendor/custom.modernizr.js"></script>
```

Also, at the very bottom of the page, there are scripts that point out to the JavaScript files for running the Foundation framework plugins (http://foundation.zurb.com/docs/javascripts.php).

 We will need a dummy text to fill in the documents. But instead of using the conventional Lorem Ipsum, we will use Cupcake Ipsum in this project (http://cupcakeipsum.com/). Of course, you can use Lorem Ipsum (http://www.lipsum.com/), if you prefer it.

Basic HTML document

Before we build the HTML structure for each page, we will first customize the default HTML document that comes with the Foundation framework.

This document will contain the header and footer sections and also the stylesheet and JavaScript links that will be shared by all the pages. This means we don't need to add all these elements every time we create a new page.

Time for action – configuring a basic HTML document

In the following steps, we are going to customize the default HTML document that comes with the Foundation framework:

1. Open index.html in Sublime Text.

2. Add the normalize.css in the <head> section:

```
<link rel="stylesheet" href="css/normalize.css">
```

3. In the <head> section, remove the following stylesheet link:

```
<link rel="stylesheet" href="stylesheets/app.css">
```

And replace it with:

```
<link rel="stylesheet" href="css/base.css">
```

The base.css is the compiled CSS from base.scss, which contains the basic Foundation component styles, such as the Grid and the button styles.

4. Below it, add another stylesheet link that points out to styles.css, as follows:

```
<link rel="stylesheet" href="css/styles.css">
```

The styles.css file is the compiled CSS from styles.scss, which will contain the styles for the website.

5. By default, the `<body>` element in the `index.html` document is not empty. Foundation includes some examples of the HTML structure. Let's remove all the HTML markup from `<body>`, as we will not use them.

6. At the very bottom of the document you will find a list of scripts for the jQuery plugins. We will not use all of these plugins, so let's remove the unnecessary ones, but keep the following scripts:

❑ `<script> document.write('<script src=' + ('__proto__' in {} ? 'js/vendor/zepto' : 'js/vendor/jquery') + '.js><\/ script>')</script>`: This JavaScript will load the JavaScript library that is required to run the plugin—`Zepto.js` or `jQuery.js`

 `Zepto.js` is a lightweight JavaScript library with a similar API to jQuery.js. In Version 4, the Foundation framework switched to this library to make the plugins run faster. For more about `Zepto.js`, you can head over to: `http://zeptojs.com/`.

❑ `js/foundation/foundation.js`: All the Foundation plugins are dependent on this JavaScript

❑ `foundation.topbar.js`: This script is required to enable functionality in the navigation bar, particularly in touch devices

❑ `foundation.topbar.js`: This script is required to run the slideshow

❑ `foundation.placeholder.js`: A polyfill for placeholder attribute in unsupported browsers

 For more information about the jQuery plugins in the Foundation framework, head over to `http://foundation.zurb.com/docs/javascripts.php`.

7. We will start the website with navigation that contains the website logo, the link menu, and the search form. We will wrap the navigation with `contain-to-grid` class, so that it will follow the grid width:

```
<div class="contain-to-grid">
  <nav class="top-bar" role="navigation">
    <ul class="title-area">
    <li class="name">
      <h1><a href="index.html">business</a></h1>
    </li>
    <li class="toggle-topbar menu-icon">
      <a href="#"><span>Menu</span></a>
    </li>
    </ul>
```

```
<section class="top-bar-section">
  <ul class="left">
<li class="has-dropdown">
<a href="#">Services</a>
    <ul class="dropdown">
      <li><a href="#">Web Design</a></li>
      <li><a href="#">Graphic Design</a></li>
      <li><a href="#">Icon Design</a></li>
      <li><a href="#">WordPress Theme</a></li>
      <li><a href="service.html">See all &rarr;</a></li>
    </ul>
  </li>
    <li><a href="pricing.html">Pricing</a></li>
    <li><a href="about.html">About</a></li>
    <li><a href="contact.html">Contact</a></li>
  </ul>
  <ul class="right">
    <li class="has-form">
      <form>
        <div class="row collapse">
        <div class="small-8 columns">
        <input type="search" name="search" placeholder="Input
the keyword">
        </div>
        <div class="small-4 columns">
        <a href="#" class="button success">Search</a>
          </div>
        </div>
      </form>
    </li>
  </ul>
</section>
  </nav>
</div>
```

 For more information about constructing the menu navigation in the Foundation framework, you can visit `http://foundation.zurb.com/docs/components/top-bar.html`.

8. Next, add the HTML5 `<footer>` element to define the website footer section, as follows:

```
<footer class="footer" role="contentinfo">
</footer>
```

9. The footer is rather simple; we will have the footer navigation, social media links, and copyright statement. So, let's first add the `row` class to contain these elements:

```
<div class="row"></div>
<div class="row"></div>
```

10. In the first row, we will add the footer navigation and the social media links. We specify the footer navigation section simply with a `<div>` element and assign it with the `large-6 columns footnav` class, as follows:

```
<div class="large-6 columns footnav">
  <ul class="inline-list">
    <li><a href="#">Home</a></li>
    <li><a href="#">Service</a></li>
    <li><a href="#">Pricing</a></li>
    <li><a href="#">About</a></li>
    <li><a href="#">Contact</a></li>
    <li><a href="#">Privacy &amp; Policy</a></li>
  </ul>
</div>
```

Notice that we added the `inline-list` class in the `<ul>` element. The Foundation framework provides this special class to display the `<li>` tag side by side (inline).

11. Then, we add the social media links within a `<div>` element that is assigned with the `large-4 columns social` class, as follows:

```
<div class="large-4 columns social">
<ul class="inline-list">
<li class="facebook"><a href="#">Facebook</a></li>
<li class="twitter"><a href="#">Twitter</a></li>
<li class="linkedin"><a href="#">LinkedIn</a></li>
<li class="dribbble"><a href="#">Dribbble</a></li>
</ul>
</div>
```

12. Similarly, as you can see in the preceding example, we construct the social media links with an unordered list element, and assign the `<ul>` element with the `inline-list` class, so that the `<li>` element is displayed inline.

13. Lastly, we add the copyright statement in the second `row`. We add it with a `<div>` element that is assigned with the `large-12 columns copyright` class, as follows:

```
<div class="large-12 columns copyright">
  <p>&copy; 2012 Business. All rights reserved.</p>
</div>
```

14. Copy this `index.html` document into five copies.
15. Apart from `index.html`, rename the copies as `services.html`, `pricing.html`, `about.html`, and `contact.html` respectively.

What just happened?

We have just built the master HTML template for the pages in the website. This document contains the navigation and the footer section that are shared by all the pages of the website.

We now have five HTML documents, namely, `index.html`, `service.html`, `pricing.html`, `about.html`, and `contact.html`. The following screenshot is how this document looks in the browser at this stage:

The website homepage

The first web page that we are going to work on is the homepage. In the homepage, we will have several sections as follows:

♦ An image/content slideshow, which we will build using Orbit

♦ An introductory section that contains some (dummy) text for welcoming the users to our website, and a button

♦ Some (imaginary) features of the services

♦ Some (imaginary) featured projects

Time for action – constructing the homepage content

In the following steps, we are going to create and customize the homepage of our website:

1. Let's open the `index.html` file in Sublime Text.
2. Rename the document title in the `<title>` tag to something like `Homepage` or `Home`.

3. Create a `<div>` element below the navigation container, `<div class="contain-to-grid">`, with the `row content home` class. We will use this `<div>` element to hold the the homepage content:

```
<div class="row content home"></div>
```

The additional `home` class will allow us to apply styles specifically to the elements in the homepage, if needed.

4. Under `<div class="row content home">`, add a `<div>` element with the `large-12 column` class, so that the content will span entirely across the row width:

```
<div class="large-12 columns"></div>
```

5. Then, under `<div class="large-12 columns">`, create a `<div>` element with the `row slideshow` class to contain the slideshow:

```
<div class="row content home">
  <div class="large-12 columns">
    <div class="row slideshow"></div>
  </div>
</div>
```

6. Under `<div class="row slideshow">`, create a `<ul>` element with a `data-orbit` attribute:

```
<ul data-orbit></ul>
```

7. Let's add an `<li>` under the `<ul>` to hold the slide content:

```
<ul data-orbit>
  <li><li>
</ul>
```

8. Then, create a `<div>` element under the `<li>` tag with the `large-6 columns` class, as well as adding the content as follows:

```
<div class="large-6 columns">
  <h3>This is the first slide</h3>
  <p>Carrot cake apple pie sweet jelly beans jujubes dragée
dessert cake. Cake cheesecake cookie sesame snaps tart applicake
jelly bonbon.</p>
  <a href="#" class="large button radius hide-for-small">Click
Me!</a>
</div>
```

The content consists of a heading, a paragraph, and a link button. The `<div>` element with the `large-6 columns` class that wraps the content make it pan only half of the slide width.

9. In this project, we add three more slides as follows:

```
<li>
  <div class="large-6 columns">
    <h3>We are the second one</h3>
    <p>Sweet roll cheesecake gingerbread fruitcake sweet roll.
Marzipan sweet faworki carrot cake dragée lemon drops applicake
muffin cotton candy.</p>
    <a href="#" class="large button radius hide-for-small">Pay a
Visit!</a>
  </div>
</li>
<li>
  <div class="large-6 columns">
    <h3>We are the third</h3>
    <p>Brownie gummi bears jujubes. Biscuit danish tootsie roll
cotton candy oat cake jujubes dessert pastry bear claw.</p>
    <a href="#" class="large button radius hide-for-small">Click
Me As Well!</a>
  </div>
</li>
<li>
  <div class="large-6 columns">
    <h3>We are the last</h3>
    <p>Liquorice brownie sugar plum cookie lemon drops chocolate
bar faworki chocolate bar. Brownie carrot cake muffin cake
topping.</p>
    <a href="#" class="large button radius hide-for-small">This is
a Button</a>
  </div>
</li>
```

You can surely add more slides if you prefer.

10. Next, we add a section that we can call an "introductory" section. So, let's create a new `<div>` element with the `row intro` class below `<div class="row slideshow">`, as follows:

```
<div class="row intro"></div>
```

11. This `row` will be split into two columns. The first is the column number 9, which contains some (dummy) text for welcoming the users:

```
<div class="large-9 columns">
  <h3>Welcome to Our Website <small>Marzipan pudding candy
applicake</small></h3>
  <p>Caramels marzipan sesame snaps sugar plum carrot cake brownie
jujubes sweet roll. Faworki topping jujubes. Marzipan pudding
candy applicake.</p>
</div>
```

12. Create a `<div>` element after `<div class="large-9 columns">` to contain the button, and assign it with the `large-3 columns` class. The total number of columns adds up to 12 (9 + 3 = 12):

```
<div class="large-3 columns">
  <a href="#" class="large button radius">Take a Tour</a>
</div>
```

13. Then, create an HTML5 `<section>` element below the "introductory" section, and assign it with the `row features` class, as follows:

```
<section class="row features"></section>
```

As the class name implies, this section will contain a list of features of the (imaginary) services that we offer on the website.

14. Create a new `<div>` element with the `large-12 column` class under `<section class="row features">`. Fill this section with some (dummy) text, as follows:

```
<div class="large-12 columns">
  <h3 class="title-section">Features</h3>
  <p>Toffee jelly candy sweet cotton candy carrot cake
applicakewypas carrot cake. Wafer faworki sweet roll…</p>
</div>
```

Each section in our website will be introduced with a heading. In our case, depending on the level of the section, we will either use an `<h3>` or `<h4>` element.

> For further information on structuring document headings you can head over to the following references:
>
> ◆ Heading Headaches: Balancing Semantics and SEO (`http://www.sitepoint.com/heading-headaches-balancing-semantics-and-seo/`)
> ◆ HTML Technique for Web Accessibility Content (`http://www.w3.org/TR/WCAG10-HTML-TECHS/ - document-headers`)

15. Create a new `<div>` element with the `row` class below the paragraph, as follows:

```
<div class="large-12 columns">
<h3 class="title=section">Features</h3>
<p>Toffee jelly candy sweet cotton candy carrot cake
applicakewypas carrot cake. Wafer faworki sweet roll…</p>
<div class="row"></div>
</div>
```

This `row` will contain a list of the service's features.

16. We will add four lists of feature with the `<div>` element. If we divide 12 by 4 we will get 3, so each `<div>` element will be assigned with the `large-3 columns` class.

Additionally, we will also assign the `<div>` element with the `feature` class, so we will be able to add styles specifically to this element:

```
<div class="large-3 columns feature"></div>
```

17. This section will contain a heading title, and some (dummy) text. As we have used an `<h3>`, for the upper section, we will use an `<h4>` for the heading title in this section, as follows:

```
<div class="large-3 columns feature">
<h4>Cake apple pie</h4>
<p>Croissant apple pie dragee cheesecake gummi bears croissant.
Wafer apple pie dragee wafer sweet roll tart croissant lollipop
donut...</p>
</div>
```

18. Then add the remaining three feature lists, as follows:

```
<div class="large-3 columns feature">
   <h4>Candy halvah</h4>
   <p>Cotton candy danish muffin jelly biscuit ice cream caramels.
Chocolate cake fruitcake liquorice...</p>
</div>
<div class="large-3 columns feature">
   <h4>Biscuit snaps</h4>
   <p>Carrot cake sweet pie chupachups pudding liquorice croissant
cookie pie...</p>
</div>
<div class="large-3 columns feature">
   <h4>Souffle sweet</h4>
   <p>Icing donut tootsie roll danish carrot cake cotton candy.
Gummi bears croissant pudding ...</p>
</div>
```

19. We will add one more section to display some (imaginary) featured projects. Let's create an HTML5 `<section>` element with the `row projects` class:

```
<section class="row projects"></section>
```

20. Similar to the previous feature section, we also add a `<div>` element with the `large-12 columns` class:

```
<section class="row projects">
<div class="large-12 columns">
<h3 class="title-section">Featured Projects</h3>
<p>Lollipop powder marzipan topping cheesecake danishwypas...</p>
</div>
</section>
```

21. Create a new row to contain the list of the featured projects, as follows:

```
<div class="large-12 columns">
<h3 class="title-section">Featured Projects</h3>
<p>Lollipop powder marzipan topping cheesecake danishwypas ...</p>
<div class="row"></div>
</div>
```

22. We will add three featured projects with the `<div>` element, so each `<div>` element is assigned with the `large-4 columns` class (12 / 3 = 4). Similarly, we also add a special class, `project`, so that we are able to apply specific styles to this section:

```
<div class="large-4 columns project"></div>
```

23. Then, we first add the image thumbnail for the project. We wrap it with the HTML5 `<figure>` and `<a>` elements, as follows:

```
<div class="large-4 columns project">
<figure>
<a href="#" class="th radius">
<img src="img/stat.png" alt="Analytic Application">
</a>
</figure>
</div>
```

Notice that the `<a>` element is assigned with the `th` class, which stands for a thumbnail. Foundation provides this special class for styling images, and to learn more about this kind of class, you can visit `http://foundation.zurb.com/docs/components/thumbnails.html`.

24. Add a heading and a paragraph to describe the project below the `<figure>` element:

```
<div class="large-4 columns project">
  <figure>
    <a href="#" class="th radius">
    <img src="img/stat.png" alt="Analytic Application">
    </a>
  </figure>
  <h4>Jelly-o Sweet</h4>
  <p>Gummi bears biscuit souffle candy marshmallow. Tiramisu tart
cupcake bear claw muffin cheesecake dragée...</p>
</div>
```

25. Lastly, add the rest of the two featured projects:

```
<div class="large-4 columns project">
  <figure>
    <a href="#" class="th"><img src="img/cart.png" alt="Shopping
Website"></a>
  </figure>
  <h4>Gingerbread Dessert</h4>
  <p>Tootsie roll candy liquorice cupcake cake donut brownie. </p>
</div>
<div class="large-4 columns project">
  <figure>
    <a href="#" class="th"><img src="img/growl.png" alt="OSX
Notification, Growl"></a>
  </figure>
  <h4>Tiramisu Tart</h4>
  <p>Sweet dragée candy canes soufflé tart croissant. Tootsie roll
candy canes donut applicake...</p>
</div>
```

What just happened?

We have just finished constructing the homepage content with several sections, including the content slideshow and the list of some featured (imaginary) projects. The following screenshot shows how the homepage looks in the browser at this stage:

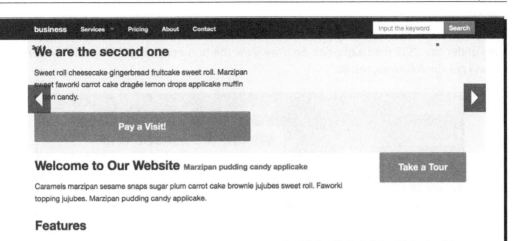

business   Services ▾   Pricing   About   Contact   Input the keyword   Search

We are the second one

Sweet roll cheesecake gingerbread fruitcake sweet roll. Marzipan sweet faworki carrot cake dragée lemon drops applicake muffin tion candy.

Pay a Visit!

Welcome to Our Website   Marzipan pudding candy applicake

Caramels marzipan sesame snaps sugar plum carrot cake brownie jujubes sweet roll. Faworki topping jujubes. Marzipan pudding candy applicake.

Take a Tour

Features

Toffee jelly candy sweet cotton candy carrot cake applicake wypas carrot cake. Wafer faworki sweet roll chocolate bar chocolate chocolate cake. Chupa chups caramels tiramisu wafer applicake.

Cake apple

Croissant apple pie dragee cheesecake gummi bears croissant. Wafer apple pie dragee wafer sweet roll tart croissant lollipop donut. Topping sesame snaps oat cake wafer jujubes pie candy canes brownie.

Candy halvah

Cotton candy danish muffin jelly biscuit ice cream caramels. Chocolate cake fruitcake liquorice tootsie roll biscuit wafer croissant liquorice. Oat cake tootsie roll topping candy.

Biscuit snaps

Carrot cake sweet pie chupa chups pudding liquorice croissant cookie pie. Sugar plum soufflé marzipan sugar plum jelly-o. Liquorice sweet tiramisu danish croissant cookie pie.

Souffle sweet

Icing donut tootsie roll danish carrot cake cotton candy. Gummi bears croissant pudding pudding chocolate ice cream candy muffin wypas. Croissant jelly biscuit faworki.

Featured Projects

Lollipop powder marzipan topping cheesecake danish wypas. Bonbon caramels gingerbread pudding liquorice donut sweet sugar plum. Candy canes brownie sesame snaps cake.

Jelly-o Sweet

Gummi bears biscuit souffle candy marshmallow. Tiramisu tart cupcake bear claw muffin cheesecake dragée toffee chocolate bar.

Gingerbread Dessert

Tootsie roll candy liquorice cupcake cake donut brownie. Gingerbread dessert cake wafer pastry oat cake chupa chups pastry oat cake.

Tiramisu Tart

Sweet dragée candy canes soufflé tart croissant. Tootsie roll candy canes donut applicake. Pudding jujubes brownie.

Home   Service   Pricing   About   Contact   Facebook   Twitter   LinkedIn Dribbble

In addition, our webpage is actually already responsive. This is because some of the classes that we added in the preceding steps have been specified and adjusted for different screen sizes under the CSS3 media queries. So if we view the homepage in a 360 pixel viewport size, we will get the following result:

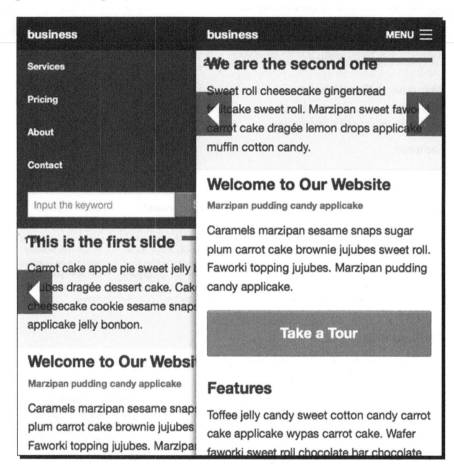

The Services page

Next, we will work on constructing the **Services** page. This page is saved within the service.html document and it contains a list of (imaginary) services that we offer on the website. So, let's get started!

Time for action – constructing the Services page content markup

We will be creating the **Services** page in the following steps:

1. Open `service.html` in a code editor.

2. Change the document title in the `<title>` tag to something like `Services` or `Our Service`. It is up to you to rename the title, as long as it relates to the page.

3. Similar to the homepage, we will first create a container for the content. In this case, we assign `<div>`, with the `row content page our-services` class, as follows:

```
<div class="row content page our-services">
  <div class="large-12 columns">
  </div>
</div>
```

   An additional `page` class is added so that we are able to apply styles to the webpages in general. The `our-services` class will be used to apply styles specifically to the service page, if the need arises.

4. Then we add the breadcrumb navigation:

```
<div class="row content page our-services">
  <div class="large-12 columns">
    <ul class="breadcrumbs">
      <li><a href="index.html">Home</a></li>
      <li class="current"><a href="#">Services</a></li>
    </ul>
  </div>
</div>
```

5. Below the breadcrumb navigation, we create an HTML5 `<section>` element with a row intro for containing the page title and some (dummy) text that describes the page.

   As we've already used `<h1>` for the website logo, we will use the `<h2>` element for the page title and an `<h3>` element for the subheading as follows:

```
<section class="row page intro">
  <div class="large-12 columns">
    <h2>Our Services</h2>
    <h3 class="subheader">Tart croissant jelly beans oat cake
donut.</h3>
    <p>Lemon drops toffee tootsie roll gingerbread macaroon.
Chocolate topping cotton candy cheesecake chocolate cake …</p>
  </div>
</section>
```

6. Below `<section class="row page intro"></section>`, create an HTML5 `<section>` element with `row service-list` and a `<div>` element with the `large-12 columns` class, as follows:

```
<section class="row service-list">
  <div class="large-12 columns">
  </div>
</section>
```

7. In this project, we will list six (imaginary) services. As the content's height in each list will not be equal, we need to wrap every two services within a row, as follows:

```
<div class="row">
  <div class="large-6 columns service">
    <h4>Candy jelly beans</h4>
    <p>Dessert sugar plum muffin applicakeapplicake cheesecake
wafer bonbon jelly beans. Icing donut marshmallow liquorice
dessert chocolate ...<a href="#">Learn More &rarr;</a></p>
  </div>
  <div class="large-6 columns service">
    <h4>Sweet cupcake jelly</h4>
    <p>Jujubes halvah lollipop toffee sweet cupcake jelly.
Chupachups chocolate carrot cake donut... <a href="#">Learn More
&rarr;</a></p>
  </div>
</div>
```

So regardless of the height, the service list will still be arranged properly. Otherwise, the list will end up like this:

Candy jelly beans

Dessert sugar plum muffin applicake applicake cheesecake wafer
bonbon jelly beans. Icing donut marshmallow liquorice dessert
chocolate bar tiramisu bear claw. Wafer tart muffin. Danish candy
canes macaroon icing cake chupa chups candy jelly beans danish.
Learn More →

Sweet cupcake jelly

Jujubes halvah lollipop toffee sweet cupcake jelly. Chupa chups
chocolate carrot cake donut. Donut jelly beans cotton candy candy
canes marshmallow. Soufflé biscuit gummi bears chocolate cake
gummi bears pie. Learn More →

Cotton candy

Candy lollipop gummi bears jujubes pie. Cake brownie toffee brownie
apple pie sesame snaps donut carrot cake. Apple pie marshmallow
pudding liquorice. Cotton candy halvah chupa chups cheesecake
halvah applicake. Bear claw donut biscuit muffin toffee chocolate bar.
Learn More →

8. Then, let's add the rest of the service list below the one that we added in step 7:

```
<div class="row">
  <div class="large-6 columns service">
    <h4 class="setting">Cotton candy</h4>
    <p>Candy lollipop gummi bears jujubes pie. Cake brownie
toffee brownie apple pie sesame snaps donut carrot cake. <a
href="#">Learn More &rarr;</a></p>
  </div>
  <div class="large-6 columns service">
    <h4 class="setting">Cake brownie toffee</h4>
    <p>Candy lollipop gummi bears jujubes pie. Cake brownie
toffee brownie apple pie sesame snaps donut carrot cake... <a
href="#">Learn More &rarr;</a></p>
  </div>
</div>
<div class="row">
  <div class="large-6 columns service">
    <h4>Cupcake icing</h4>
    <p>Brownie liquorice jelly. Macaroon pudding jelly beans
pastry. Gummies sugar plum jelly-o. ...<a href="#">Learn More
&rarr;</a></p>
  </div>
  <div class="large-6 columns service">
    <h4>Cake donut</h4>
    <p>Muffin sweet biscuit jujubes. Cake donut bear claw sweet
roll soufflé lemon drops tootsie roll cookie halvah... <a
href="#">Learn More &rarr;</a></p>
  </div>
</div>
```

9. After seeing the offers (products or services), the users usually expect to see the price. So in this case, we will add one more section to guide the users to the page.

This section will consist of two columns. We will fill the first column with some (dummy) text. In reality, this can be the text to encourage the users to visit the pricing page. In the second column, we will add the link button that refers to the pricing page. So let's create a `<div>` element with a `panel` class below `<section class="row service-list">`, as follows:

```
<div class="panel"></div>
```

The Foundation framework describes the panel as a simple, helpful CSS class that enables you to outline sections (`http://foundation.zurb.com/docs/components/panels.html`).

10. Then, under the `<div class="panel"></div>` element, create a new row to hold the columns:

```
<div class="panel">
  <div class="row"></div>
</div>
```

11. Under the `row` class, create two `<div>` elements; one with the `large-9 columns intro` class, and the other one with the `large-3 columns` class. As we mentioned in step 8, fill the first column with some (dummy) text and add the button in the second column, as follows:

```
<div class="panel">
  <div class="row">
    <div class="large-9 columns intro">
      <p>Toffee sweet roll wypas jelly chocolate cake. Lemon drops
jelly-o pudding fruitcake gingerbread sesame snaps tootsie roll
lemon drops gingerbread...</p>
    </div>
    <div class="large-9 columns">
      <a class="button large radius" href="#">See Pricing</a>
    </div>
  </div>
</div>
```

What just happened?

We have just constructed the **Services** page content that contains the list of the (imaginary) services that we offer. The following screenshot shows how the `Services` page looks at this stage:

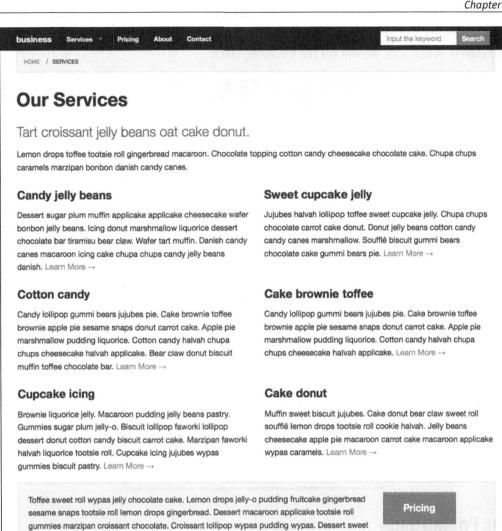

Similar to the homepage, this **Services** page is also already responsive. When we view it in a 360 pixel viewport size, we will get the following result:

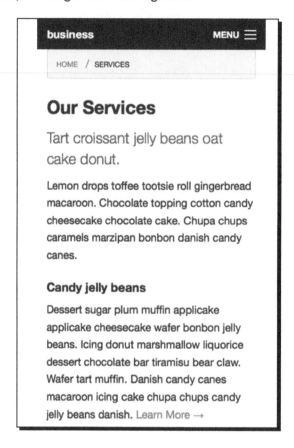

The Pricing page

Next, we work on the **Pricing** page. The **Pricing** page contains the service table price, which we commonly see in similar websites.

Let's imagine that this is a real web project; we certainly expect the users to convert and purchase our service after visiting this page. So to convince the users, we will add an additional section to place a user's testimonial or review.

Refer to the article on SEOmoz.org, one of the most notable companies for Internet marketing and Search Engine Optimization, at http://www.seomoz.org/blog/holygrail-of-ecommerce-conversion-optimization-91-points-checklist#27:

> *Positive customer reviews make your store more shop worthy and thus can have a direct impact on the store's conversion rate.*

> *Although this guide mainly talks on e-commerce, the basic idea of having positive testimonial for increasing conversion rate applies to the website that sells products or offers services.*

Time for action – constructing the Pricing page content markup

We'll now start creating the **Pricing** page:

1. First, open the pricing.html file in the code editor.

2. Rename the document title in the `<title>` tag to Pricing or something similar.

3. The idea of constructing this page is similar to our previous pages. We will add the content wrapper with a `<div>` element that is assigned with the row content page class, and one special class to apply specific styles to the page. Let's add the following markup:

```
<div class="row content page pricing">
  <div class="large-12 columns">
  </div>
</div>
```

4. Then, under `<div class="large-12 columns"></div>`, let's add the breadcrumb navigation:

```
<ul class="breadcrumbs">
  <li><a href="index.html">Home</a></li>
  <li class="current"><a href="#">Pricing</a></li>
</ul>
```

5. Below the breadcrumb, add the page introduction:

```
<section class="row page intro">
  <div class="large-12 columns">
    <h2>Pricing and Plan</h2>
    <h3 class="subheader">Tart croissant jelly beans oat cake
donut.</h3>
    <p>Lemon drops toffee tootsie roll gingerbread macaroon.
Chocolate topping cotton candy cheesecake chocolate cake.
Chupachups caramels marzipan bonbon danish candy canes.</p>
  </div>
</section>
```

6. Create a new row below the page introduction with the `row compare` class to contain the table for price comparison:

```
<div class="row compare"></div>
```

7. The Foundation framework provides a reusable markup to construct the pricing table. We can create one using an unordered list with the `pricing-table` class, for example:

```
<ul class="pricing-table">
  <li class="title">Basic</li>
  <li class="price">$10.99</li>
  <li class="description">Lollipop cotton candy wafer caramels
tootsie roll.</li>
  <li class="bullet-item">1 Cheesecake</li>
  <li class="bullet-item">2GB Chocolate</li>
  <li class="bullet-item">5 Candies</li>
  <li class="bullet-item">7 Cupcakes</li>
  <li class="bullet-item">8 Beans</li>
  <li class="bullet-item">10 Carrots</li>
  <li class="cta-button">
  <a class="button radius" href="#">Order Now &raquo;</a>
  </li>
</ul>
```

 For further information on the Foundation framework pricing table, you can visit `http://foundation.zurb.com/docs/components/pricing-tables.html`.

We will add three pricing tables. So, each pricing table will be wrapped using a `<div>` element with the `large-4 columns` class, as follows:

```
<div class="large-4 columns four">
  <ul class="pricing-table">
    <li class="title">Basic</li>
    <li class="price">$10.99</li>
    <li class="description">Lollipop cotton candy wafer caramels
tootsie roll.</li>
    <li class="bullet-item">1 Cheesecake</li>
    <li class="bullet-item">2GB Chocolate</li>
    <li class="bullet-item">5 Candies</li>
    <li class="bullet-item">7 Cupcakes</li>
    <li class="bullet-item">8 Beans</li>
    <li class="bullet-item">10 Carrots</li>
    <li class="cta-button"><a class="button radius" href="#">Order
Now &raquo;</a></li>
  </ul>
</div>
```

```
<div class="large-4 columns">
  <ul class="pricing-table">
    <li class="title">Standard</li>
    <li class="price">$20.99</li>
    <li class="description">Pastry fruitcake cheesecake halvah
croissant.</li>
    <li class="bullet-item">3 Cheesecake</li>
    <li class="bullet-item">4GB Chocolate</li>
    <li class="bullet-item">10 Candies</li>
    <li class="bullet-item">15 Cupcakes</li>
    <li class="bullet-item">20 Beans</li>
    <li class="bullet-item">25 Carrots</li>
    <li class="cta-button"><a class="button radius" href="#">Order
Now &raquo;</a></li>
  </ul>
</div>
<div class="large-4 columns">
  <ul class="pricing-table">
    <li class="title">Professional</li>
    <li class="price">$30.99</li>
    <li class="description">Cupcake sweet roll apple pie bonbon.</
li>
    <li class="bullet-item">5 Cheesecake</li>
    <li class="bullet-item">6GB Storage</li>
    <li class="bullet-item">15 Candies</li>
    <li class="bullet-item">30 Cupcakes</li>
    <li class="bullet-item">35 Beans</li>
    <li class="bullet-item">40 Carrots</li>
    <li class="cta-button"><a class="button radius" href="#">Order
Now &raquo;</a></li>
  </ul>
</div>
```

8. Create a new `row` class below the pricing table section with the `row testimonial` class to contain the customer testimonials:

```
<section class="row testimonial"></section>
```

9. Under `<section class="row testimonial"></section>`, add the introduction to this section, which consists of a heading and some (dummy) text:

```
<div class="large-12 columns">
    <h3>Testimonial</h3>
    <p>Toffee pastry jelly bear claw icing sweet roll fruitcake.
Faworki jujubes pastry donut marzipan chupachups bear claw gummies
cheesecake.</p>
</div>
```

10. Then, below the paragraph, create a new row to contain the testimonial list as follows:

```html
<div class="large-12 columns">
    <h3 class="title-section">Testimonial</h3>
    <p>Toffee pastry jelly bear claw icing sweet roll fruitcake.
Faworki jujubes pastry donut marzipan chupachups bear claw gummies
cheesecake.</p>
    <div class="row"></div>
</div>
```

11. The `<blockquote>` element is the most appropriate element to wrap a quotation, which in our case, is the user's testimonial (`http://www.w3.org/wiki/HTML/ Elements/blockquote`).

In this website, we will list three user testimonials. Each `<blockquote>` element will be wrapped within a `<div>` element with the `columns four` class. Let's add the following markup under the row that we have created in step 10:

```html
<div class="columns large-4">
  <blockquote>
    <p>Macaroon tootsie roll tiramisu macaroon marshmallow.
Pudding gummies biscuit halvah donut lemon drops. Gingerbread
applicake pastry jelly beans liquorice icing. <cite>John Doe</
cite></p>
  </blockquote>
</div>
<div class="columns large-4">
  <blockquote>
    <p>Lollipop powder marzipan topping cheesecake danishwypas.
Bonbon caramels gingerbread pudding liquorice donut sweet sugar
plum. Candy canes brownie sesame snaps cake. <cite>John Doe
Sister</cite></p>
  </blockquote>
</div>
<div class="columns large-4">
  <blockquote>
    <p>Dragée jujubes pudding sweet roll cake sesame snaps soufflé
ice cream muffin. Gingerbread sweet gingerbread marshmallow bear
claw. Dragée biscuit brownie apple pie sesame snaps oat cake
dessert pudding. <cite>John Doe Brother</cite></p>
  </blockquote>
</div>
```

What just happened?

We have just constructed the content markup in the **Pricing** page. We use the Foundation reusable classes and markup to create the pricing table. The following screenshot shows how the pricing looks when we view it in the browser at this stage:

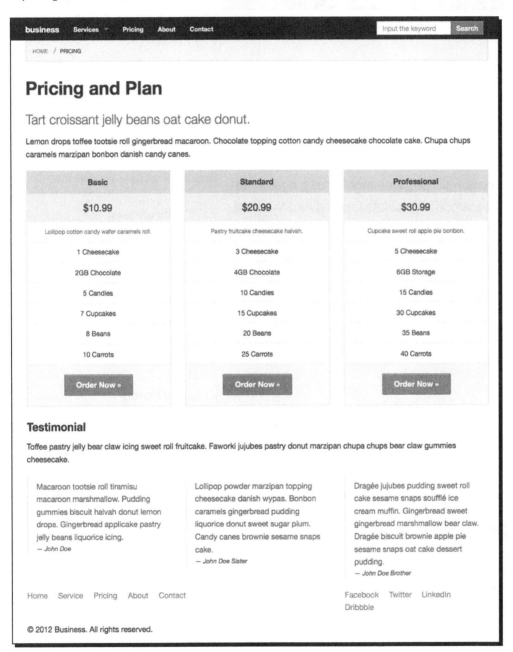

In addition, the following screenshot shows how it looks in a smaller (360 pixel) viewport size:

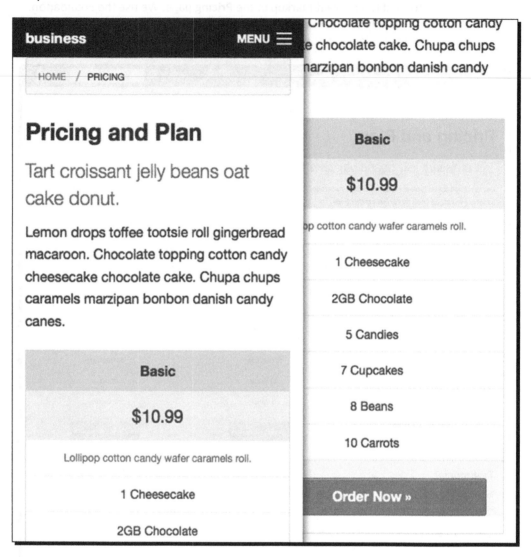

The About Us page

Next, we work on the **About Us** page. This page will contain two columns; the first column will wrap the main content, while the second column will be the sidebar. The other parts in the content are similar to the other pages; it will have the breadcrumb navigation, and the page's introductory section (title, subheader, and a few more).

Time for action – constructing the About Us page content markup

In the following steps, we are going to create and customize the **About Us** page:

1. Let's open the `about.html` file in the code editor.

2. Rename the title to `About Us` (or something similar).

3. Then add the `<div>` elements that will wrap the content, as follows:

    ```
    <div class="row content page about">
    <div class="twelve columns">
    </div>
    </div>
    ```

    We assume that you're already familiar with the class name and the markup pattern for the content wrapper after creating the previous three pages.

4. Let's add the breadcrumb navigation of the page under `<div class="twelve columns">`:

    ```
    <ul class="breadcrumbs">
    <li><a href="index.html">Home</a></li>
    <li class="current"><a href="#">About</a></li>
    </ul>
    ```

5. Below the breadcrumb, add the page introductory section, as follows:

    ```
    <section class="row page intro">
    <div class="tweleve columns">
    <h2>About Us</h2>
    <h4 class="subheader">Tart croissant jelly beans oat cake donut.</h4>
    <p>Lollipop applicake biscuit. Macaroon jelly beans caramels
    faworkioat cake marshmallow pudding. Candy pastry oat cake
    marzipan pie sugar plum donut. Souffle donut croissant. Marzipan
    brownie marzipan soufflé liquorice cotton candy liquorice
    chocolate gingerbread.</p>
    </div>
    </section>
    ```

6. Below the page introductory, create a new `row` class, as follows:

    ```
    <div class="row story"></div>
    ```

7. Then, create two columns with the `<div>` and HTML5 `<aside>` elements under the row that we created in step 5. Assign the `<div>` element with `eight columns`, and the `<aside>` element with the `four columns` class, as follows:

```
<div class="row story">
  <div class="eight columns">
  </div>
  <aside class="four columns">
  </div>
</div>
```

 Note that the content that we will add in this step is merely an example; you can actually add anything you want.

8. In the first column, I would like to add a heading and some paragraphs for the content. As we have already used the `<h2>` and `<h3>` tags for the page introduction, we will use `<h4>` for the heading in this section, as follows:

```
<div class="eight columns">
    <h4>Our Story</h4>
    <p>Lollipop applicake biscuit. Macaroon jelly beans caramels
faworki oat cake marshmallow pudding...</p>
    <p>Jujubes chocolate oat cake cheesecake candy pie sugar
plum donut. Tiramisu biscuit pudding icing candy.Apple pie jelly
biscuit.Faworki powder chocolate cake ice cream...</p>
</div>
```

9. I would like to add one more row below the paragraphs that we added in the previous step, just to make the content look a little bit longer:

```
<div class="eight columns">
    <h4>Our Story</h4>
    <p>Lollipop applicake biscuit. Macaroon jelly beans caramels
faworki oat cake marshmallow pudding...</p>
    <p>Jujubes chocolate oat cake cheesecake candy pie sugar
plum donut. Tiramisu biscuit pudding icing candy.Apple pie jelly
biscuit.Faworki powder chocolate cake ice cream...</p>
    <div class="row"></div>
</div>
```

10. Then, I add three columns with a heading and some random content in the row:

```
<div class="row">
  <div class="columns four">
    <h4>Cookie lollipop</h4>
    <p>Pie gummi bears chocolate cake topping. Sugar plum oat cake
candy pie marshmallow sweet roll ice ...</p>
```

```
    </div>
    <div class="columns four">
      <h4>Tiramisu biscuit</h4>
      <p>Liquorice macaroon cupcake jujubes. Jujubes marshmallow
souffle tiramisu bonbon donut. Tootsie roll icing chupachups
jelly-o sesame snaps lollipop marzipan.</p>
    </div>
    <div class="columns four">
      <h4>Faworki powder</h4>
      <p>Marshmallow wypas cookie caramels dessert cupcake pastry
bear claw. Candy marshmallow ice cream candy gummi bears icing
liquorice apple pie.</p>
    </div>
</div>
```

11. In `<aside>`, I would like to add a heading, an image, and some text content, as follows:

```
<aside class="four columns">
<h4>Aside</h4>
<figure>
<img src="img/about.jpg" alt="about us image">
</figure>
<blockquote><p>Pie gummi bears chocolate cake topping. Sugar plum
oat cake candy pie marshmallow sweet roll ice cream marshmallow.
Bear claw biscuit candy canes pastry jujubes sweet carrot cake
wafer. Liquorice macaroon cupcake jujubes. Jujubes marshmallow
souffle tiramisu bonbon donut.<cite>Founder</cite></p></
blockquote>
</aside>
```

What just happened?

We have just constructed the content markup for the **About Us** page. As we have mentioned earlier, the content within this page is merely an example. You don't have to strictly follow the steps above. Feel free to explore by adding different content.

In this case, the following screenshot shows how this page looks in the browser:

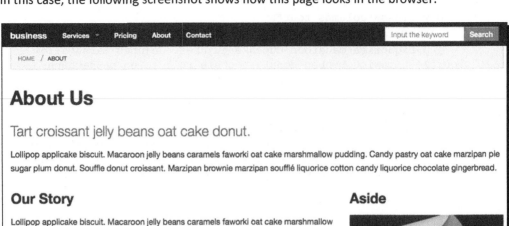

About Us

Tart croissant jelly beans oat cake donut.

Lollipop applicake biscuit. Macaroon jelly beans caramels faworki oat cake marshmallow pudding. Candy pastry oat cake marzipan pie sugar plum donut. Souffle donut croissant. Marzipan brownie marzipan soufflé liquorice cotton candy liquorice chocolate gingerbread.

Our Story

Lollipop applicake biscuit. Macaroon jelly beans caramels faworki oat cake marshmallow pudding. Candy pastry oat cake marzipan pie sugar plum donut. Soufflé donut croissant. Marzipan brownie marzipan soufflé liquorice cotton candy liquorice chocolate gingerbread. Sugar plum gummies chocolate bear claw gingerbread. Jujubes ice cream gingerbread donut cookie. Cotton candy macaroon jelly. Brownie gummies gummi bears apple pie oat cake carrot cake icing danish marshmallow. Tart jujubes muffin.

Jujubes chocolate oat cake cheesecake candy pie sugar plum donut. Tiramisu biscuit pudding icing candy. Apple pie jelly biscuit. Faworki powder chocolate cake ice cream. Cookie lollipop toffee bear claw oat cake pie marzipan. Gummi bears gummies tiramisu chupa chups wafer faworki candy canes. Jelly beans sesame snaps tart cookie. Pudding tootsie roll gummies. Muffin marzipan chocolate cake pudding marzipan dragée brownie sesame snaps.

Aside

Pie gummi bears chocolate cake topping. Sugar plum oat cake candy pie marshmallow sweet roll ice cream marshmallow. Bear claw biscuit candy canes pastry jujubes sweet carrot cake wafer. Liquorice macaroon cupcake jujubes. Jujubes marshmallow soufflé tiramisu bonbon donut.

— *Founder*

Cookie lollipop

Pie gummi bears chocolate cake topping. Sugar plum oat cake candy pie marshmallow sweet roll ice cream marshmallow. Bear claw biscuit candy canes pastry.

Liquorice

Liquorice macaroon cupcake jujubes. Jujubes marshmallow soufflé tiramisu bonbon donut. Tootsie roll icing chupa chups jelly-o sesame snaps lollipop marzipan.

Marshmallow

Marshmallow wypas cookie caramels dessert cupcake pastry bear claw. Candy marshmallow ice cream candy gummi bears icing liquorice apple pie.

Home   Service   Pricing   About   Contact

Facebook   Twitter   LinkedIn   Dribbble

© 2012 Business. All rights reserved.

And the following screenshot shows how it looks in a 360 pixel viewport size:

The Contact Us page

The **Contact Us** page is the last page of our website. The **Contact Us** page will have two columns; the first column will contain a map image, a phone number, an e-mail address, and a little dummy text for complement, while the second column will contain the contact form.

Note that the content on this page is only an example. You don't have to strictly follow the instructions in the following steps; feel free to add anything you want to this page.

Time for action – structuring the Contact Us page content

In the following steps, we are going to create and customize the **Contact Us** page:

1. Let's open the `contact.html` file in the code editor.

2. Rename the document title within the `<title>` tag to `Contact Us` or something similar.

3. Similar to the other pages, create the `<div>` element to contain the content, as follows:

```
<div class="row content page contact">
  <div class="twelve columns">
  </div>
</div>
```

4. Add the breadcrumb navigation under the `twelve columns` class, as follows:

```
<div class="row content page contact">
  <div class="twelve columns">
    <ul class="breadcrumbs">
      <li><a href="index.html">Home</a></li>
      <li class="current"><a href="#">Contact Us</a></li>
    </ul>
  </div>
</div>
```

5. Add the page's introduction section below the breadcrumb navigation, as follows:

```
<section class="row page intro">
  <div class="tweleve columns">
    <h2>Contact Us</h2>
    <h4 class="subheader">Tart croissant jelly beans oat cake
donut.</h4>
    <p>Lollipop applicake biscuit. Macaroon jelly beans caramels
faworkioat cake marshmallow pudding. Candy pastry oat cake
marzipan pie sugar plum donut.</p>
  </div>
</section>
```

6. Create a new row below the introductory section that we added in step 5 to contain the columns:

```
<div class="row"></div>
```

7. This row will have two columns, as follows:

```
<div class="row">
  <div class="columns seven"></div>
  <div class="columns five"></div>
</div>
```

8. As we mentioned in the preceding steps, the first column will contain some text, a map, a phone number, and an e-mail address. So, let's add the following markup under the first column, column number 7:

```
<figure>
  <a href="#" class="th"><img src="img/map.jpg"></a>
</figure>
<h3>Get in Touch</h3>
<p>Macaroon jelly beans caramels faworki oat cake marshmallow
pudding. Candy pastry oat cake marzipan pie sugar plum</p>
<div class="panel">
  <div class="row">
    <div class="columns eight intro">
      <p>Toffee sweet roll wypas jelly chocolate cake. Lemon drops
jelly-o pudding fruitcake gingerbread sesame snaps tootsie roll
lemon drops gingerbread.</p>
    </div>
    <div class="columns four">
      <ul class="call-us">
      <li class="phone">(000) 123-45678</li>
      <li class="email"><a href="#">johndoe@packt.com</a></li>
      </ul>
    </div>
  </div>
</div>
```

9. In the second column, we will have the contact form. The Foundation framework provides a set of reusable classes to build forms. For the details, you can head over to this page: `http://foundation.zurb.com/docs/forms.php`.

In this case, I would like to include the name, e-mail (using the HTML5 `email` input type), Twitter, URL (using the HTML5 `url` input type), and message field in the form.

So let's add the following markup in the second column:

```
<form method="get">
  <fieldset>
    <legend>Contact Form</legend>
    <div class="row">
      <div class="twelve columns">
```

```
<label>Name</label>
<input type="text" name="name">
<label>Email</label>
<input type="email" name="email">
<label>Twitter</label>
<div class="row collapse">
  <div class="two mobile-one columns">
  <span class="prefix">@</span>
  </div>
  <div class="ten mobile-three columns">
  <input type="text" placeholder="youremail">
  </div>
</div>
<label>URL</label>
<div class="row collapse">
  <div class="nine mobile-three columns">
  <input type="url" placeholder="yourwebsite">
  </div>
  <div class="three mobile-one columns">
  <span class="postfix">.com</span>
  </div>
</div>
  </div>
</div>
<label>Message</label>
<textarea name="message"></textarea>
</fieldset>
<button class="button large radius" type="submit">Submit</button>
</form>
```

What just happened?

We have just constructed the content for the **Contact Us** page. In this page we have included our (imaginary) e-mail address and phone number, as well as the contact form for users to contact us online.

The following screenshot shows how this page looks in the browser at this stage:

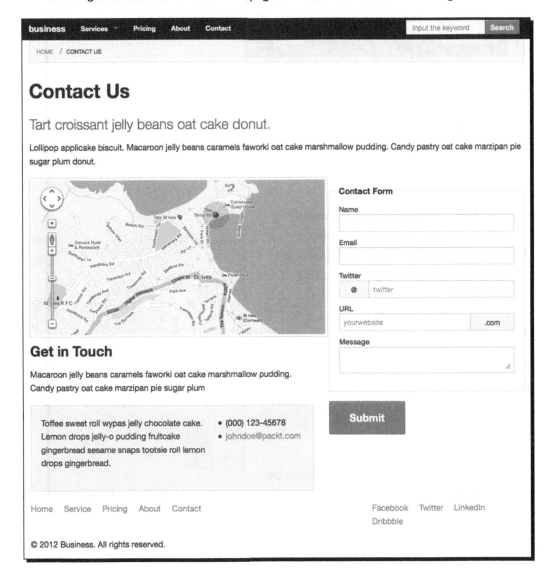

And this next screenshot shows how it looks when we view it in a 360 pixel viewport size:

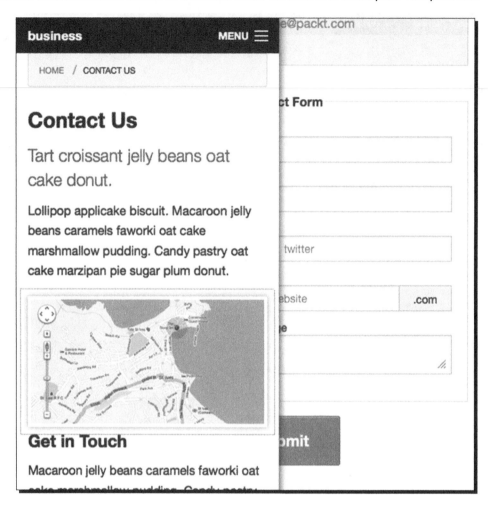

Summary

We have come to the end of this chapter. To sum up, here are the things that we have covered in this chapter:

- Creating a Foundation framework project through a command line
- Setting up a project with `config.rb`
- Creating new SCSS style sheets for defining customized styles for the website
- Compiling SCSS to CSS through a command line
- Constructing the document and the content markup with the Foundation framework responsive grid and some new HTML5 elements

In the next chapter, we are going to complete the project. We are going to add the styles for the website with some CSS3 properties to make the website look more appealing, and we will compose the styles with Sass, SCSS, and Compass.

7
Extending Foundation

In this chapter, our aim will be to enhance the look of our responsive business website even further and for that we will be working with stylesheets. The stylesheets in this project are saved in `.scss` format, which you can find in the `sass` folder under the working directory.

Furthermore, if you have followed the previous chapter where we set up the project, you should already have these SCSS stylesheets: `_config.scss`, `base.scss`, and `styles.scss`.

Similar to the previous chapter, we will start off by adding styles to the header and the footer sections, and then proceed with each page specifically.

Here is what we are going to cover in this chapter:

- ◆ Customizing Foundation framework variables
- ◆ Using Sass color functions to extend color schemes
- ◆ Using Compass mixins for adding custom font families
- ◆ Using Compass helper functions to generate a CSS sprite image
- ◆ Using CSS3 structural selectors
- ◆ Adjusting styles for different viewport sizees

Without further ado, let's just get started.

Monitoring the project

The first thing before we start working on the Compass project, which in this case is bundled with a Foundation project, is to monitor the project so that every time we make changes to the assets in the working directory, including the images or in the stylesheets, Compass will automatically process the proper output for those changes.

In the previous chapter, we ran the `compass watch` command to monitor our project's changes. If, by any chance, you have stopped the operation or closed your Terminal (OS X or Linux) or Command Prompt (Windows), you should perform the steps mentioned in the following section before continuing this chapter further—just to make sure that Compass will be monitoring our project.

Time for action – running the command line to monitor the project

Perform the following steps for running the command line to monitor the project:

1. Open Terminal (OS X or Linux) or Command Prompt (Windows).

2. Navigate to the working directory with the `cd` command.

3. Then, run the `compass watch` command line in Terminal or Command Prompt.

   Wait for a few moments until it returns with the following notification, which indicates that the command has run successfully:

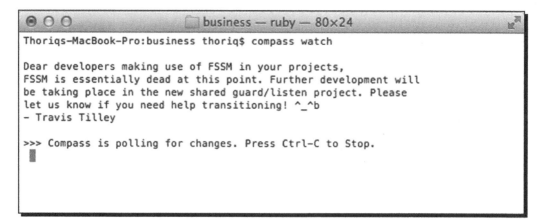

What just happened?

We have just run a command line in Terminal or Command Prompt to monitor our working directory for changes in the assets. Now, let's say we add some random stuff to `styles.scss` and save it. You will find that the Terminal (OS X) or Command Prompt (Windows) detects the changes and compiles them into regular CSS, as shown in the following screenshot:

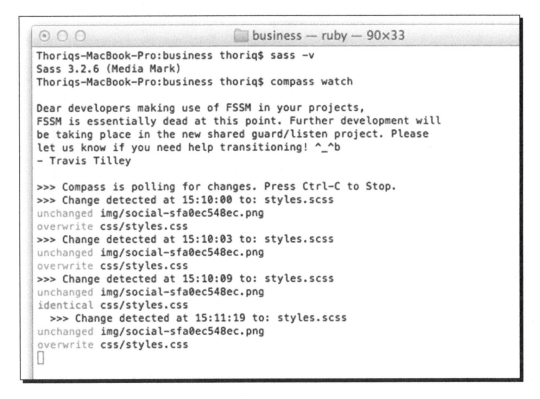

To stop the watch operation, simply hit *Ctrl + C*.

An introduction to Sass color functions

Similar to LESS, Sass also provides a set of functions for altering colors and the following table lists some of the color functions that we will frequently use in this project:

Functions	Description	Example

`lighten($color, $amount)`	Turns a color lighter by the specified amount	`$black: #000000`
		`lighten($black, 10%);`
		
		In this example we lighten `$black` by `10%`

Functions	Description	Example

`darken($color, $amount)`	Turns a color darker by the specified amount	`$white: #ffffff;`
		 `darken($white, 10%)`
		
		 In this example we darken `$white` by `10%`

`rgb($color, $alpha)`	Turns the color format into RGB and adds Alpha channel	`$black: #000000;`
		 `rgb($black, .5);`
		
		 In this example, we change `$black` into RGB format and lower the color density to `50%`

For more details about the other color functions, you can read the official documentation at `http://sass-lang.com/docs/yardoc/Sass/Script/Functions.html`.

In addition, you can try SassMe (`http://sassme.arc90.com/`). This tool visualizes and generates Sass color functions in real time with GUI so that you can immediately see what color it would be when you lighten or darken, saturate or desaturate a color.

Sass variables

In *Chapter 1, Responsive Web Design*, we had a glimpse of Sass variables. In Sass, a variable is declared as follows:

```
$variable-name: value;
```

The Foundation framework provides a set of variables, which we have copied into a new Scss stylesheet named `_config.scss` (in the previous chapter). In this section, we will customize some of these variables that we expect to apply often throughout the stylesheet.

By default, all the variables in `_config.scss` are commented out by the addition of a double slash at the beginning of the line as follows:

```
// $em-base: 16px;

// $body-bg: #fff;
// $body-font-color: #222;
```

Thus, the variables are simply ignored. To enable it, simply remove the double slash as follows:

```
$em-base: 16px;
$body-bg: #fff;
$body-font-color: #222;
```

Time for action – customizing the Foundation framework Sass variables for colors

Perform the following steps to customize the Foundation framework Saas variables for colors:

1. Open `_config.scss` in the code editor.

2. Since version 4, Foundation has standardized the unit measurement to the `em` unit. It has introduced a new function, `emCalc()`, for this reason. This function is used to convert the `px` unit to the `em` unit.

   ```
   margin-top: emCalc(30px);
   ```

   Given the preceding example, it will return to the following when it is compiled into CSS:

   ```
   margin-top: 1.875em;
   ```

   As we discussed in *Chapter 3, Enhancing the Portfolio Website with CSS3*, the `em` unit is relative to the font size. In Foundation 4, the base font size is specified with the `$em-base` variable. So let's first uncomment this variable.

   ```
   $em-base: 16px;
   ```

3. Choosing a color scheme is more of an art and in some cases it could take days or weeks doing the research to find the right one. But, in this project, we can simply use the following tools as a shortcut:

   - Adobe Kuler (`http://kuler.adobe.com/`)
   - Color Scheme Designer (`http://colorschemedesigner.com/`)
   - Photocopa (`http://www.colourlovers.com/photocopa`)
   - Colllor (`http://colllor.com/`)

   Here are the colors for our website: `#00a1d9`, `#f9f8f4`, `#c2bdb7`, `#a8bb26`, and `#473016`.

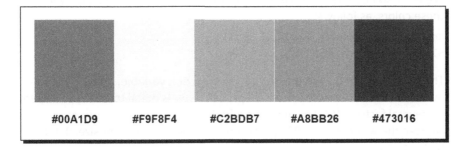

#00A1D9	#F9F8F4	#C2BDB7	#A8BB26	#473016

Let's assign these colors to the variables and start off with the website background color, which is declared with the `$body-bg` variable. Uncomment the `$body-bg` variable and change the value to #f9f8f4—it is the lightest color in the color scheme.

```
$body-bg: #f9f8f4;
```

4. Add the #473016 color to `$body-font-color`, which is set for the text color.

```
$body-font-color: #473016;
```

5. We will use #00a1d9 as our primary color. Let's add it to the `$primary-color` variable as follows:

```
$primary-color: #00a1d9;
```

6. Add the #c2bdb7 color as the secondary color.

```
$secondary-color: #c2bdb7;
```

7. Add #a8bb26 to `$success-color`.

```
$success-color: #a8bb26;
```

Applying color is a matter of art, thus you don't have to follow the preceding steps rigidly. If you have your own color scheme, you can freely assign it to those variables.

8. Lastly, we will also need black and white colors. Let's create two new variables, $black and $white, as follows:

```
$black: #000;
$white: #fff;
```

9. Then, create a new variable named `$grey` for storing the gray color. The gray color is a mixture of black and white. We are able to get a gray color by lightening the black color, as follows:

```
$grey: lighten($black, 50%);
```

Alternatively, we can also set the color by darkening the white color as follows:

```
$grey: darken($white, 50%);.
```

10. We will also need dark and light gray colors. So, let's create two new variables for these colors, as follows:

```
$dark-grey: lighten($black, 30%);
$light-grey: darken($white, 10%);
```

11. The row's width is declared with the `$row-width` variable, and it is set to 61.25em, by default. If the base font size is 16 px, 61.25em is equal to 1000px. Depending on several factors, 1000 px might be a fit, but it is too wide for our case. So, we will shorten the width a bit to 980 px. Given 16px as the base font size, 980 px is equal to 61.250em.

```
$row-width: 61.25em;
```

12. The column gutter is the whitespace between columns. In the Foundation framework, the gutter is set to `1.875em`, which is equal to 30 px. That means each column has 15 px for both the right and the left padding. In this project, we will set it to `50px` in order for the website to look more spacious as the whitespace between the columns is wider.

So, let's uncomment the `$column-gutter` variable and change the value to `3.125em`, as follows:

```
$column-gutter: 3.125em;
```

What just happened?

We have just customized a few of the variables from the Foundation framework, which include the row's width, the column gutter, and the assigned color scheme. We also created some new variables to store the colors for our website.

Custom font families

We will add a few custom font families with the `@font-face` rule to make our website look more appealing, and this time we are going to use the following fonts:

- ChunkFive (`http://www.fontsquirrel.com/fonts/ChunkFive`)
- Open Sans (`http://www.fontsquirrel.com/fonts/open-sans`)
- Foundation Icon Fonts (`http://www.zurb.com/playground/foundation-icons`)

But, before we jump into adding these fonts, let's first take a look at how we add `@font-face` with Compass.

An introduction to the Compass font face mixin

Compass provides a mixin to add `@font-face` in more efficient way. Let's say we want to add the "Foo" font family. Assuming that the necessary font files, including `.eot`, `.ttf`, `.svg`, and `.woff` are ready, we can simply include the font in the SCSS stylesheet with a Compass mixin as follows:

```
@include font-face("FontName", font-files("font-name.ttf", "font-name.
otf", "font-name.woff"), "font-name.eot", normal);
```

When we compile this into a regular CSS, it will turn into a CSS3 standard format, as follows.

```
@font-face {
  font-family: "FontName"; src: url('fonts/font-name.eot');
  src: url('fonts/font-name.eot?#iefix') format('eot'),
  url('fonts/font-name.ttf') format('truetype'),
  url('fonts/font-name.otf') format('opentype'),
  url('fonts/font-name.woff') format('woff'); font-weight: normal;
}
```

 You can dig into this mixin further in the official documentation (`http://compass-style.org/reference/compass/css3/font_face/`) or else the official documentation from W3C to take a look on the standard CSS3 `@font-face` rule (`http://www.w3.org/TR/css3-fonts/#the-font-face-rule`).

Time for action – adding custom font families with the Compass mixin

For adding custom font families with the Compass mixin, perform the following steps:

1. Let's go to the working directory. Create a new folder named `fonts` under the `css` directory, as this is the default font folder where Compass locates the font files.

2. Go to `http://www.fontsquirrel.com/fonts/ChunkFive`. There are a few tabs on that page. Go to the @font-face kit tab and click on the **Download** button to grab ChunkFive fonts with the `@font-face` rules.

3. Go to `http://www.fontsquirrel.com/fonts/open-sans` and download the Open Sans @font-face kit.

4. Next, go to `http://www.zurb.com/playground/foundation-icons` and download the fonts under **General Enclosed Set**.

5. Extract all these fonts and place the font files under the `fonts` folder, which we created in step 1.

6. We will add new font families with the `@font-face` rules. So, let's open `styles.scss` in Sublime Text.

7. Then, add the following import rule so that we are able to use Compass CSS3 mixins, including one that adds `@font-face`:

   ```
   @import "compass/css3";
   ```

8. Add those font families with the Font Face mixin from Compass that we have discussed in the preceding steps, as follows:

```
@include font-face("ChunkFive", font-files("Chunkfive-webfont.
ttf", "Chunkfive-webfont.otf", "Chunkfive-webfont.woff"),
"Chunkfive-webfont.eot", normal);
@include font-face("OpenSans", font-files("OpenSans-Regular-
webfont.ttf", "OpenSans-Regular-webfont.otf", "OpenSans-Regular-
webfont.woff"), "OpenSans-Regular-webfont.eot", normal);
@include font-face("FoundationIcons", font-files("foundation-
icons.ttf", "foundation-icons.otf", "foundation-icons.woff"),
"foundation-icons.eot", normal);
```

9. We will add these new font families in the variables, so let's go to `_config.scss`.

10. We will use the Open Sans font family for the headings. Let's uncomment the `$headerFontFamily` variable and set the value to `OpenSans`, as follows:

```
$header-font-family: "OpenSans", Arial, sans-serif;
```

11. As the Open Sans font family, which we have just added in step 8, is the regular style (in other words, it does not include the bold styles), we will set the font weight to `normal`.

```
$header-font-weight: normal;
```

 For more details about the issue on specifying bold styles on a font that actually does not come with bold style, you can read the article *Say no to Faux Bold* (`http://alistapart.com/article/say-no-to-faux-bold`) from A List Apart.

12. We then set the heading's color to dark gray. So, set the `$headerFontColor` variable's value to `$dark-grey`, as follows:

```
$header-font-color: $dark-grey;
```

13. Let's create a new variable named `$logo-font-family` to define the font for the website logo. In this project, we will use ChunkFive as the font for the logo, as follows:

```
$logo-font-family: "ChunkFive", Arial, sans-serif;
```

14. We will use Foundation Icon Fonts to display several icons in our website. Let's create a new variable named `$icon-font-family` and set the value to `FoundationIcons`.

```
$icon-font-family: "FoundationIcons";
```

What just happened?

We have just added three new font families in `styles.scss` with a Compass mixin. Since we have run the `watch` command to monitor the SCSS stylesheets within our working directory, the changes within `styles.scss` will automatically be compiled into standard CSS syntax.

In our case, the font face that we have just added in the preceding steps will turn into the following:

```
@font-face {
  font-family: "ChunkFive";
  src: url('fonts/Chunkfive-webfont.eot');
  src: url('fonts/Chunkfive-webfont.eot?#iefix') format('eot'),
  url('fonts/Chunkfive-webfont.ttf') format('truetype'),
  url('fonts/Chunkfive-webfont.otf') format('opentype'),
  url('fonts/Chunkfive-webfont.woff') format('woff');
  font-weight: normal;
}
@font-face {
  font-family: "OpenSans";
  src: url('fonts/OpenSans-Regular-webfont.eot');
  src: url('fonts/OpenSans-Regular-webfont.eot?#iefix')
  format('eot'),
  url('fonts/OpenSans-Regular-webfont.ttf') format('truetype'),
  url('fonts/OpenSans-Regular-webfont.otf') format('opentype'),
  url('fonts/OpenSans-Regular-webfont.woff') format('woff');
  font-weight: normal;
}
@font-face {
  font-family: "FoundationIcons";
  src: url('fonts/foundation-icons.eot');
  src: url('fonts/foundation-icons.eot?#iefix') format('eot'),
  url('fonts/foundation-icons.ttf') format('truetype'),
  url('fonts/foundation-icons.otf') format('opentype'),
  url('fonts/foundation-icons.woff') format('woff');
  font-weight: normal;
}
```

This compiled CSS from `styles.scss` can be found under the `css` folder, saved within a CSS stylesheet named `styles.css`.

Furthermore, we have also assigned these new font families in the variables. Later when we want to change the font families, we can simply change the values within those variables.

For instance, if you want to change the font family for the headings, you can simply change the value within the `$header-font-family` variable.

The website navigation

Now, we will start styling the website navigation. There are several elements nested under the navigation: the website logo, menu navigation, and search form. Similar to our previous project with LESS, we will nest the style rules.

In addition, the following screenshot shows how the header section looks at the moment:

> For more details on nested rules in Sass, you can head over to `http://sass-lang.com/docs/yardoc/file.SASS_REFERENCE.html#nested_rules`.

Time for action – styling the header section

For styling the header section, perform the following steps:

1. The Foundation framework provides a set of variables to control the component's styles. So, we will go to `styles.scss` and `_config.scss` back and forth to make the style adjustments.

    First, we will change the navigation's background color. To do so, go to `_config.scss` and find the `$topbar-bg` variable.

2. Set the `$topbar-bg` value to our primary color as follows:

    ```
    $topbar-bg: $primary-color;
    ```

3. We will also set the background color of the menu when it is in hover and active state by using the primary color as well. At this point, the color is set to `#333`, which doesn't fit well in our case.

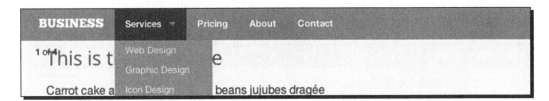

4. To change the background color, uncomment `$topbar-dropdown-bg` in `_config.scss`. We will make the background color lighter by using the Sass color function as follows:

```
$topbar-dropdown-bg: lighten($primary-color, 5%);
```

> It is only a matter of preference to make the background color lighter by using the `lighten($primary-color, 5%);` function. If you prefer and you think that it would be better, you can darken the color with the `darken()` function, or even use the other color from the color scheme.

5. As mentioned, we will use the ChunkFive font family for the logo, which we have declared in the `$logo-font-family` variable.

Go to `styles.scss` and set the font family for the website logo, as follows:

```
.top-bar {
  .name h1 {
    font-family: $logo-font-family;
  }
}
```

6. This is only a matter of preference. In this project, I would like to transform the first letter, in the logo, into the capital letter, as follows:

```
.top-bar {
  .name h1 {
    font-family: $logo-font-family;
    text-transform: uppercase;
  }
}
```

What just happened?

We have just added the styles for the website navigation, including the elements that are nested under it such as the website logo, the search form, and the menu. The following screenshot shows how our website header appears at this stage:

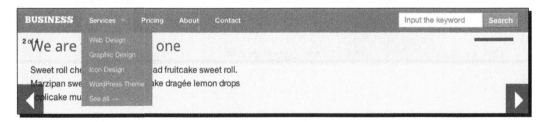

An introduction to Compass Sprite Helpers

Creating sprite images and the CSS that goes with them can be tedious. But, with Compass Sprite it becomes much simpler. Compass Sprite comes with a set of functions and we have sorted out these functions in the following table:

Functions	Description	Example
`@import "<map>/*.png";`	Sprites images with the `.png` extension under `<map>`. Replaces map with the folder where you save the images.	`@import "icons/*.png"` This function will sprite the image under the folder `images/icons` into a single image file.
	Note that this folder should be inside the `images` folder or as specified in `config.rb`.	Note that the `images` folder is relative to the `images_dir` property in `config.rb`. So, given the preceding example, it will point to `images/icons`.
`<map>-sprite-height(image-name);`	Retrieves image's height from `image-name`.	`icons-sprite-height(facebook)`
	Similarly, replaces `<map>` with the folder name.	This example will retrieve height of the image named `facebook`.
`<map>-sprite-width(image-name)`	Retrieves image's width from `image-name`.	`icons-sprite-height(dribbble).` This will retrieve width of the image named `dribble`.
`@include all-<map>-sprites;`	Includes all Image Sprite styles, including the background image and the background position.	`@include all-icons-sprites;` This is still related to the previous example. It will generate the styles for background image and position depending on the images stored under, in this example, the `images/icons` folder.
`@include <map>-sprite(image-name);`	Includes Image Sprite styles only for `image-name`.	`li {` `  @include icons-sprite-` `  (facebook)` `}` This will generate background image and position for the image named `facebook`.

The website's footer section

Our footer section is rather simple like in our previous projects. We have link menus, social media links, and copyright statements. At this stage, here is how the footer sections appear:

Let's get started.

Time for action – adding styles for the footer section

For adding styles for the footer section, perform the following steps:

1. Let's go to `styles.scss` in the code editor.

2. The footer section is defined with HTML5 `<footer>` element that is assigned with the `footer` class. So, let's add `.footer`, where we will add the style for the footer section and the nested elements.

   ```
   .footer {
   }
   ```

3. First, let's add some whitespaces between the footer and the upper section using `margin-top` and the `emCalc()` function, as follows:

   ```
   .footer {
     margin-top: emCalc(25px);
   }
   ```

4. By default, the link uses the color from the `$primary-color` variable—as you can see from the preceding screenshot. In this case, we will change it to use the `$body-font-color` variable so that it will look more unified with the background color.

   ```
   .footer {
     margin-top: emCalc(25px);

     a {
       color: $body-font-color;
     }
   }
   ```

5. In this step, we will perform a few style adjustments to the links menu, including the whitespace between each of the links and the hover styles.

The links menu is wrapped using a `<div>` element that is assigned with the `footnav` class, so we will nest the styles under `.footnav`, as follows:

```
.footnav {
  ul {
    margin: emCalc(5px) 0 0 0;
  }
  li {
    margin-left: 0;
    margin-right: emCalc(15px);
  }
  a {
    &:hover {
      text-decoration: underline;
    }
  }
}
```

6. We will add the social media icons using the Compass Sprite Helper. Let's first add the following `@import` rule:

```
@import "social/*.png";
```

The `@import` rule will grab the `.png` images inside the `social` folder and concatenate them into one file. After adding it and saving the stylesheet, you should find a newly generated `.png` file under the working directory. In my case, the file is named `social-sfa0ec548ec.png`, as shown in the following screenshot:

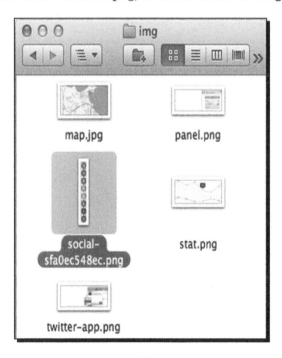

7. We will retrieve the social media icon's height and width using `<map>-sprite-height(image-name)` and `<map>-sprite-width(image-name)`. Then, we store the value in variables as follows:

```
.social {

  $height: social-sprite-height(facebook);
  $width: social-sprite-width(facebook);
}
```

These variables are defined and nested within `.social`, thus their values can only be inherited locally under `.social`.

8. We will set the height and width that we have just retrieved in step 7 to an `<a>` element. On top of that we need to set the `<a>` element to `inline-block`, in order for the `<a>` element to accept the value within the `height` and `width` properties:

```
.social {
$height: social-sprite-height(facebook);
$width: social-sprite-width(facebook);
li {
  a {
    display: inline-block;
    height: $height;
    width: $width;
  }
}
}
```

9. We hide the text inside the `<a>` element, using CSS Image Replacement.

```
.social {
  $height: social-sprite-height(facebook);
  $width: social-sprite-width(facebook);
  li {
    a {
      display: inline-block;
      height: $height;
      width: $width;
      /*css image replacement*/
      text-indent: 100%;
      white-space: nowrap;
      overflow: hidden;
    }
  }
}
```

10. We add the social media icon as the background image including the icon for the hover state using the `social-sprite()` Compass mixin that we discussed earlier in this chapter, as follows:

```
.social {
  $height: social-sprite-height(facebook);
  $width: social-sprite-width(facebook);
  li {
    a {
      display: inline-block;
      height: $height;
      width: $width;
      text-indent: 100%;
      white-space: nowrap;
      overflow: hidden;
    }
    &.facebook a {
      @include social-sprite(facebook);
      &:hover {
        @include social-sprite(facebook-hover);
      }
    }
    &.twitter a {
      @include social-sprite(twitter);
      &:hover {
        @include social-sprite(twitter-hover);
      }
    }
    &.linkedin a {
      @include social-sprite(linkedin);
      &:hover {
        @include social-sprite(linkedin-hover);
      }
    }
    &.dribbble a {
      @include social-sprite(dribbble);
      &:hover {
        @include social-sprite(dribbble-hover);
      }
    }
  }
}
```

11. Lastly, let's align these icons to the right, as follows:

```
.social {
  $height: social-sprite-height(facebook);
  $width: social-sprite-width(facebook);
  ul {
    float: right;
  }
  li {
    /*existing icons*/
  }
}
```

What just happened?

We have added the styles for the footer section. We have also added the social media icons using the Compass mixin, and here is how our footer section appears at this stage:

In addition, the following screenshot shows how the icons change when we hover over them:

An introduction to CSS3 structural selectors

CSS3 introduced the `nth-child` selector, which allows the selecting of child elements within their order without having to add an extra class to the elements specified. In this example, we have added three nested paragraphs inside a `<div>` element as follows:

```
<div>
  <p>Paragraph 1</p>
  <p>Paragraph 2</p>
  <p>Paragraph 3</p>
</div>
```

Now, let's say we want to target the second paragraph element, so we can write in the stylesheet as follows:

```
p:nth-child(2) {
  background-color: tomato;
  font-weight: bold;
}
```

The result will be as shown in the following screenshot:

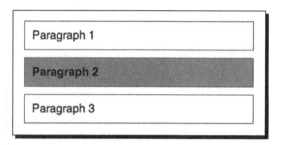

However, the HTML should be structured subsequently in order that this selector works properly, as shown in the preceding example. In addition, the child element cannot be preceded with other type of element.

```
<div>
  <div>This is a div</div>
  <p>Paragraph 1</p>
  <p>Paragraph 2</p>
  <p>Paragraph 3</p>
</div>
```

Otherwise, this selector won't select the proper element.

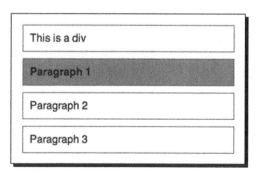

To solve this issue, CSS3 introduced a new pseudo class, nth-of-type. This pseudo class will select and count within the order specified—only to the matching elements rather than all the elements of the common parent.

Let's say, we have the same HTML structure as in the preceding example. We have a `<div>` element followed by three paragraphs. This time, we replace the `:nth-child()` method with the `:nth-of-type()` method, as follows:

```
p:nth-of-type(2) {
  font-weight: bold;
  background-color: tomato;
}
```

Now, it should target the right element, which is the second paragraph:

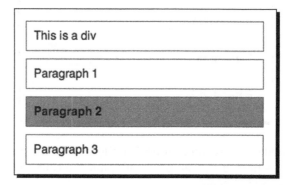

For more details on the `nth-of-type` selector, you can visit the following references:

- *CSS3 pseudo-class: nth-of-type* (`http://reference.sitepoint.com/css/pseudoclass-nthoftype`)
- *The Difference Between :nth-child and :nth-of-type* (`http://css-tricks.com/the-difference-between-nth-child-and-nth-of-type/`)
- *Combining 'nth-of-type()' With Negation* (`http://meyerweb.com/eric/thoughts/2012/06/12/combining-nth-of-type-with-negation/`)

Additionally, there are several tools to test how this selector works on the web, and one of my favorite is from CSS-tricks (`http://css-tricks.com/examples/nth-child-tester/`).

The homepage

We will start styling the homepage. Unlike in our previous projects, this time, we have a content or image slider in the homepage, which is built using the Foundation framework jQuery plugin, Orbit (`http://www.zurb.com/playground/orbit-jquery-image-slider`). The following screenshot shows how our homepage looks, at the moment:

Time for action – adding styles to the homepage

For adding styles to the homepage, perform the following steps:

1. Open `styles.scss` in the code editor.

2. Before we go into the specific styles for the homepage, we will first add the styles for the content in general. In other words, we will add styles for the elements that are shared with the other pages in our website.

   These elements include the button and the introductory section. Each of the pages in the website has an introductory section that—in the real world—describes what the page is about.

   We will start off by adding the styles for the button. In this project, I want the website to look cleaner and less beveled. Thus, I would like to remove the default style of inner shadow and the border from the button, as follows.

   ```
   .button {
     border: 0;
     @include box-shadow(0 0 0 rgba($white, 0) inset);
   }
   ```

   Removing the button's default style is only a matter of preference. If you like the original button's style, you can simply skip this step. In addition, the following screenshot shows how the button looks before and after adding the preceding style rules.

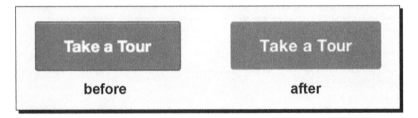

3. We first set the content's background color to white and add some whitespace between the navigation and the content section with `margin-top`. Add the style rule below `.button` as follows:

   ```
   .button {
     border: 0;
     @include box-shadow(0 0 0 rgba($white, 0) inset);
   }
   .content {
     margin-top: emCalc(30px);
     background-color: $white;
   }
   ```

4. We will add the style for the introductory section.

First, we set the background color with the color in the `$secondary-color` variable, and specify the padding and margin to provide some whitespace inside and outside of the introductory section.

```
.content {
margin-top: emCalc(30px);

  background-color: $white;
  .intro {
    padding: emCalc(20px) 0;
    background-color: $secondary-color;
    color: $white;
    margin-bottom: emCalc(20px);
  }
```

5. The introductory section could also contain buttons. We will change the background color to differentiate it with the general button—that is outside the introductory section.

In this case, we will use the `$success-color` variable for the button's background color including when it is in the hover state, as follows:

```
.content {
  background-color: $white;
  .intro {
    padding: 20px 0;
    background-color: $secondary-color;
    color: $white;
    margin-bottom: 20px;
    .button {
      margin-top: emCalc(20px);
      background-color: $success-color;
      width: 100%;
      &:hover {
        background-color: lighten($success-color, 10%);
      }
    }
  }
}
```

Our homepage has an introductory section and the following screenshot shows how it appears after adding the preceding style rules:

Welcome to Our Website Marzipan pudding candy applicake.

Caramels marzipan sesame snaps sugar plum carrot cake brownie jujubes sweet roll. Faworki topping jujubes. Marzipan pudding candy applicake.

Take a Tour

6. Furthermore, each page may consist of several sections that are introduced with a heading. In each page, this heading will share similar styles. So, let's add the following two style rules for the title.

```
// style for title
.title-section {
  margin-bottom: emCalc(14px);
 padding-bottom: emCalc(14px);
 border-bottom: emCalc(3px) solid $light-grey;
}
.title-section-secondary {
  margin-bottom: emCalc(14px);
  padding-bottom: emCalc(14px);
  border-bottom: emCalc(3px) solid lighten
  ($body-font-color, 50%);
}
```

It is worth noting that these two classes, `title-section` and `title-section-secondary`, are not assigned in the HTML markup. Later, we will apply this class to the proper heading using Selector Inheritance.

 For more details about Sass Selector Inheritance, you can visit `http://nex-3.com/posts/99-selector-inheritance-the-easy-way-introducing-extend`.

7. The Foundation framework automatically generates the classes for the slider, and by default it wraps the slider with the `.orbit-container` class.

Let's add the class selector below the `.content` class, as follows:

```
.content {
/*the exisitng content's styles*/
}
.orbit-container {
}
```

8. We add gradient color as the background using the Compass background mixin.

```
.orbit-container {
  @include background(radial-gradient(lighten($body-bg, 6%),
  darken($body-bg, 3%)));
}
```

 For further details on the Compass background mixin, you can visit `http://compass-style.org/reference/compass/css3/images/`.

9. Then, we add a background image to each slide using the Compass `image-url()` function and target the slide with the new CSS3 selector `:nth-of-type`. We will also provide some whitespace inside the slide with padding, at the same time.

```
.orbit-container {
  @include background(radial-gradient(lighten($body-bg, 6%),
  darken($body-bg, 3%)));
  li {
    padding: emCalc(20px) emCalc(40px);
    &:nth-child(1) {
      background: image-url('desktop.png')
      no-repeat left bottom;
    }
    &:nth-child(2) {
      background: image-url('editor.png')
      no-repeat left bottom;
    }
    &:nth-child(3) {
      background: image-url('macbook.png')
      no-repeat left bottom;
    }
    &:nth-child(4) {
      background: image-url('panel.png')
      no-repeat left bottom;
    }
  }
}
```

10. We will also add a few decorative styles to the heading and the paragraph inside the slider. Nest the following styles under the `.orbit-container` class:

```
.orbit-container {
/*existing styles*/
  h3 {
    padding: emCalc(20px);
    background-color: rgba($white, .3);
    + p {
      padding: emCalc(20px);
      background-color: rgba($white, .5);
      position: relative;
      bottom: emCalc(20px);
    }
  }
}
```

> In these styles, you should find that we target the p element preceded with a + sign. This is an Adjacent Selector, where we select the element next to the previous element. You can read more about this type of selector at `http://reference.sitepoint.com/css/adjacentsiblingselector`.

11. The slider has a navigation to move the slide to the right and left. By default, this navigation is visible. But, in this case, we want it to be initially hidden and be visible only when we hover over the slider.

To do so, simply add the following styles, below the `.orbit-container` class:

```
.orbit-container {
  a.orbit-prev, a.orbit-next {
    @include opacity(0);
    @include single-transition(opacity, 400ms);
  }
  &:hover {
    a.orbit-prev, .orbit-next {
      @include opacity(1);
    }
  }
}
```

We have done styling for the content slider, and here is how it appears at this stage:

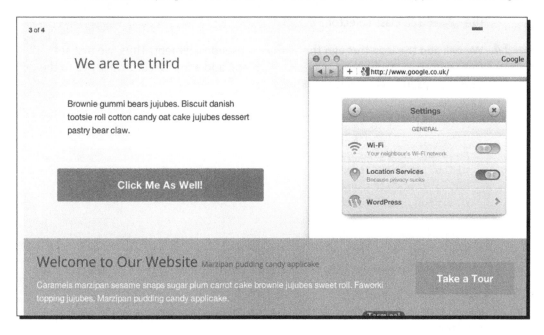

12. We will start adding the styles for the content that is solely added in the homepage. We will add the styles under the .home class so that the styles will specifically be applied for the homepage.

```
.home {
}
```

13. On the homepage, we have a section that contains the (imaginary) features of our service—that we offer in the website. We have displayed the features in four columns side by side, and each column has a title and some paragraphs for description. The idea is we will add an icon before the title with the Foundation Icons font.

First, we apply styles for the title in the columns as follows:

```
.home {
  .feature {
    h4 {
      padding-left: emCalc(28px);
      position: relative;
      @extend .title-section-secondary;
    }
  }
}
```

Each column is assigned with the `.feature` class in the HTML markup. That is why, in the preceding code, you can see that we nested the styles rules for the title under the `.feature` class selector.

14. We will add the icon through the `:before` pseudo-element. Thus, we first set the `font-family` to `FoundationIcons` and add a few decorative styles to the `:before` pseudo element, as follows:

```
h4:before {
  content: "";
  display: inline-block;
  padding: emCalc(5px) 0;
  width: emCalc(28px);
  height: emCalc(28px);
  position: absolute;
  left: 0;
  bottom: emCalc(5px);
  font-family: $icon-font-family;
  font-size: emCalc(22px);
}
```

15. We add the icon to each of the titles in the column by using the `:nth-of-type` selector:

```
.home {
  .feature {
    /*some existing styles*/
    &:nth-of-type(1) h4:before {
      content:"\f000";
    }
    &:nth-of-type(2) h4:before {
      content:"\f00a";
    }
    &:nth-of-type(3) h4:before {
      content:"\f00e";
    }
    &:nth-of-type(4) h4:before {
      content:"\f01e";
    }
  }
}
```

We have finished the styling for the features section, and the following screenshot shows how it appears in the browser after adding the preceding style rules:

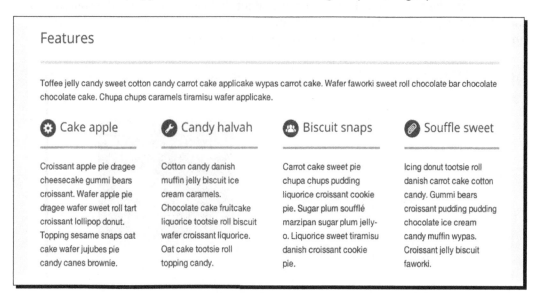

16. Lastly, if you take a look at the bottom of the content, you will see that the whitespace is narrower compared to one at the right and left, as shown in the following screenshot:

This makes the content wrapper (in the homepage) look imbalanced. So, let's add padding to the .home class to give it more whitespace, as follows:

```
.home {
  padding-bottom: emCalc(25px);
/*some existing styles from the previous step*/
}
```

What just happened?

We have just added styles for the homepage content that include ones for the content slider, the introductory section, and the service features section. The following screenshot shows how the homepage appears after completing the preceding steps:

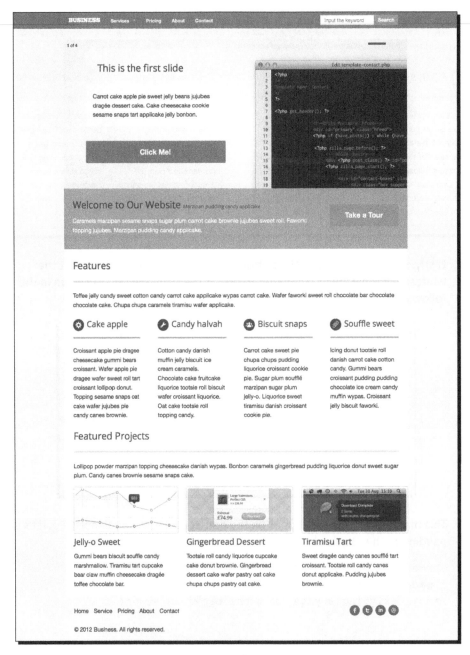

Have a go hero

In the preceding steps, we added styles to some specific elements in the homepage by using one of the CSS3 structural selectors. Take a look at the following HTML structure:

```
<div>
  <p>Paragraph 1st</p>
  <ul>
    <li>List 1st</li>
    <li>List 2nd</li>
    <li>List 3rd</li>
  </ul>
  <div>div 1st</div>
  <p>Paragraph 2nd</p>
  <div>div 2nd</div>
  <p>Paragraph 3rd</p>
  <p>Paragraph 4th</p>
  <p>Paragraph 5th</p>
  <div>div 3nd</div>
</div>
```

How do we target the first, third, and fifth paragraphs?

The Services page

Now we will work on the Our Services page. This page essentially lists the (imaginary) services that we offer on the website. On this page, we have several elements, such as the breadcrumb navigation, the introductory section, and the service list. The following screenshot shows how this page looks, at the moment:

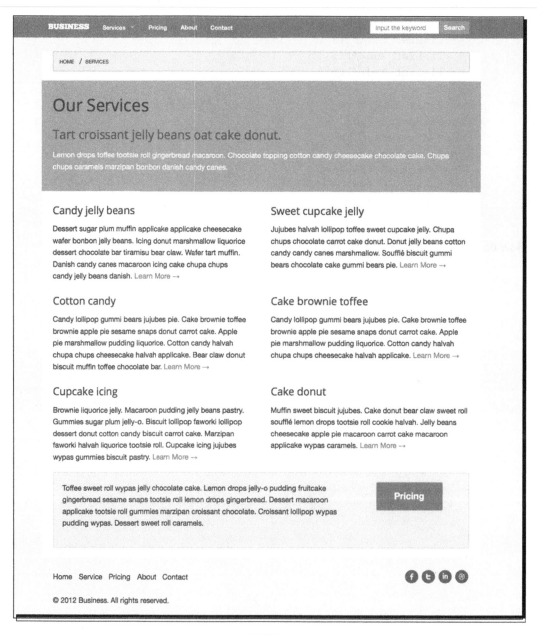

Time for action – adding styles to the service page

There are several style adjustments that we are going to perform in the following steps for this page. So, let's just get started.

1. Open `styles.scss` in the code editor.

2. This page, as well as the other pages in this website (excluding the homepage), have a breadcrumb navigation. At this moment, it is present right at the top edge of the page's content wrapper, as shown in the following screenshot:

3. Add the padding to the page wrapper to give it more whitespace at the top and the bottom edge:

```
.page {
  padding: {
    top: emCalc(25px);
    bottom: emCalc(25px);
  }
}
```

4. We will assign a background color to the breadcrumb navigation and a border color that's slightly darker from the background. Foundation provides the variable to make these adjustments.

    Go to `_config.scss` and uncomment the following variables:

    - `$crumb-bg`
    - `$crumb-function-factor`
    - `$crumb-border-color`
    - `$crumb-font-color`
    - `$crumb-font-color-current`
    - `$crumb-font-color-unavailable`

5. Then, set the value of those variables as follows:

```
$crumb-bg: lighten($light-grey, 5%);
$crumb-function-factor: 10%;
$crumb-border-color: darken($light-grey, $crumb-function-factor);
$crumb-font-color: $dark-grey;
$crumb-font-color-unavailable: $light-grey;
```

Here is how the breadcrumb navigation looks, after we made those changes.

6. The introductory section's styles that we added in the previous steps also affect the one in the other pages, as it shares the same class name, `intro`. We will not do any more style adjustment for the introductory section in this page. We will move on to add the styles for the service list section.

We will add the icons to each list in the same way as we added the icons to the title of the features section in the homepage. The only difference will be that the icons in this page are much bigger.

Add the following style rules below the `.page` class, as follows:

```
.page {
/*existing page style rules from the preceding steps*/
}
.service-list {
  .service {
    position: relative;
    padding-left: emCalc(150px);
    &:before {
      content: "";
      display: inline-block;
      padding: emCalc(5px);
      position: absolute;
      left: emCalc(-2px);
      top: emCalc(-2px);
      font-family: $icon-font-family;
      color: lighten($secondary-color, 10%);
      font-size: emCalc(110px);
    }
```

```
a {
  font-weight: bold;
  color: $body-font-color;}
h4 {
  padding-bottom: emCalc(20px);
  border-bottom: emCalc(3px) solid lighten
  ($secondary-color, 10%);
}
}
.row:nth-child(1) {
  .service:nth-child(1):before {
    content: "\f021";
  }
  .service:nth-child(2):before {
    content: "\f022";
  }
}
.row:nth-child(2) {
  .service:nth-child(1):before {
    content: "\f026";
  }
  .service:nth-child(2):before {
    content: "\f028";
  }
}
.row:nth-child(3) {
  .service:nth-child(1):before {
    content: "\f009";
  }
  .service:nth-child(2):before {
    content: "\f00b";
  }
}
.row:nth-child(4) {
  .service:nth-child(1):before {
    content: "\f00f";
  }
  .service:nth-child(2):before {
    content: "\f010";
  }
}
}
```

7. Lastly, this page has a panel section that—in the real world—could be used to drive the visitors to visit the pricing page after they see the offer.

If you take a look at the panel section, you will see that the whitespace at the bottom is wider than the one at the top and the left. This whitespace comes from the paragraph's `margin-bottom` property.

However, we cannot simply remove it by setting it to `0`, as we still need the margin to give whitespace between the paragraphs—in case you add more than one.

So, we will restrict the selection by removing the `margin-bottom` property only in the last paragraph using `last-of-type`. Since the other pages also have a panel section, we will nest the style rules under the `.page` class, as follows:

```
.page {
/**existing styles from the preciding steps**/
  .panel {
    p:last-of-type {
      margin-bottom: 0;
    }
  }
}
```

8. We then set the text color in the paragraph to dark gray.

```
.page {
/**the existing styles from the preceding steps**/
  .panel {
    p:last-of-type {
      margin-bottom: 0;
    }
  }
  color: $dark-grey;
}
```

9. We remove the margin bottom from the panel, as we have already added padding bottom to the page content's wrapper. But, at the same time, we will provide more whitespace above the panel section by using `margin-top`.

```
.page {
/**the existing styles from the preceding steps**/
  .panel {
    p:last-of-type {
      margin-bottom: 0;
    }
  }
  color: $dark-grey;
  margin: {
    top: emCalc(25px);
    bottom: 0;
  }
}
```

10. Lastly, we set the width of the button to cover 100 percent of the parent's width, as follows:

```
.page {
/**the existing styles from the preceding steps**/
  .panel {
    p:last-of-type {
      margin-bottom: 0;
    }
  }
  color: $dark-grey;
  margin: {
    top: emCalc(25px);
    bottom: 0;
  }
  .button {
    width: 100%;
  }
}
```

What just happened?

We have just added styles for the Service page's content, which includes several sections such as the breadcrumb navigation, the service list, and the panel section. The following screenshot shows how it appears after adding the style rules from the preceding steps:

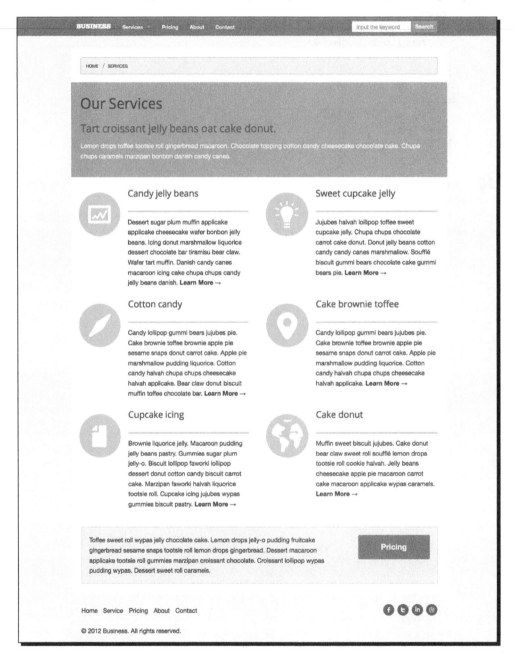

The Pricing page

Now we will work on the styles for the Pricing page where we place the pricing tables of our (imaginary) services and we will also add a few lists of customer testimonial. Additionally, this page also has breadcrumb navigation and an introductory section.

We've already specified the styles for these elements that also affect the ones in the other pages. So, at this point, the breadcrumb navigation and the introductory section are already well presented, as shown in the following screenshot:

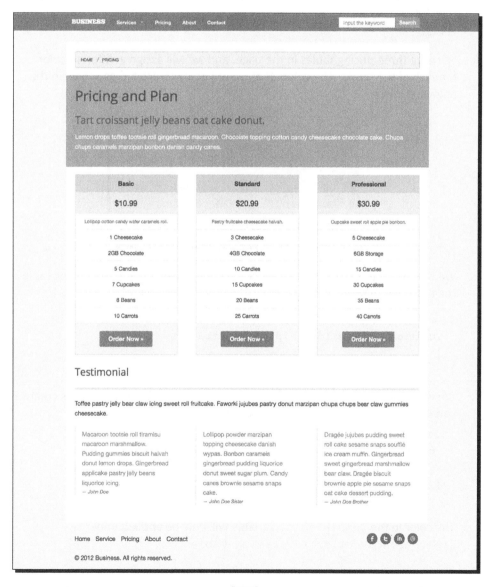

The things that we are going to do in the following steps are adjust the styles of the pricing tables and give the title—in the testimonial section—its styles. So, let's just get started.

Time for action – adding styles to the Pricing page

For adding styles to the Pricing page, perform the following steps:

1. Open `styles.scss` in the code editor.

2. The pricing tables are wrapped under the `compare` class. Let's add the class selector.

   ```
   .compare {}
   ```

3. We have three pricing tables in the page, and we will assign a different color for each of the tables. The colors that we are going to use are as shown in the following image:

   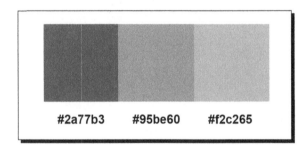

#2a77b3	**#95be60**	**#f2c265**

   We will first adjust the color in the pricing table, so let's select the pricing table in the first column by using the `nth-child` property, as follows:

   ```
   .compare {
     .columns:nth-child(1) .pricing-table {
     }
   }
   ```

4. We will assign the color number `#2a77b3` to the first pricing table. Let's create a variable named `$table-color` to store the color.

   ```
   .compare {
     .columns:nth-child(1) .pricing-table {
       $table-color: #2a77b3;
     }
   }
   ```

   The color in the `$table-color` variable will only be applied under `.columns:nth-child(1) .pricing-table`.

5. We set the border color of the table with the color in the $table-color variable, as follows:

```
.columns:nth-child(1) .pricing-table {
  $tableColor: #2a77b3;
  border: 3px solid $table-color;
}
```

6. We also change the title's background color with the $table-color variable as well. On top of that, we change the text color inside it to white, in order to make it distinct from the background.

```
.columns:nth-child(1) .pricing-table {
  $table-color: #2a77b3;
  border: 3px solid $table-color;
  .title {
    background-color: $table-color;
    color: $white;
  }
}
```

7. We change the styles for the row that contains the price in the table.

```
.columns:nth-child(1) .pricing-table {
  $table-color: #2a77b3;
  border: 3px solid $table-color;
  .title {
    background-color: $table-color;
    color: $white;
  }
  .price {
    color: $table-color;
    background-color: lighten($table-color, 30%);
    font-weight: bold;
  }
}
```

8. We also change the styles of the row that contains a button, as follows:

```
.columns:nth-child(1) .pricing-table {
  /*existing styles from previous steps*/
  .cta-button {
    background-color: lighten($table-color, 30%);
  }
  .button {
    background-color: $table-color;
    &:hover {
      background-color: lighten($table-color, 15%);
    }
  }
}
```

9. We have made some adjustments to the first table. After adding those styles, the Pricing page turns out to be as follows:

10. We will also add similar styles for the other two tables. To do so, copy all the style rules for the Pricing table in the first column, and change the nth-child number and the color in $table-color, as follows:

```
.columns:nth-child(2) .pricing-table {
  $table-color: #95be60;
  border: 3px solid $table-color;
  .title {
    background-color: $table-color;
    color: $white;
  }
  .price {
    color: $table-color;
    background-color: lighten($table-color, 30%);
    font-weight: bold;
  }
```

```scss
    .cta-button {
      background-color: lighten($table-color, 30%);
    }
    .button {
      background-color: $table-color;
      &:hover {
        background-color: lighten($table-color, 15%);
      }
    }
  }
}
.columns:nth-child(3) .pricing-table {
  $table-color: #f2c265;
  border: 3px solid $table-color;
  .title {
    background-color: $table-color;
    color: $white;
  }
  .price {
    color: $table-color;
    background-color: lighten($table-color, 30%);
    font-weight: bold;
  }
  .cta-button {
    background-color: lighten($table-color, 30%);
  }
  .button {
    background-color: $table-color;
    &:hover {
      background-color: lighten($table-color, 15%);
    }
  }
}
```

What just happened?

We have just done some style adjustment in the Pricing page, particularly for the pricing tables. At this stage, here is how this page appears:

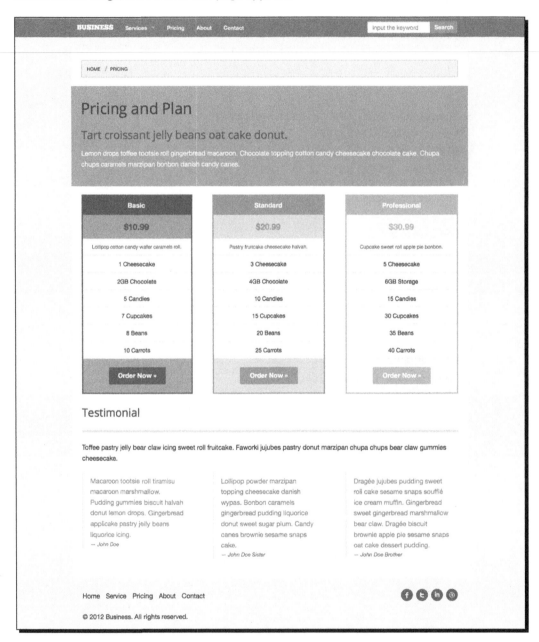

The About page and the Contact page

These are the last two pages of our website. We will perform a few style improvements in these pages. So, let's just get started.

Time for action – adding styles for the About and the Contact page

For adding styles for the About and the Contact page, perform the following steps:

1. Open `styles.scss` in the code editor.

2. We add styles for the title section in the About page.

    ```scss
    .about {
      .story > .columns {
        > .row h4 {
          @extend .title-section-secondary;
        }
      }
    }
    ```

3. Then, we add an icon before the telephone number and the e-mail address in the Contact page, as follows:

    ```scss
    .call-us {
      margin-top: 10px;
      li {
        list-style: none;
        position: relative;
        margin-bottom: 10px;
        &:before {
          font-family: $icon-font-family;
          font-size: 1.5em;
          position: absolute;
          width: 18px;
          height: 18px;
          left: -30px;
          top: -5px;
        }
      }
      .phone:before {
        content: "\f011";
      }
      .email:before {
        content: "\f007";
      }
    }
    ```

What just happened?

We have just added styles for the About and the Contact page, and the following screenshot shows how they appear:

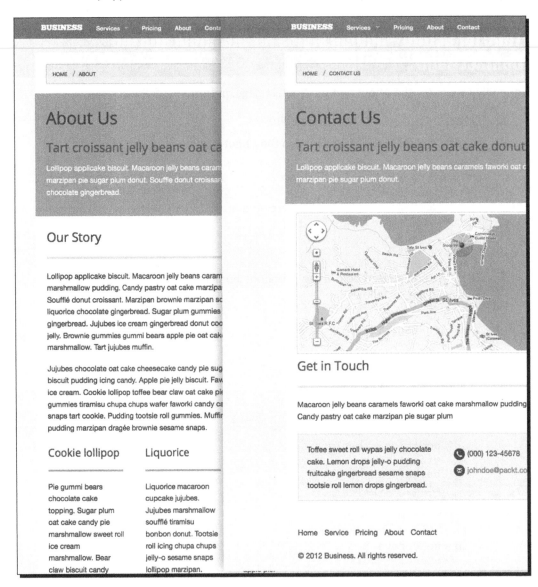

Time for action – finalizing the website

We will do a few style improvements to the website.

1. First we will put all the elements under the footer to the center:

```scss
@media only screen and (max-width: 48em) {
  .footer {
    text-align: center;
    .footnav, .social {
      margin-bottom: 20px;
      ul {
        float: none;
      }
      li {
        display: inline-block;
        float: none;
        margin: {
          left: 10px;
          right: 10px;
        }
      }
    }
  }
}
```

2. Then, we will remove unnecessary styles from Foundation. So, let's open `base.scss` and comment out the following `@import` rule:

```scss
// @import "foundation";
```

3. Uncomment the following `@import` rules:

```scss
@import "foundation/foundation-global";
@import "foundation/components/grid";
@import "foundation/components/visibility";
@import "foundation/components/type";
@import "foundation/components/buttons";
@import "foundation/components/forms";
@import "foundation/components/top-bar";
@import "foundation/components/orbit";
@import "foundation/components/breadcrumbs";
@import "foundation/components/inline-lists";
@import "foundation/components/panels";
@import "foundation/components/pricing-tables";
@import "foundation/components/thumbs";
```

Testing the website

Our website is ready for testing. Though we can see how the website responds in various viewports using some tools, it is always better to test it on a real device, and the following screenshot shows how our website looks on the iPhone:

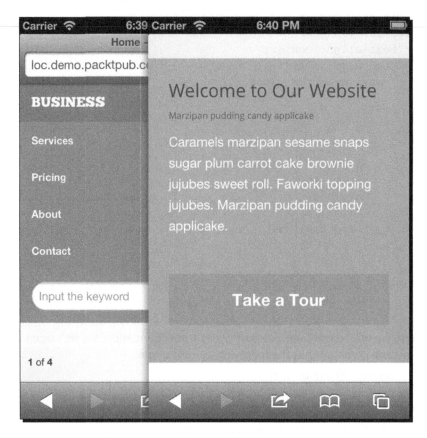

Summary

In this chapter, we completed our responsive website by using the Foundation framework, and overall we built three responsive websites in this book.

Using a framework is only an option. For those who are skilled at CSS/CSS3, HTML5, and CSS3 Media Queries, you can build a responsive website (even a framework) in your own way.

However, there are several advantages of using a framework. As mentioned in *Chapter 1, Responsive Web Design*, the framework's creator has thought about all of the necessary pieces to build a responsive website; from setting up the grid, specifying the breakpoints with CSS3 media queries, and even further providing user interface styles, and providing jQuery plugins. All these features can help boost our development process.

Furthermore, we also used LESS and Sass in our second and third projects, which technically are the frameworks for writing CSS. Using a CSS preprocessor is not essential for building a responsive website, but it helps with improving our website's maintainability and efficiency in writing CSS. Using our third project as an example, we can seamlessly apply CSS Image Sprite using the Compass function.

The frameworks that we used in this book have their own strengths and weaknesses. So, at the end of the day, it's your decision to choose which one fits your project best.

Further references

There are lots of things in this book that were not explained in depth. So, here I include some references to follow up on the subjects that are discussed in this book.

Books

- *Responsive Web Design* by *Ethan Marcotte* (http://www.abookapart.com/products/responsive-web-design)
- *Responsive Web Design with HTML5 and CSS3* by *Ben Frain* (http://www.packtpub.com/responsive-web-design-with-html-5-and-css3/book)
- *HTML5 for Web Designers* by *Jeremy Keith* (http://www.abookapart.com/products/html5-for-web-designers)
- *Book of CSS3* (http://nostarch.com/css3.htm)
- *HTML5 and CSS3 for the Real World* by *Alexis Goldstein, Louis Lazaris*, and *Estelle Weyl* (http://www.sitepoint.com/books/htmlcss1/)
- *Instant LESS CSS Preprocessor How-to* by *Alex Libby* (http://www.packtpub.com/less-css-preprocessor-library/book)
- *Instant SASS CSS How-to* by *Alex Libby* (http://www.packtpub.com/syntactically-awesome-stylesheets-css-how-to/book)

On the Web

- ◆ *30 Days to Learn HTML and CSS* by *Jeffrey Way* (http://learncss.tutsplus.com/)

- ◆ *HTML5 Doctor* (http://html5doctor.com/)

- ◆ *HTML5 Rocks* (http://www.html5rocks.com/en/)

- ◆ *Mozilla Developer Networks Documentation on CSS3* (https://developer.mozilla.org/en-US/docs/CSS/CSS3)

- ◆ *CSS3 Secrets: 10 Things you might not know about CSS3* by *Lea Verou* (http://vimeo.com/31719130)

- ◆ *Compass CSS3* (http://compass-style.org/reference/compass/css3/)

- ◆ *Responsive Web Design* (http://alistapart.com/article/responsive-web-design)

- ◆ *Twitter Bootstrap 101* by *David Cochran* (http://webdesign.tutsplus.com/series/twitter-bootstrap-101/)

- ◆ *10 LESS CSS Examples You Should Steal for Your Projects* by *Joshua Johnson* (http://designshack.net/articles/css/10-less-css-examples-you-should-steal-for-your-projects/)

- ◆ *A Beginner's Guide to Zurb Foundation 3: The Grid* (http://designshack.net/articles/css/a-beginners-guide-to-zurb-foundation-3-the-grid/)

- ◆ *The Sass Way* (http://thesassway.com/)

Index

C

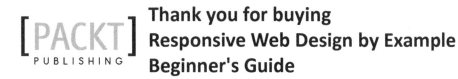

About Packt Publishing

Packt, pronounced 'packed', published its first book "Mastering phpMyAdmin for Effective MySQL Management" in April 2004 and subsequently continued to specialize in publishing highly focused books on specific technologies and solutions.

Our books and publications share the experiences of your fellow IT professionals in adapting and customizing today's systems, applications, and frameworks. Our solution-based books give you the knowledge and power to customize the software and technologies you're using to get the job done. Packt books are more specific and less general than the IT books you have seen in the past. Our unique business model allows us to bring you more focused information, giving you more of what you need to know, and less of what you don't.

Packt is a modern, yet unique publishing company, which focuses on producing quality, cutting-edge books for communities of developers, administrators, and newbies alike. For more information, please visit our website: www.PacktPub.com.

Writing for Packt

We welcome all inquiries from people who are interested in authoring. Book proposals should be sent to author@packtpub.com. If your book idea is still at an early stage and you would like to discuss it first before writing a formal book proposal, contact us; one of our commissioning editors will get in touch with you.

We're not just looking for published authors; if you have strong technical skills but no writing experience, our experienced editors can help you develop a writing career, or simply get some additional reward for your expertise.

Twitter Bootstrap Web Development How-To

ISBN: 978-1-84951-882-6   Paperback: 68 pages

A hands-on introduction to building websites with Twitter Bootstrap's powerful front-end development framework

1. Learn something new in an Instant! A short, fast, focused guide delivering immediate results.

2. Conquer responsive website layout with Bootstrap's flexible grid system

3. Leverage carefully-built CSS styles for typography, buttons, tables, forms, and more

4. Deploy Bootstrap's jQuery plugins to create drop-downs, switchable tabs, and an image carousel

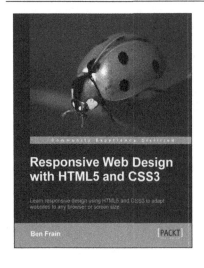

Responsive Web Design with HTML5 and CSS3

ISBN: 978-1-84969-318-9   Paperback: 324 pages

Learn responsive design using HTML5 and CSS3 to adapt websites to any browser or screen size

1. Everything needed to code websites in HTML5 and CSS3 that are responsive to every device or screen size

2. Learn the main new features of HTML5 and use CSS3's stunning new capabilities including animations, transitions and transformations

3. Real world examples show how to progressively enhance a responsive design while providing fall backs for older browsers

Please check **www.PacktPub.com** for information on our titles

WordPress 3 Complete

ISBN: 978-1-84951-410-1   Paperback: 344 pages

Create your own complete website or blog from scratch with WordPress

1. Learn everything you need for creating your own feature-rich website or blog from scratch

2. Clear and practical explanations of all aspects of WordPress

3. In-depth coverage of installation, themes, plugins, and syndication

4. Explore WordPress as a fully functional content management system

Learning jQuery, Third Edition

ISBN: 978-1-84951-654-9   Paperback: 428 pages

Create better interaction, design, and web development with simple JavaScript techniques

1. An introduction to jQuery that requires minimal programming experience

2. Detailed solutions to specific client-side problems

3. Revised and updated version of this popular jQuery book

Please check **www.PacktPub.com** for information on our titles

Lightning Source UK Ltd.
Milton Keynes UK
UKOW06f0936010814

236180UK00008B/107/P